Charles A. Beard

and

American Foreign Policy

Charles A. Beard
and
American Foreign Policy

Thomas C. Kennedy

A University of Florida Book

The University Presses of Florida
Gainesville • 1975

Library of Congress Cataloging in Publication Data

Kennedy, Thomas C.   1932–
    Charles A. Beard and American foreign policy.

    "A University of Florida book."
    Bibliography: p.
    Includes index.
    1. Beard, Charles Austin, 1874–1948. 2. United
States—Foreign relations—20th century—Historiography.
I. Title.
E175.5.B385   327.73   77–186324
ISBN 0–8130–0354–7

PRINTED BY THE ROSE PRINTING COMPANY, INCORPORATED
TALLAHASSEE, FLORIDA

Acknowledgments

THERE is no substantial collection of "Charles A. Beard Papers" in the accepted sense of the term. Consequently, this study is based principally on Beard's prodigious printed record, including monographs, textbooks, pamphlets, essays, articles, book reviews, letters to editors, printed lectures, speeches, and testimony before congressional committees, not to mention numerous forewords, prefaces, and introductions to the works of other scholars. Nonetheless, I have been privileged to see and to utilize unpublished correspondence to a greater degree than the author of any previous published work on Beard. It is necessary to extend recognition to the many persons and institutions which made this possible.

Especially I wish to acknowledge the prompt and courteous responses to my inquiries by William Beard, Miriam Beard Vagts, and Alfred Vagts. Mr. and Mrs. Vagts were very gracious in recommending corrections and new insights for parts of the manuscript which they read. William Beard and Miriam Beard Vagts also granted me permission to quote from many of their father's unpublished letters and from the following published works covered by the copyrights listed below: *The American Party Battle* (1928), copyright renewed 1955 by William Beard and Mrs. Miriam B. Vagts; *Contemporary American History* (1914), copyright renewed 1942 and transferred by bequest to William Beard and Mrs. Mir-

v

327.73
B38ZK

iam B. Vagts; *The Idea of National Interest* (1934), transferred by bequest to William Beard and Mrs. Miriam B. Vagts; *The Open Door at Home* (1934), transferred by bequest to William Beard and Mrs. Miriam B. Vagts; *Cross Currents in Europe Today* (1922), copyright renewed 1950 by Mrs. Miriam B. Vagts.

Publishers who granted permission to quote from works by or about Charles A. Beard are as follows: Doubleday, Doran and Company, *A Basic History of the United States* (1944) by Charles and Mary Beard; Ginn and Company, *The Development of Modern Europe* (1907–8 and 1930) by Charles Beard and James Harvey Robinson; Harper and Brothers, *The Navy: Defense or Portent?* (1932); Alfred A. Knopf, Inc., *A Foreign Policy for America* (1940), *The Economic Basis of Politics* (1945), and *Charles A. Beard: The Economic Basis of Politics and Related Writings* (1957), compiled by William Beard; The Macmillan Company, *American Government and Politics* (1910), *The Rise of American Civilization* (1927) by Charles and Mary Beard, *America in Midpassage* (1939) by Charles and Mary Beard, *The American Spirit* (1942) by Charles and Mary Beard; University of Kentucky Press, *Charles A. Beard: An Appraisal*, edited by Howard K. Beale; Vanguard Press, *The Devil Theory of War* (1936); and Yale University Press, *American Foreign Policy in the Making, 1932–1940* (1946), *President Roosevelt and the Coming of the War, 1941* (1948), *The Pragmatic Revolt in American History: Carl Becker and Charles Beard* (1958) by Cushing Strout.

I have received permission to quote from the writings of Charles A. Beard, and of those who wrote about Beard, from these periodicals: *American Historical Review, Harper's, Nation,* and *New Republic.* The publishers of the *Historian, Mid-America,* and *Military Affairs* have kindly consented to let me incorporate passages from articles I wrote for their journals.

I am particularly grateful for the assistance and authorizations I have received from the librarians or directors of institutions containing Beard materials or correspondence by and to Charles A. Beard. These include the DePauw University Archives; Western History Research Center, University of Wyoming; Yale University; State Historical Society of Wisconsin; Franklin D. Roosevelt Library; and Harry S Truman Library. Quotations from Charles A. Beard's letters to Oswald Garrison Villard are by permission of the Houghton Library, Harvard University.

In the course of my research, I have corresponded with numerous individuals who have supplied valuable leads and information. I want to single out for special thanks Professors Merle Curti and William L. Langer, and Dr. E. Bernard Noble, director of the Historical Office of the Department of State. Finally, I would like to express my gratitude to my mentor, Professor Thomas A. Bailey of Stanford University, for recommending such a challenging topic and for his warm encouragement and judicious advice.

Preface

Following the death of Charles Austin Beard (1874–1948), numerous tributes testified to his formidable influence upon American thought and institutions as a result of his multifaceted career as a historian, political scientist, teacher, educator, and champion of progressive-liberal causes. But Beard's death also occasioned pointed allusions to what had been, in the opinion of some friends as well as hostile critics, a decline in Beard's reputation as "the dean of American historians." As one historian suggested in 1954, "It is indisputable that his prestige was higher ten or twelve years before his death than it has been since."[1]

The fundamental reason for this development may be found in the extent of unfavorable response to Beard's last two volumes on President Franklin D. Roosevelt's conduct of American diplomacy prior to World War II.[2] But his waning prestige also coincided

1. Robert E. Burke, review of Howard K. Beale, ed., *Charles A. Beard: An Appraisal*, hereafter cited as *Beard Appraisal*, in *American Historical Review* 60 (October 1954):116. Full citations of references appear in the Bibliography, which is divided into three main parts. The first is made up of references to Beard's works, subdivided into (1) books, pamphlets, and edited works, and (2) articles, essays, and book reviews. The second contains works referring to or about Beard. The third has general works, including manuscript collections.
2. Charles A. Beard, *American Foreign Policy in the Making, 1932–1940: A Study in Responsibilities*, hereafter cited as *Foreign Policy in the Making*; Beard, *President Roosevelt and the Coming of the War, 1941: A Study in Appearances and Realities*, hereafter cited as *Roosevelt and the War*.

with the period (roughly from 1934 to 1948) when Beard's writings on foreign policy reflected an almost doctrinaire isolationist point of view, or "continentalism," as he preferred to call it.

Most scholars have tended to identify Beard's isolationism only with this period and have further suggested that this was something of an aberration on the part of Beard. That is, during this period, he presumably departed radically from his liberal internationalist outlook of the first three decades of the twentieth century. The generalization has some merit in terms of the volume of Beard's isolationist writings during the last decade and a half of his career. My research, however, uncovered a number of pre-1930s roots and expressions of what became Beard's fully matured isolationism. This was especially evident during the 1920s. But Beard held some beliefs and assumptions prior to World War I that would reappear in, and were consistent with, his isolationist works of the 1930s and after.

This study, then, is an examination of Beard's views on American foreign policy throughout his adult life, including considerations of those persons, ideas, events, and personal experiences that might have shaped his thinking and writing about foreign affairs. But the essential focus is on the last phase of his life, in which I have sought answers to the question of why Beard formulated his thesis of "continentalism," and why he embraced a revisionist interpretation of America's intervention in World War II.

Contents

1. The Formative Years, 1874–1904 / 1

2. Years of Academic Achievement and Controversy, 1904–1914 / 15

3. The War Years, 1914–1919 / 28

4. The Peace Settlement to the Great Depression, 1919–1930 / 40

5. Formulating a Philosophy of Isolationism, 1931–1935 / 58

6. Waging the Cause of Neutrality, 1935–1941 / 78

7. Beard during World War II, 1941–1945 / 105

8. The Efforts to Confirm a Thesis, 1945–1948 / 128

9. Epilogue / 154

Appendix / 169

Bibliography / 175

Index / 193

To BARBARA ANNE
and the children
DOUGLAS, ELIZABETH, DAVID

1

The Formative Years, 1874–1904

CHARLES AUSTIN BEARD, the youngest of the two sons of Mary
Payne and William Henry Harrison Beard, was born on November 27, 1874. The birth site was a modest family farm north of
Knightstown, Indiana, approximately forty miles east of Indianapolis. His forebears came from a long line of English and Scotch-
Irish colonists and included two Pilgrims. By the eighteenth
century, some Beards from Nantucket, Massachusetts, had settled
in North Carolina, with some of their descendants making their
way to Indiana during the nineteenth century.[1]

One of the relatives who might have influenced the development
of Charles Beard's character was his grandfather, Nathan Beard,
who often displayed an independence of mind and action that was
a hallmark of his grandson's career as a scholar, educator, publicist,
and reformer. Though reared in the Quaker faith, for example,
Beard's grandfather rejected a doctrinaire approach to religious
questions, an attitude boldly expressed in his decision to marry a
Methodist. Nathan Beard, who participated in the "underground
railway" of North Carolina which aided runaway slaves in their

1. Peter A. Soderbergh, "Charles A. Beard, the Quaker Spirit, and North
Carolina," p. 19; Paul L. Schmunk, "Charles Austin Beard: A Free Spirit, 1874–
1919," p. 7.

1

flights to freedom,[2] was also a man of courage and humanitarian-
ism, and these traits were conspicuously manifest in Charles Beard's
private and public life.

Beard's father also contributed to what would become a lifelong
concern about encroachments on civil liberties and civil rights.
When a visiting Negro bishop was denied lodging in the local hotel
near Beard's home in Indiana, the elder Beard risked public censure by taking him in as his guest.[3]

Charles Beard's maternal grandmother, Sarah Wilson Payne, died
when he was eight years old. But this formidable frontierswoman
left an indelible imprint on the impressionable youngster. Many
years after her death, Beard nostalgically remembered her as "an
unforgettable apparition" who "knew just what to bring, to do,
and to say in enhancing her mystic powers over my imagination."[4]

The family's antislavery convictions, plus a reluctance to swear
allegiance to the Confederacy, prompted William Henry Harrison
Beard to move from North Carolina to Indiana in 1861. For a time
he worked at a number of odd jobs, including carpentry and teaching in a country school. Three years after his marriage in 1863,
William Beard purchased the farm near Knightstown where the
Beards resided until 1880, when the family moved a short distance
to a sixty-acre farm in the vicinity of a Quaker community in
Spiceland, Indiana. The move was prompted, in part, by the
father's desire to have his children educated at the highly regarded
Spiceland Academy. Simultaneously, he branched out into real
estate speculation and other economic ventures, including management of the Knightstown Bank and a successful building and con-
tracting firm. The senior Beard's success in the marketplace brought
him sufficient wealth to permit "a life of the most pleasing luxury
and ease."[5]

2. Mary R. Beard, *The Making of Charles A. Beard: An Interpretation*, p. 9;
Bernard C. Borning, *The Political and Social Thought of Charles A. Beard*,
pp. xvi–xvii.

3. Eric F. Goldman, *Rendezvous with Destiny: A History of Modern American Reform*, p. 149, hereafter cited as *Rendezvous with Destiny*.

4. C. A. Beard, "An Unforgettable Woman," pp. 8–9, ms., n.d. (probably
1942), in "A Collection of Materials on Charles A. and Mary R. Beard," Microfilm No. 139, DePauw University Archives, hereafter cited as "The Charles A.
Beard File."

5. Soderbergh, "Beard, the Quaker Spirit," p. 21; Schmunk, "Beard: A Free
Spirit," p. 11; M. Beard, *Making of Charles A. Beard*, pp. 10–11.

In his youth, Charles Beard was also able to take advantage of his father's rather good private library. But it was the exposure to his father's gospel of property-conscious conservatism which had the greatest impact on his later scholarly interest in the juxtaposition of economic motives and political behavior as they might affect a nation's domestic and foreign policies. "People ask me," Beard once remarked, "why I emphasize economic questions so much. They should have been present in the family parlor, when my father and his friends gathered to discuss public affairs."[6]

Until his early manhood, Beard's political and social thought —by his own admission—was influenced by a Federalist-Whig-Republican outlook.[7] During his adult life, Beard was variously labeled a Populist, Progressive, Socialist, and Democrat. But while he was in the mainstream of the progressive-liberal tradition of the twentieth century, he was not a partisan in the usual sense. His wife, Mary Ritter Beard, claimed that Charles was not a "party Republican" after their marriage and that they were both "independent politically."[8] This would confirm Beard's penchant for playing the role of a maverick, meting out praise or criticism of any particular political leader, party, or program in keeping with his convictions about those public issues or programs he deemed necessary and desirable to fulfill his vision of America's destiny. The notion of political partisanship, therefore, had no discernable effect upon his analyses of American foreign policy.

Richard Hofstadter observed that Beard's "social criticism is that of a man who belongs, both morally and materially, to the possessing classes" of the United States.[9] Like his father, Beard had a modest stake in the American economy, which included the ownership and management of dairy farms in Connecticut.[10] Thus, as he

6. Quoted in Eric F. Goldman, "Charles A. Beard: An Impression," in Beale, *Beard Appraisal*, p. 2.

7. See, for example, his review of Andrew C. McLaughlin's *Constitutional History of the United States* in *New Republic*, September 15, 1937, p. 163; and C. A. Beard, *The Republic: Conversations on Fundamentals*, pp. 287–88, hereafter cited as *The Republic*. Beard's father was born in 1840, the same year his namesake was elected president on the Whig ticket.

8. M. R. Beard to Merle Curti, March 2, 1952, Curti Papers, Box 5, Folder 3, State Historical Society of Wisconsin.

9. *The Progressive Historians: Turner, Beard, Parrington*, p. 168, hereafter cited as *Progressive Historians*.

10. William Beard, comp., *Charles A. Beard: The Economic Basis of Politics and Related Writings*, p. xi.

became increasingly critical of America's foreign economic involve-
ments by the 1930s, it was not surprising that he would be concerned about the nature of "the American stake abroad."[11]

The nearly two decades Beard spent in a rural environment have
been the source of speculation concerning his possible Jeffersonian-
agrarian outlook. There is the temptation to read into Beard's
thoughts on foreign policy during the 1930s a reversion of sorts to
some of the attitudes that have been ascribed to Middle Western
isolationism. Matthew Josephson, a Connecticut neighbor and frequent guest of the Beards during the 1920s and 1930s, contended
that Beard "came to believe with Jefferson that a life spent close
to the land, producing food, was the better way and gave deeper
satisfaction than urban existence." In 1938, while reminiscing
about his childhood in Indiana, Beard conceded that it was a hard
life, but that it was one that "seems beautiful against the background of wars, hatred, and intolerance of this age; and the best
of the old days I should like to recover for America and for the
world."[12]

Beard undoubtedly had a certain fondness for the rural life which
had nurtured him in his youth. Yet, there is sufficient evidence to
contradict the notion that he had a deep-seated antipathy toward
urban civilization or that he was a constant champion of Thomas
Jefferson's yeoman-farmer ideal. Much of Beard's life was spent in
or near metropolitan centers, and he traveled widely in Europe
and the Orient before the 1930s. He once attributed his cosmo-
politan outlook to these travels, adding, "I feel as much at home
among the headhunters of Formosa and the paving pounders of
Berlin as in the villages of the Middle West."[13] His writings and
activities in municipal administration and reform also suggest that

11. C. A. Beard and George H. E. Smith, *The Idea of National Interest: An
Analytical Study in American Foreign Policy*, pp. 196–310, hereafter cited as
The Idea of National Interest.
12. "Charles A. Beard: A Memoir," p. 590; quoted in Clifton J. Phillips, ed.,
"Charles A. Beard's Recollections of Henry County, Indiana," p. 17. See also
Ray A. Billington, "The Origins of Middle Western Isolationism."
13. Quoted in Fred B. Millett, *Contemporary American Authors*, p. 237.
Charles Beard's daughter, Mrs. Miriam Beard Vagts, informed the author that
her father "bought into a studio cooperative building . . . in New York City
BEFORE we got the farm. He kept this [apartment] until the 1930s. . . . Father
certainly did love that farm [in Sherman, Conn.] (which I now have) and was
enthusiastic about agriculture, but it was not his whole life": Miriam Beard
Vagts to author, February 16, 1971.

he entered enthusiastically into the cultural mainstream of urban civilization. There were instances during his life when he was critical of some of the Populist attacks on the American business system. Beard viewed Jefferson's goal of an agrarian democracy as unrealistic, and took sharp exception to his view of the city as an inherent menace to civilization. "On the contrary," Beard said in the late 1920s, "it is from the urban centers that the national economy of the future will be controlled . . . and it is the culture of urbanism that promises to dominate the future."[14] Summarily, it would be misleading to associate Beard's writings on foreign policy during the last two decades of his life with an ingrained rural provincialism or to label them a reflection of Middle Western isolationism.

Following Beard's graduation from Knightstown Academy in 1892, his father purchased the *Knightstown Banner* for him and his older brother, Clarence, to run. For nearly three years, they cooperated in the management of the newspaper and turned it into a profit-making enterprise. In the spring of 1895, shortly before his twenty-first birthday, Beard enrolled at DePauw University in Greencastle, Indiana, a Methodist-affiliated school. For a time Beard might have contemplated entering the ministry, a possibility suggested by occasional requests for him to speak at local churches on such topics as temperance.[15]

But Beard's attention and conscience were diverted into more secular channels by the domestic and foreign crises through which the nation was moving and by the influence of outstanding teachers at DePauw. During his undergraduate years, Beard's Republican orthodoxy was challenged by the farmer-labor discontent of the 1890s, which he was able to observe directly in the course of a field trip to Chicago in the summer of 1896. On this occasion, he was shocked by the problems stemming from the rapid industrialization and urbanization of the country during the "Gilded Age," problems such as political corruption, low wages, the unsanitary living and working conditions of laborers, and the indifference of many respectable members of the community to the plight of the poor.

14. Quoted in *New York Times*, October 16, 1928, p. 14. See also C. A. Beard, "Jefferson and the New Freedom"; Luther Gulick, "Beard and Municipal Reform," in *Beard Appraisal*, pp. 47–60.

15. W. Beard, *Charles A. Beard*, p. xii; Schmunk, "Beard: A Free Spirit," p. 35; C. J. Phillips, "The Indiana Education of Charles A. Beard," p. 5.

In Chicago, the first stirrings of Beard's reform impulse were generated by visits to Jane Addams' Hull House, where he could hear prominent spokesmen for various programs aimed at adjusting American society to the new industrial order, and where he could participate in heated discussions between Populists and Socialists.[16]

Beard's undergraduate years were also bracketed by the war crises —one with Great Britain in 1895 over her boundary dispute with Venezuela, and another, the Spanish-American War in 1898. Opportunities for publicly expressing his opinions on both foreign and domestic affairs were afforded by his editorship in 1897–98 of the college paper, the *DePauw Palladium*. A few months before the Cuban crisis ended in war between the United States and Spain, Beard justified American meddling in foreign affairs by stressing the importance of our vital commercial relations with Europe, regardless of the noninterventionist principle embodied in what he called the "antiquated" Monroe Doctrine. Similarly, he did not object to American diplomatic pressures against Spain in the spring of 1898. As was true of many Americans, he was impelled by idealism to sympathize with the Cuban people. After war was declared, however, Beard wondered aloud, "How an intelligent rational man can be for war with all its dire consequences is beyond comprehension . . . it is a gory path to glory." Two weeks later, he noted with apparent satisfaction that the earlier campus enthusiasm for the war had subsided. He added that only if the war began to go badly for the United States should students contemplate fighting for the country. Indeed, shortly after his graduation that spring, he and a DePauw classmate volunteered for military service, only to be turned away because of a surfeit of men in the army.[17]

In view of Beard's well-known criticisms of war and imperialism after he became an established scholar, this minor episode in his life has inspired a number of generalizations about the impact it had upon him. Samuel Eliot Morison ventured the opinion that Beard's aversion to war, his tendency to minimize its results, and his ridiculing of military men were mainly a result of this experi-

16. Goldman, *Rendezvous with Destiny*, p. 150; Hofstadter, *Progressive Historians*, pp. 170–71; Schmunk, "Beard: A Free Spirit," p. 59; Phillips, "Indiana Education," p. 2.

17. Schmunk, "Beard: A Free Spirit," pp. 54–55; Phillips, "Indiana Education," pp. 13–14; Hofstadter, *Progressive Historians*, p. 171.

ence. Mary Beard suggested that it was about this time that "[William Jennings] Bryan's anti-imperialism took root in Beard's soul." Beard himself, in an allusion to the meat-poisoning scandals in the Quartermaster Corps during the Spanish-American War, once quipped, "They wouldn't take us. They had more men than they had embalmed beef." Two years before his death in 1948, Beard told Arthur M. Schlesinger that he "left the G.O.P. on imperialism in 1900 and . . . found no home anywhere since that year."[18]

But is it possible that, many years after the events, Beard and others may have magnified and overly dramatized the immediate effect upon him of the Spanish-American War and America's acquisition of an overseas empire? However critical he might have been of militarism and the involvement of the United States in particular wars, Beard was not a pacifist in a philosophical or religious sense.[19] As will be noted shortly, more than two years after the annexation of the Philippines, Beard was not unalterably opposed to the *idea* of imperialism.

Unquestionably, Beard's personal observations of, and direct involvement in, some of the nation's domestic and foreign issues from 1895 to 1898 were made more meaningful through his contact with DePauw professor of political science James Riley Weaver, who served as a catalyst to Beard's mind and a gadfly to his conscience. It was Weaver who introduced Beard to *The Federalist* and the works of John Stuart Mill, Karl Marx, and John Ruskin. In the study of economics, politics, and diplomacy, Weaver could also draw upon his experiences from 1869 to 1895 as an American consul at Brindisi, Italy, Antwerp, and Vienna. In light of Beard's subsequent preoccupation with the subjective factors that enter into the historian's writing of history, it is of more than passing interest that Weaver's instruction stressed the presence of class, religious, political, and economic biases in public affairs.[20]

18. Samuel Eliot Morison, "Did Roosevelt Start the War? History Through a Beard," p. 91; M. Beard, *Making of Charles A. Beard*, p. 15; quoted in Hubert Herring, "Charles A. Beard: Freelance among the Historians," p. 642; quoted in Hofstadter, *Progressive Historians*, p. 171n3.
19. More than four months before his death on September 1, 1948, Beard expressed annoyance over a remark in *Newsweek* magazine that "sets me down as an old-time 'pacifist.' I have been many things," he added, "but never a pacifist or any other kind of absolutist"; Beard to George Morgenstern, April 11, 1948, Morgenstern Papers, Western History Research Center, University of Wyoming Library.
20. Merle Curti, "A Great Teacher's Teacher," pp. 264–66.

After earning his Ph.B. from DePauw University in June 1898, Beard received financial aid and encouragement from his father to undertake the study of English history at Oxford University. In close association with Frederick York Powell, Regius Professor of Medieval and Modern History, Beard was thoroughly grounded in the theory of the Teutonic origins of Anglo-American constitutional government. He was also exposed to the German seminar methods inspired by Leopold von Ranke and exemplified in the writings of the British constitutional historian William Stubbs. In addition, he read widely in the works of most of the major English historians, such as Carlyle, Macaulay, Maitland, Freeman, and Buckle.[21]

Of more immediate significance than the formal aspects of Beard's graduate study in England was his intimate contact with the leaders and reform activities of the British trade union movement, cooperative societies, temperance organizations, and the Fabian Society. His most notable achievement during this period of his life was his establishment, with the help of Kansas socialist Walter Vrooman, of Ruskin Hall, a college for the laboring class at Oxford University. Beard suggested that the college be named after John Ruskin, a famous English art critic. This was a result of the fact that, after 1860, Ruskin trenchantly attacked the prevailing doctrines of laissez-faire economics, acquisitive values, and social abuses of industrialism in Great Britain. Ruskin's humanistic credo was set forth persuasively in *Unto This Last: Four Essays on the First Principles of Political Economy* (1862), a slender volume which Beard is said to have carried around with him for many years as an inspiration. Beard served as director of the Ruskin Hall Extension Service, contributed articles to the Ruskin Hall periodical, *Young Oxford*, and lectured extensively in such industrial centers as London, Liverpool, Manchester, and Birmingham.[22]

Most of Beard's lectures and published writings in connection with his Ruskin Hall activities were directed largely to the prob-

21. Burleigh T. Wilkins, "Frederick York Powell and Charles A. Beard: A Study in Anglo-American Historiography and Social Thought"; Max Lerner, "Charles Beard's Political Theory," in *Beard Appraisal*, pp. 26–27.
22. Harlan B. Phillips, "Charles Beard, Walter Vrooman, and the Founding of Ruskin Hall," hereafter cited as "Beard and Vrooman"; B. T. Wilkins, ed., "Charles A. Beard on the Founding of Ruskin Hall"; Roger Stein, *John Ruskin and Aesthetic Thought in America, 1840–1900*, pp. 259–60; H. B. Phillips, "Charles Beard: The English Lectures, 1899–1901."

lem of ameliorating the lot of the working man in England. Yet, some of his analyses and recommendations were soon to be applicable to society in the United States. As was true of many contemporary American reformers, Beard "assumed that an international industrial revolution had made both America and England similar so that diagnosis and therapy for one patient applied as a matter of course to the other."[23]

Beard also began to formulate at this time a few principles of international relations which would be incorporated into some of his writings before he adopted an isolationist viewpoint during the 1930s. He was impressed, for example, with the way in which international trade and finance seemed to promote the economic and political interdependence of the world, accompanied by the prospect of a downgrading of nationalism. In a revised edition of *The Industrial Revolution*, Beard maintained that "the ties of patriotism, racial and national, are being snapped asunder in the stress of profit-making."[24]

Residing in a country which possessed an extensive colonial empire, Beard understandably reflected upon the nature of imperialism. His interest in the subject probably was enhanced by the recent territorial acquisitions of the United States in the Pacific and Caribbean. With the passage of time, he would refer to this episode as part of an "imperialist racket." In 1901, however, he suggested that imperialism might have benign aspects. "In the broader and truer sense," he observed, "Imperialism is the world-creating process." If it was wrong, "then history since the beginning of time, and especially since the beginning of the seventeenth century, has been wrong, a mistake to be deplored." Pointing to the founding of the United States as one consequence of this imperialism, he asked, "Is their existence to be regretted?" He answered, "The average, rational, healthy man who does not suffer from Imperial word-phobia will agree that the imperialism which produced the United States and the colonies is good."[25]

Beard did concede that there were some individuals engaged in international commerce and finance who, for their own "self-aggrandizement and self-enrichment," had corrupted the more con-

23. Arthur Mann, "British Social Thought and American Reformers of the Progressive Era," pp. 689–90, 691.
24. Pages 52, 88–89.
25. C. A. Beard, "A Living Empire. I," p. 24.

structive aspects of imperialism. In particular, he lamented the fact that imperialism was not being undertaken in such a way as to redound to the ethical credit of the colonizing nations. Clearly anticipating his lifelong concern about the close connection between domestic and foreign policies, he believed that unenlightened imperialism flowed from the failure of imperial nations to resolve many of their domestic social and economic problems.[26]

One of Beard's more fascinating proposals for imperial nations engaged in "world-creating activities" proceeded from the assumption of Anglo-Saxon superiority. Members of the white race, he suggested, should guard against a drastically declining birth rate at home. As a corollary, he would not sanction miscegenation and integration in the colonial system he envisioned. Nevertheless, and possibly with the American suppression of the Filipino rebellion in mind, he would tolerate "no murder, no brutality, no outrages" against subject peoples "which degrade the survivors and hurl the world downward toward brutedom." In a more positive vein, he argued that, if the imperial nations could. establish proper priorities in solving their own economic, social, political, and educational problems, then "vast settlements from various white countries would be transplanted, not as individuals, but as communities, over the rich plains of northern and central Asia and southern South America, while the United States and England would use the same methods in distributing needed population over the great western plains of America and of South Australia and South Africa."[27]

Beard interrupted his sojourn in England for about one year, from 1899 to 1900, during which time he enrolled in a semester of graduate study under Moses Coit Tyler at Cornell University. In March 1900, Beard married a former classmate at DePauw, Mary Ritter of Indianapolis. That summer, during their honeymoon in Europe, the newlyweds took walks through the German countryside. By the time Beard was prepared to resume his Ruskin Hall activities in England, he was, according to Eric F. Goldman, "amused at the pretensions of German professors and fuming at Prussian soldiers who forced him into the gutter rather than share

26. Ibid., p. 25; C. A. Beard, "A Living Empire. II," p. 39.
27. "A Living Empire. II," pp. 39–43.

the sidewalk."[28] These experiences may well have colored Beard's vigorous denunciations of Prussian militarism during World War I.

In the course of his second stint in England, Beard wrote his first book, *The Industrial Revolution*, originally published in 1901, with a corrected edition in 1902. A tone of righteous indignation permeates the volume, as Beard protested throughout against the inefficiency and human costs in the economic affairs of an industrialized society. Offsetting the severe moral indictments was a note of optimism. This optimism, wedded to the idea of progress, was characteristic of Beard's temperament throughout his life. However great his sense of outrage over particular domestic or foreign policies, however severe his censure of certain groups or individuals, he was unwilling to resign himself for any length of time to total pessimism or despair. With very few exceptions, he consistently believed that rational, humane men and women could shape the vast potential of machine technology to bring about a beneficent material and spiritual transformation in which each individual, "in seeking the fullest satisfaction of his own nature . . . will harmoniously perform his function as a member of a corporate society" (pp. 104–5).

The nature of Beard's activities in England seemed to establish, or at least foreshadow, a pattern that was evident in much of his later career. This pattern, or life style, was one in which the potential tensions and contradictions between the life of the activist reformer and the life of the contemplative scholar were never fully resolved. "Even in his Oxford days," Richard Hofstadter has penetratingly observed, "we can see in him an uncomfortable duality that was always to haunt him—a duality between the aseptic ideal of scientific inquiry and his social passions."[29]

In pursuing his studies, Beard aspired to that quality of emotional detachment which Professor Frederick York Powell deemed vital to scholarship. At the same time, he was keenly aware of the more than fine distinction between the historian and the pamphleteer or publicist. In an article for the *Young Oxford* evaluating William Cobbett's contribution to the cooperative movement in England, Beard admitted that he did not "intend to pose as an

28. M. Beard, *Making of Charles A. Beard*, p. 20; Goldman, *Rendezvous with Destiny*, p. 150.
29. *Progressive Historians*, p. 178.

historian; for it is his duty to leave ethics alone. . . . I am not," he added, "going to attempt the obviously impossible task of making an impartial and dispassionate judgment of [Cobbett's] character." In a passage which might be viewed as an unintentional forerunner of his writings of the 1930s on historical relativism, in which he argued that the historian selected those facts which were in keeping with the particular social purpose he had in mind, Beard wrote, "I will take from his life and works such examples as will serve to guide us in shaping our own personalities in such a way as to contribute to the moral and social power of the race."[30]

Beard might have been able to resolve the sort of duality Hofstadter detected had he chosen to remain in England. This was a prospect which Beard and his wife considered, briefly, but seriously, owing in part to their affection for the country and people. But the possibility of becoming an expatriate might have been encouraged because of the favorable impression he made upon some prominent labor leaders. Ramsay MacDonald, for example, is reported to have asked him to serve in the cabinet of a Labor government, which he confidently expected to be a reality in the very near future.[31]

In early 1902, however, the Beards reluctantly decided to return to the United States. Perhaps, as one student of Beard's Ruskin Hall venture has suggested, the young reformer had become impatient with his failure to achieve immediate and dramatic success in his effort "to marshall mankind in one mighty crusade against ignorance."[32] On the other hand, maybe the scholarly impulse had not been adequately satiated, an impulse which had been a primary motive in his decision to go to England in 1898.

By continuing his graduate studies at Columbia University, Beard's quest for more knowledge and further professional training were more than amply satisfied, for this was the "golden age of the Columbia Faculty of Political Science."[33] He was thus afforded an

30. C. A. Beard, "Men Who Have Helped Us. I: William Cobbett, Friend of Man," p. 172. For Beard's most well known expressions on the theory of historical relativism, see "Written History as an Act of Faith," and "That Noble Dream."

31. Wilkins, "Beard on the Founding of Ruskin Hall," p. 284; Alexander Ware, "The Beards, Chroniclers of the Times," p. 5; Goldman, *Rendezvous with Destiny*, pp. 150–51.

32. H. Phillips, "Beard and Vrooman," p. 191.

33. Arthur Macmahon, "Charles Beard, the Teacher," in *Beard Appraisal*, p. 225.

opportunity to study under and work with such renowned authorities in public, constitutional, and international law as Frank J. Goodnow, John W. Burgess, and John Bassett Moore. He did not long adhere to the Teutonic theory of the evolution of Anglo-Saxon political institutions embraced by these scholars. But other professors, in whose seminars he enrolled, encouraged him to strike out in new directions of historical inquiry during what has been characterized as "the revolt against formalism" in many disciplines before World War I.[34] These professors included James Harvey Robinson and his "New History" school of historiography and E. R. A. Seligman with his emphasis on the economic interpretation of history.

Shortly after enrolling for the spring semester in 1902, Beard distinguished himself by winning the George William Curtis Fellowship for his prize essay, "The Present Duty of Every American." The general principles which he believed should guide each American citizen "in the discharge of his civic responsibilities" included a brief consideration of foreign affairs. The Spanish-American War had altered the nature and scope of America's international relations, especially in foreign commerce. "Never again," he asserted, "can the United States assume the isolated position which was once held to be the national destiny." Echoing a theme in his *Young Oxford* articles on imperialism, he added that "the coming race struggle for the planet will force the United States into the assumption of new obligations." These would "involve perils and difficulties," and "public intelligence and courage . . . of a high order" were necessary to avoid such perils as corruption and the "usurpation of power" in government. Moreover, the "proper fulfillment" of America's "delicate task of governing alien dependents" had to be carried out with a "clear appreciation of the fact that the standards and institutions of our civilization are only relatively good, and ought not and cannot be arbitrarily forced upon alien people."[35]

Beard received his master's degree in political science in 1903 for a thesis on Civil Service reform. The next year he was awarded his doctorate. His published dissertation, *The Office of the Justice of the Peace in England in Its Origins and Development* (1904),

34. Morton G. White, *Social Thought in America: The Revolt against Formalism.*
35. C. A. Beard, "The Present Duty of Every American."

represented the culmination of the formal training received, and the research begun, in England, when he examined county records bearing on the powers and functions of this office.

At the age of thirty, Beard stood on the threshold of a multiple career as a teacher, political scientist, historian, and reformer. This was a career that would exercise a tremendous influence on the study and teaching of American history and politics. In reaching this plateau, his family background, education, and activities in England implanted in him a number of convictions and traits which he retained throughout his life. Notably, Beard had demonstrated an ambivalence toward the requirements of detached scholarship and committed reformism. In addition, he had outlined in broad terms his vision for the American future, namely, the ideal of what he would one day term a "collectivist democracy."[36] Both of these early developments would subsequently figure prominently in his writings about American foreign policy.

36. "Written History as an Act of Faith," p. 228.

2

Years of Academic Achievement and Controversy, 1904-1914

C HARLES A. BEARD's appointment in 1904 as a Lecturer in History at Columbia University inaugurated a distinguished thirteen-year association with an institution that was one of the outstanding intellectual centers of the nation during the Progressive Era. Beard himself became one of the "galaxy of teachers" who adorned the faculty of the college on Morningside Heights in New York City. To employ the felicitous phrase of Richard Hofstadter, Beard's "energies of demonic intensity" resulted in a prodigious publication record and participation in manifold reform activities, particularly in municipal administration and reform. These achievements were more than matched by his outstanding skills as an orator (the fruition, perhaps, of extensive debating experience even before he went to England) and his consistent popularity as a teacher.[1]

This period was marked also by writings and activities that continued to underscore the tensions between Beard's desire to be a

1. Irwin Edman, *Philosopher's Holiday*, pp. 129–31; Arthur E. Soderlind, "Charles A. Beard and the Social Studies," p. 28; Hofstadter, *Progressive Historians*, p. 292; R. Gordon Hoxie et al., *A History of the Faculty of Political Science, Columbia University*, p. 84; Josephson, "Charles A. Beard: A Memoir," pp. 585–86; Macmahon, "Charles Beard, the Teacher," in *Beard Appraisal*, pp. 213–30.

dispassionate scholar and his inclination toward passionate involvement in public affairs. The result was that he gained a reputation which he would carry through life, as a person who could both generate controversy, and be the object of it, in assessing the past, present, and future of American civilization.

At this time, he began to delineate those who would continue to be the principal targets of his sometimes devastatingly sarcastic criticism. These included advocates of rugged individualism and laissez-faire economics, abstract theorists of political behavior, and, during the last decade of his career, proponents of extensive American involvement in world affairs. The essential style of Beard as a controversialist has been described as that of one who "was truculently confident and self-assertive. The thesis he attacked was not merely disproved: it was shredded, and stamped upon, and its proponents exhibited by implication as fools and knaves."[2] But consistent with his graduate training and research in both England and the United States, Beard, while at Columbia, frequently revealed his attachment to the ideals of objectivity, to the eschewing of moral judgments, and to temperateness of language in the writing of history.[3]

During the decade after he received his doctorate, Beard showed an increasing interest in the theoretical and practical aspects of international affairs. The bulk of his published work relating to this topic dealt with the historical and contemporary diplomacy of European nations. In his general studies of American history and politics, however, a few noteworthy interpretations of American foreign policy appeared. Some of the themes briefly considered during this period, such as America's foreign trade, national defense, and the diplomatic powers of the president, would, of course, take on heightened importance and increased space in his writings from the 1930s until his death.

Through his provocative, revisionist study of the American Constitution in 1913, Beard became prominently identified in academic and public circles with the economic interpretation of history. But many years before this, he had begun tentatively to formulate his thinking on the influence of economic factors in shaping foreign and domestic affairs and the interaction between the two. Thus,

2. Peter R. Levin, "Charles A. Beard: Wayward Liberal," p. 36.
3. Merle Curti, "Beard as Historical Critic," in *Beard Appraisal*, pp. 186–200.

in a lecture course on American expansion, which he offered in 1904, his students were advised that "The territorial expansion resulting from the Spanish-American war and the recent unprecedented development of foreign commerce have brought new and important problems before the people of the United States and stimulated their interest in international affairs. The relation of these new issues to domestic policies promises to become of increasing concern. A necessity has therefore been created for a careful consideration of imperial questions apart from party politics."[4] The course itself was designed to show that these events were not unique in American history, since American involvement in world affairs "has always extended as far as American interests." The "unprecedented commercial development of the decade before the Spanish war prepared the way for the American invasion" of Cuba and the Philippines. The connection between imperialism and industrial nations with surplus goods and capital also was to be covered. The inclusion of John Hobson's *Imperialism: A Study* (1901) in a general bibliography, with the remark that it made "short work of many current fallacies," suggested an important source of Beard's emphasis on an economic interpretation of imperialism at this early date.[5]

There were no comments in the course syllabus to indicate that Beard strenuously objected to America's overseas empire and expansion of foreign trade, or that he regarded them as necessarily contrary to America's national interest. But similar to his remarks about imperialism in the previous two years, he indicated his concern that the expansionist thrust might have unfavorable consequences for the country. Among these consequences were an increasing war spirit and the providing of "certain classes" with an opportunity to divert the nation's attention from "problems of national life" that were "of greater importance than the mission of civilization."[6] Thus, three decades before he consistently and vigorously espoused an isolationist position, Beard had reflected briefly upon some of the major arguments which he would use to buttress that position.

Further encouragement for Beard to apply an economic interpretation to foreign affairs came from two studies of the French Revo-

4. *Syllabus on the Expansion of the United States*, p. 2.
5. Ibid., pp. 2, 12.
6. Ibid., p. 13.

lution by the French Socialist scholars Gabriel Deville and Jean Juarès. In a lengthy book review in 1906, Beard agreed with the authors that "the fundamental force in history is economic," but he praised them for not reducing "the complex phenomena of social life . . . to an economic formula. . . . Thus restricted," he added, "the economic interpretation of history will doubtless be accepted by most scholars who avowedly aim at objectivity, though they may not agree that the historian should assume the duties of an ethical teacher—for when he undertakes such a function, he usually degenerates into a partisan."[7]

Beard, nonetheless, was disappointed that Juarès had not made his economic thesis relevant to the causes of the wars of the French Revolution. Rather, he had "fallen into the habit of those historians who imagine that history can be written from diplomatic notes and parliamentary speeches," by stressing such things as treaty guarantees between England and France and France's revolutionary propaganda. Far more vital in Beard's mind were the previous one hundred years of "determined struggle for colonial and commercial dominion" between the two nations.[8]

Later that same year, in a book of readings on English history, Beard wrote that "the international politics of Europe for the last three centuries can be understood solely in the light of the economic interests engendered in the race for markets and territorial dominion." He conceded that the urge for colonization included political and religious motives, but that "the main impulse in the work of colonization was economic." In addition, the domestic politics of every contemporary European country were "complicated by questions involved in securing new markets for manufacturers and new areas for the profitable investment of capital."[9]

In the two-volume college text *The Development of Modern Europe: An Introduction to the Study of Current History* (1907, 1908), written with his Columbia colleague James Harvey Robinson, the stress upon the economic factor in contemporary international relations was even more pronounced. This work was also unique in the deliberate effort of the authors to break with the

7. "A Socialist History of France." The books reviewed were G. Deville, *Histoire socialiste: du 9 thermidor au 18 brumaire,* and J. Juarès, *Histoire socialiste jusqu'au 9 thermidor,* 4 vols.
    8. Ibid., p. 116.
    9. *An Introduction to the English Historians,* pp. 423, 429, 623.

tradition of the historical guild, which held that the proper concern of the historian was the remote past, unconnected with the present. Explaining the basic tenets of the "New History" in the introduction, Beard and Robinson indicated that their primary interest had been to enable the reader to understand the present and, implicitly, improve it through an examination of the recent past. In pursuit of this goal, they emphasized that, while much less space was devoted "to purely political and military events" than was customary in histories of the nineteenth century, they had treated generously the "more fundamental economic matters," such as the Industrial Revolution, commerce, and colonization.[10]

In their treatment of these economic matters, Beard and Robinson claimed that two powerful forces—factories seeking markets and capital seeking investment—were "shaping the foreign and commercial policies of every important European country. *They alone explain* why the great industrial nations are embarking on what has been termed a policy of 'imperialism,' which means a policy of adding distant territories for the purpose of controlling their products, getting the trade with the natives, and investing money in the development of natural resources."[11]

Given their conviction that the international rivalries for colonies in the preceding two centuries had been the major cause of constant warfare, the two scholars expressed apprehension about the possible fruits of this continuing process of colonization into the twentieth century. They noted that the seemingly inexorable necessity for industrial nations to pursue policies of imperialism resulted in their development of large military and naval establishments beyond the requirements of national defense. The resulting armaments race, involving increasingly sophisticated weapons, had enhanced the risk and potential destruction of warfare. Moreover, the tremendous cost of maintaining huge standing armies and navies was draining away resources vital to improving the social and economic condition of the masses in each country. They, nonetheless, placed their faith in the possibility that these costly instruments of death and devastation might serve as a deterrent to warfare as statesmen came to recognize that all nations would suffer greatly from their use. Indeed, even those who had a role in pro-

10. 1:iii–iv.
11. Ibid., 2:328, 366 (italics added).

moting imperialism, including the "financial interests," had a stake in avoiding the disastrous effects of international conflict upon trade and industry. Accordingly, the authors optimistically believed that such interests were using their influence in the "movement for the peaceful settlement of international disputes and the reduction of armaments."[12]

The latter idea was an updating of Beard's belief, fostered when he was in England, that international trade and finance could reduce national rivalries and promote a spirit of cooperation that would minimize the risk of war between civilized industrial nations. It was also a view of international affairs which commanded the support of many thoughtful American businessmen in the decade or so before World War I.[13] Augmenting Beard's own conviction that the world was a "great economic unity"[14] was his faith in the potentialities of science and technology in furthering international amity. "So far as our political economy is concerned," he said in a 1908 lecture, "Japan is as much a part of the United States as Oregon." He thought that steam and electricity might be able to achieve "what neither the armies, nor the law, nor the faith of Rome could accomplish—that unity of mankind which rests on the expansion of a common consciousness of rights and wrongs through the extension of identical modes of economic activity."[15]

Beard's general acceptance of the idea that foreign commercial activities might be a positive force for peace clearly illustrated his optimism and his belief in progress. This thesis implicitly maintains that rational men of good will will pursue rational goals, particularly when their economic self-interest is involved. Distinctively characteristic of most of Beard's historical analyses, this thesis may account, in part, for his tendency to give inadequate weight to chance, ideas, individuals, and even irrational behavior in shaping or defining the course of history. Certainly, he was aware of these forces and occasionally went out of his way to note their

12. Ibid., 1:80, 2:367–69.

13. C. Roland Marchand, *The American Peace Movement and Social Reform, 1898–1918*, pp. 74–98.

14. Review of Achille Viallate, ed., *La Vie politique dans les deux mondes*, in *Political Science Quarterly* 24 (March 1909):165.

15. *Politics: A Lecture Delivered at Columbia University in the Series on Science, Philosophy, and Art*, p. 30.

importance, especially during the latter years of his life. But his writings seldom reflected a consistent and balanced presentation of these factors. The general framework within which his historical evaluations were made rested upon a rationalist interpretation of economic behavior.

Beard could be ambivalent in his view of the role of economic motivation in history. In the Robinson and Beard volumes, for example, their analysis of imperialism had a pronounced deterministic thrust. Manufacturers, merchants, and financiers were depicted as having to support expansionist policies owing to the necessities of an economic system which required foreign outlets for surplus goods and investment capital. Economic behavior was thus presented as essentially a matter of compulsion rather than of rational choice.

It was not until 1913 that Beard's ambivalence in interpreting economic behavior would significantly appear in a major work on American history, *An Economic Interpretation of the Constitution of the United States*.[16] Until that time, a substantial portion of his published work dealt with European civilization, with much of it to be found in numerous book reviews on British, French, and German history and contemporary politics. From 1905 to 1909, he compiled, with his Columbia colleagues Alvin Johnson and Carleton J. H. Hayes, a semiannual survey of world affairs in the *Political Science Quarterly*. Beard was responsible for the sections on foreign events.[17]

In some of his book reviews, as well as in his comments in the survey of world affairs, Beard demonstrated a keen appreciation of the actual or potential conflict inherent in rivalries for trade

16. Many scholars have commented on this aspect of Beard's study of the Constitution. Major critiques are summarized in Lee Benson, *Turner and Beard: American Historical Writing Reconsidered*. Benson attributes the ambivalence, or dualism, in Beard's thought to his failure to make a sufficient distinction between James Madison's "economic determinist theory of politics" in *Federalist No. 10* and E. R. A. Seligman's explanation of "the economic interpretation of history" in a book of the same title published in 1902. Madison's view of the sources of political conflict, Benson points out, rested on the assumption that human nature is static in a changing environment. Seligman's theory, on the other hand, was a more open-ended system in which free will could operate in a larger framework of environmental forces. In short, Beard did not deal squarely with the perhaps unresolvable dilemma of compulsion versus choice (Benson, pp. 96–109).

17. Alvin Johnson, *Pioneer's Progress: An Autobiography*, pp. 155–56.

and colonies. He often reflected upon the workings of the European power alignments that had been developing since the 1890s, but did not seem to regard them as unduly provocative, and, on at least one occasion, appeared to be skeptical of the relative importance of the Alliance System as it affected world affairs for good or ill. When he reviewed a book on Franco-German relations in 1907, for example, Beard faulted the author for his lack of impartiality and for his careful selection of statistical data. But his most biting criticism was directed at the author's presumptuousness in predicting that an increased rapprochement among Russia, France, and Great Britain would encircle Imperial Germany which, in turn, might increase the prospect of hostilities. "Whether [this] thesis is a prophecy or delusion," Beard wrote, "the future alone can decide."[18]

The future seemed at hand the following year when the Austrian annexation of Bosnia and Herzegovina in October 1908 touched off a diplomatic crisis that created consternation in the foreign offices of all the major European capitals. Notwithstanding the rashness of Austria's act, Beard noted in an essay for the Association for International Conciliation that the act did not lead to the military clash that might have been expected. "The governments of all the great nations," he observed, "took a judicial attitude." This restraint, which owed much to the understandings among England, France, and Russia, "conclusively demonstrated their realization of the responsibilities resting upon the power making the first belligerent move." Because of this realization, "no country is willing to take the huge risk of plunging Europe into war."[19]

Beard did not think it important to speculate as to whether this admirable display of prudent statesmanship was due to a concern for economic interests, the fear of war itself, a belief in the folly of war, or the reluctance of Europe's leaders to incur the blame for making a decision in which the "hasty action on the part of some minor power . . . might bring on a local conflict whose larger implications could scarcely be apprehended." It was sufficient, he believed, that moderation and good sense had prevailed during the negotiations that (temporarily, as it turned out) resolved rivalry between nations over the Balkans. "This happy escape from crisis,"

18. Review of Victor Bérard, *La France et Guillaume II*, in *American Historical Review* 12 (July 1907):897.
19. *European Sobriety in the Presence of the Balkan Crisis*, pp. 9–10.

he concluded, "may be deemed a triumph for the cause of peace."[20] Like many men and women of good will on both sides of the Atlantic, Beard simply did not want to accept the grim prospect of Western civilization tearing itself apart over quarrels that could be settled by reason and conciliation.

Soon after this essay appeared, Beard published his first extensive analysis of American political history, *American Government and Politics*, supplemented by a book of readings. The first edition of this highly successful college text appeared in 1910 and went through ten editions before Beard's death. Devoted principally to a survey of domestic political institutions and practices, he included a chapter on American foreign relations that touched briefly upon a number of topics that would be of vital concern to him in the 1930s and 1940s.

In both the text and volume of readings, Beard stressed the commanding position of the president as the only official of the government "authorized to speak with authority for the United States on the conduct of foreign affairs." The diplomatic functions of the president as explicitly set forth in the Constitution were noted. But, in the text, Beard forcefully argued and illustrated the point that the president's "real achievements are not set by the letter of the law." Rather, they are "determined . . . by his personality, the weight of his influence, his capacity for managing men, and the strength and effectiveness of the party forces behind him."[21]

As early as 1910, Beard was anxious that these inherent presidential powers be exercised in a responsible fashion, and he would eventually demonstrate this feeling in his criticisms of Franklin D. Roosevelt's dynamic role in directing American foreign policy. The president, he observed, had the implied constitutional authority to make executive agreements with other nations which, for at least his term of office, were as binding as a treaty. Polk's diplomacy toward Mexico and McKinley's diplomacy during the Cuban crisis were briefly considered to dramatize the point that the president could dispatch troops and ships without specific congressional authority, and could do this in a way that might provoke war. In time of war, Beard concluded, "the President, having possession of the military power, can readily close the courts in any district

20. Ibid., pp. 7, 10–11, 13–14.
21. *Readings in American Government and Politics*, p. 183; *American Government and Politics*, pp. 187, 344.

. . . and as a matter of fact, a practically absolute power must be vested in the commander-in-chief."[22]

Beard continued to regard the Spanish-American War as an extremely significant event, which, because of the subsequent expansion of America's foreign commerce, "was drawing us more and more into the current of world politics." Contrary to the widely held view, however, this did not constitute a violation of the alleged "splendid isolation" of the United States "from the rest of the powers of the world." The frequent, vigorous military and diplomatic defense of America's commercial interests since the administration of George Washington refuted the claim that we had enjoyed a truly isolated position with respect to other nations in Europe and Asia.[23]

American power had been a key factor in challenging a policy of true isolationism. "It is sufficient to say," Beard remarked, "that we have been a world power, as far as has been necessary, from the beginning of our history. In a word, the protection of our government has steadily advanced with the extension of our material interests, and the foreign policy of the last ten years is no breach of our historical development." He predicted that the continued safeguarding of newly acquired commercial interests in the Far East might require occasional military cooperation with foreign powers, as during the Boxer Rebellion at the turn of the century. Consequently, "no political doctrines with regard to our independence from the rest of the world are strong enough to overcome those material and moral forces which are linking our destinies to the world at large."[24]

The question of the extent of America's military establishment had taken on greater urgency and dimensions in the wake of the Spanish-American War. The protection of overseas dependencies and the increase in our foreign trade seemed to require a "rapid increase in expenditures for warlike preparations." Although this would appear to contradict "a strong tradition in the United States that we are preeminently a peaceful people," Beard thought otherwise. Somewhat wryly he noted that Americans usually had pointed "with pity to the nations of Europe staggering under their enormous military burdens." Distinguishing the appearances from the

22. *American Government and Politics*, pp. 196–97, 354.
23. Ibid., pp. 330–31.
24. Ibid., pp. 331–33.

realities, Beard deftly presented the following statistics: 41 per cent of all the federal revenues for fiscal year 1908 had been spent on the army, navy, and fortifications; 31 per cent of all revenue went for pensions, interest, and other charges stemming from past wars.[25]

Consistent with his earlier expressions of concern about military expenditures which diverted funds from domestic projects, Beard was not encouraged by this trend. Nevertheless, in a balanced analysis, he set forth the arguments of those who endorsed these increased outlays for the army and navy. Indeed, in his discussion of Theodore Roosevelt's message to Congress in December 1907, Beard did not find fault with the president's "pointing out that in every foreign war which we have waged an enormous cost in men and money could have been avoided, if in time of peace we had taken wise precautions to maintain the regular army at a high standard of efficiency."[26]

A similar tendency on the part of Beard not to object to Theodore Roosevelt's boldness in foreign policy matters may be inferred from his first major survey in American history, *Contemporary American History, 1877–1913* (1914).[27] Since the volume appeared shortly after his controversial study on the Constitution, it probably attracted more scholarly commentary than was normally given to a college text. Like his early work on European history with James Harvey Robinson, however, the methodological approach Beard employed was another reason for the acclaim and criticism with which it was received. "In its quiet way," Morton White contends, this book "helped shape the historical imagination of the coming generation. It drew the picture which became a religious icon to the readers of the *New Republic* and *The Nation* and which later was adopted by the *New Masses* after it had been slightly retouched."[28]

In the preface to the aforementioned survey, Beard said he was planning to treat matters which seemed "important from the modern point of view." Though he confessed that his account was "impressionistic," he had "endeavored to be accurate and fair" (p. v). One reviewer suggested, however, that Beard's interpretations were colored by the intellectual climate of the reform move-

---

25. Ibid., p. 355.
26. Ibid., pp. 356–57.
27. Pages 279–81, hereafter cited as *Contemporary American History*.
28. White, *American Social Thought*, pp. 32–33.

ment.[29] In his treatment of certain domestic and foreign issues, Beard reflected two of the characteristics of the Progressive mind delineated by Richard Hofstadter: a compulsion to expose and an ambiguity about the motives of human behavior.[30]

In his most detailed analysis of the causes of the Spanish-American War to date, Beard mentioned the idealistic impulses and crusading zeal of the American people in regard to Spain's treatment of the Cuban people. Yet, a few pages earlier he had remarked somewhat cynically, "Contrary to their assertions on formal occasions, the American people enjoy wars beyond measure, if the plain facts of history are allowed to speak." In the discussion of the negotiations to resolve the Cuban crisis, Beard did not directly charge the McKinley administration with fomenting war hysteria. But hinting at a possible conspiracy, he wrote, "It was fortunate for the conservative interests that the quarrel with Spain came shortly after McKinley's election, and they were able to employ that ancient political device, 'a vigorous foreign policy,' to divert the public mind from domestic difficulties."[31]

More bluntly, Beard located the fundamental cause of the war, not in idealism, yellow journalism, partisan advantage, or blind chance, but in the "frank acknowledgments of the new emphasis on world policy which the economic interests demanded." Following the renewal of the Cuban insurrection in 1895, American capitalistic interests were "strong enough to induce interference" on the part of the federal government in order to prevent any further loss of trade and American property on the island. "Powerful economic interests" following the defeat of Spain, he asserted, "were busy impressing the public mind with the advantages to be derived from the retention of the distant Pacific Islands," not only as an area for trade and investment in their own right, but as a base for expanding American commercial endeavors throughout the Orient.[32]

But Beard continued to be ambivalent. He did not reconcile this economic interpretation in which economic interest groups

29. Review of *Contemporary American History* by Raymond G. Gettell, in *Annals of the American Academy of Political and Social Science* 54 (July 1914): 329.

30. "Charles Beard and the Constitution," in *Beard Appraisal*, pp. 83–87.

31. Beard, *Contemporary American History*, p. 199 (order of quotations reversed).

32. Ibid., pp. 204, 213, 214–15.

self-consciously sought to use the government for private gain with his more general analysis of the "newer imperialism" of the 1890s. The latter rested upon the assumption of economic determinism. This was evidenced in his assertion about the *"inexorable necessity of the present economic system,"* which meant that "markets and safe investment opportunities *must be found* for surplus products and accumulated capital." There was an "inevitability" behind the more advanced countries engaging in rivalries over the "economically backward countries" in Asia, Africa, and Latin America. *"Economic necessity,"* he concluded, "thus overrides American isolation and drives the United States into world politics."[33]

One prominent student of Beard's historiography considered his view of imperialism at this time as being "very close to the Marxists." For that reason, Beard was "armed with an interpretation when the First World War broke out" and presented "in popular form an economic approach to war which was to become almost commonplace in the twenties and thirties, and to be forgotten by some in the forties of this century."[34]

On the eve of World War I, Beard had established a national reputation as a scholar, teacher, reformer, and controversialist. In so doing, he displayed incredible physical energy, wide-ranging intellectual curiosity, and admirable humanitarian impulses. His approach to the writing of history was informed by a conviction that the study of the past should be undertaken with a view to progressively improving man's present political, social, and economic environment. The most fruitful way of achieving this aim, he believed, was through an appreciation of the fundamental importance of economic forces in interpreting men's ideas, institutions, and actions. A growing knowledge of the theory and practice of international relations and American foreign policy, buttressed by the assumption of the possible benevolent role of world-wide economic interdependence, also contributed to Beard's decidedly internationalist point of view at this time.

33. Ibid., pp. 202–3 (italics added).
34. White, *American Social Thought*, p. 43.

3

The War Years, 1914-1919

W HEN WAR broke out in Europe in the summer of 1914, Charles Beard was extremely well informed on many of the forces and events which had led up to the clash between two great power blocs. Even so, less than two years after the conflict began, he and James Harvey Robinson admitted that "the most terrible and destructive war in the history of Europe . . . came as a horrible surprise," largely because the statesmen of Europe knew in advance that such a war "would involve untold woe and destruction." This struggle, they contended with great insight, "is the most important single event in the whole history of Europe and perhaps the world."[1]

In their effort to account for this calamity, Beard and Robinson said that the exact causes were still a matter of dispute. But they pointed to such factors as the naval armaments race between Germany and Great Britain, the Alliance System, and the economic forces which had propelled the most industrialized countries of Europe into competition for colonies. Although the latter explanation received the greatest notice, the authors described it simply as "one of the causes of the great European war," without claiming that it was the most important.[2] On the issue of national responsi-

1. Beard and Robinson, *Outlines of European History*, 2:677.
2. Ibid., 2:456, 592, 680–81.

bility for precipitating the crisis, Beard and Robinson suggested where their own sentiments lay when they asserted that "Prussia has been the military schoolmaster of Europe." When discussing the Balkan imbroglio, the authors believed that Austria had to bear a large degree of blame because of its provocative annexationist policies and the intolerable conditions of its ultimatum to Serbia on July 23, 1914.[3]

It is perhaps not surprising that Beard rather quickly and publicly expressed his personal sympathy and support for the Triple Entente, or the Allied Powers. In the autumn of 1914, he delivered a speech at the City College of New York in which he attacked the Central Powers so sharply that, as he later recalled, the college president forbade him to speak again at that institution on that subject.[4] The relative speed and the depth of feeling with which Beard condemned the Central Powers seemed to be the culmination of earlier experiences when he was in Germany. They were also the culmination of scholarly studies which had made him extremely suspicious of the nature and aims of German militarism, very critical of Kaiser Wilhelm's diplomacy before 1914, and harsh in his judgments of the autocratic nature of the Imperial German government.[5]

In the first of a series of four lectures delivered at Amherst College in 1916, Beard alluded to the war in Europe and, in a pessimistic vein, said to his audience, "The present plight of the world seems to show that mankind is in the grip of inexorable forces which may destroy civilization if not subdued to humane purposes. It may be that in the end we must . . . confess the futility of our quest." While the carnage of the war sorely tried his faith in progress, Beard's essential optimism asserted itself in a statement which suggested that mankind should not cease to seek ways out of its current dilemma: "Even though every door be slammed in our faces, still we must knock."[6]

In keeping with his own counsel, Beard had already indicated his support of a "Congress of Nations." At the Friends' Meeting House in New York City in January 1916, he spoke of the need for a postwar international legislative body. A major international

3. Ibid., 2:677, 684, 691–93.
4. *New York Times*, January 26, 1919, p. 8.
5. Beard and Robinson, *The Development of Modern Europe*, 2:148–50.
6. *The Economic Basis of Politics* (1922 ed.), pp. 2–3.

organization, the Hague Tribunal, had proved inadequate because it was unrepresentative and inflexible. It was more interested in settling disputes than in preventing them. Lasting peace, Beard said, must come through an international legislature composed of delegates elected by the people of the nations they represent.[7]

But Beard was finding it personally difficult to restrict himself to endorsing programs for international peace in which it was assumed that the United States would commit itself only after the war ended. The following recollection of a former student of his at Columbia underscored the extent to which Beard had accepted the necessity of American intervention on the side of the Allies and had rejected the notion of pacifism as a justification for continuing American neutrality:

Throughout 1916, Professor Beard urged America's entry into the war. He warned us in class that Germany was a danger to civilization. It was an illusion, he said, to think of Americans as pacific people; they are and always have been one of the most violent peoples in history. . . . One morning, when the press reported the sinking of a merchant vessel by German submarines, Dr. Beard came into the classroom pale and stern. He looked at us for a long time in silence, then closed his eyes.

"Gentlemen," he said, "the history of the world was altered today. It will now be impossible for the United States to stay out of the war. German autocracy will have to be destroyed." He opened his eyes and they were full of tears.[8]

Nevertheless, "Uncle Charley," as he was now widely referred to by the Columbia student body, did not let these intense convictions override a realistic appraisal of what could reasonably be achieved by defeating the Central Powers. His skeptical reaction to President Woodrow Wilson's "peace without victory" speech on January 22, 1917, for example, indicated that he was far from satisfied with its idealistic rhetoric. In an interview for the *New York Times*, Beard was sharply critical of Wilson's intentions in even making the speech. In particular, he took issue with Wilson's generalities which, in the case of self-determination of peoples, left unanswered

7. *New York Times*, January 21, 1916, p. 9.
8. Joseph Freeman, *An American Testament*, p. 107.

some politically embarrassing questions about such countries as Ireland and India, not to mention Haiti and Santo Domingo. The address, Beard told his interviewer, was "not much of a basis for negotiations." Unless the president was acting "on the basis of some information which he has received from one or the other conflicting party," he was "just preaching a sermon—just a sermon."[9]

Nearly four weeks after Germany had announced its campaign of unrestricted submarine warfare on January 31, 1917, President Wilson went before a joint session of Congress to secure authority to arm American merchantmen. In another *New York Times* interview, when asked what he thought about this request, Beard told the reporter, "Personally I favor more drastic action than the President has taken up to date. I have thought for some time that this country should definitely align itself with the Allies and help eliminate Prussianism from the earth. Even without authorization of Congress, the President can now take a stand where he will compel Germany to rescind her illegal orders or admit defeat."[10] The *Times'* account of the interview, however, did not state exactly what Beard might have had in mind beyond "armed neutrality." In any event, a Senate filibuster eventually forced Wilson to issue an executive order arming American merchant ships.

News of the torpedoing of the first armed American merchantman, the *Aztec*, was made public on Sunday, April 1, 1917. A group of pacifists in New York City planned a mass protest demonstration for the next day against any possible vigorous response of the United States government. At Columbia University, however, a committee of interventionist professors prepared to engage in a counterdemonstration. On behalf of this committee, Beard issued a statement that read, in part, "The hour has struck to put an end to the Prussian oligarchy. . . . Every advocate of peace at any price . . . is now playing into the hands of Prussian militarism."[11] On April 2, President Wilson presented his war message to Congress.

9. Quoted in *New York Times*, January 23, 1917, p. 2.
10. Quoted ibid., February 27, 1917, p. 2. Slightly more than two months after the armistice, Beard was still adamant in his disagreement with the president's policies before April 1917. In late January 1919, he asserted that he had not belonged to "Mr. Wilson's sweet neutrality band." Further, he had simultaneously taught his students that "war has been one of the most tremendous factors in the origin of the State and the progress of mankind," although he had never "advocated war for war's sake." Quoted ibid., January 26, 1919, p. 8.
11. Quoted in Walter Millis, *The Road to War, 1914–1917*, pp. 428–29.

The war resolution was approved in the Senate and the House on April 4 and 6, respectively.

For some time prior to America's entrance into World War I, the *New Republic* had adopted the editorial position that American interests would be jeopardized by a victory of the Central Powers.[12] Beard shared this belief of most of the editors of this liberal periodical to which he had contributed a number of articles and book reviews since its founding in 1914. Less than two weeks after the United States became a belligerent, one of the editors may very well have had Beard, among others, in mind when he declared, "College professors headed by a President who had himself been a college professor contributed more effectively to the decision in favor of war than did the farmers, the businessmen, or the politicians."[13]

Beard's efforts did not cease with the declaration of war. In his published statements supporting the belligerent status of the United States, he usually emphasized the major role the nation would have to play in halting unbridled German militarism and in promoting postwar stability. He did not, however, completely succumb to the heady idealism implicit in the shibboleth that the world was to be made "safe for democracy." Of primary concern to him were Germany's threats to the interests and values of the United States.

Beard's contributions to the war effort came under the heading of propaganda activities. One rumor, which he would neither confirm nor deny, was that President Wilson had asked him to make speeches in the West and Middle West.[14] He was briefly associated with the Division of Civic and Educational Publications, an agency of George Creel's Committee on Public Information. Under the direction of University of Minnesota historian Guy Stanton Ford, this division was responsible for literature that presented "the Wilsonian war doctrine in a reasoned, accurate, authoritative statement that would appeal to educated people everywhere." One of the noteworthy volumes produced by this agency was *The War Cyclopedia*, "a handbook for ready reference on the Great War."

12. Richard H. Gentry, "Liberalism and the *New Republic*, 1914–1960," p. 84.
13. "Who Willed American Participation?" *New Republic*, April 14, 1917, p. 308.
14. *New York Times*, October 11, 1917, p. 24.

Edited by Professors Frederick L. Paxson and Edward S. Corwin, many prominent historians contributed to its compilation, including Charles A. Beard, Carl L. Becker, Sidney B. Fay, and J. Franklin Jameson.[15]

A month before the armistice, *Harper's Magazine* published a fervent appeal by Beard to support the fourth Liberty Bond Drive. It contained what was probably his most passionate printed analysis of German responsibility for the war and is quoted at length for comparison with the more judicious statements he made during the war and with his revised opinions in subsequent years: "America and her allies are now pitted against the most merciless military despotism the world has ever seen. Surely all those who hoped for the conversion of Germany and the House of Hohenzollern to ways of peace and decency are cured of their delusion by this time. Equipped by forty years of preparation for armed conquest, fortified by forty years of conspiracy against the democratic nations of the earth, supported by all the engines of destruction that science can devise, the German military machine threatens all mankind. It has made a religion of brutality; it has despised everything that savors of democracy; it has willed to impose its cruel might upon all who refuse to accept its yoke. Let whoever doubts this ponder upon Belgium, the 'Lusitania,' and Brest-Litovsk. A German victory means the utter destruction of those ideals of peace and goodwill which have been America's great reliance, ideals which make life worth living in America or anywhere else."[16]

A more temperate, balanced expression of Beard's estimate of the nature of the German threat and Allied war aims is to be found in a letter, written in June 1917, to the editor of the *New Republic*. The communication reflected his confidence in the ultimate military success of the Allies and anticipated the spirit of Woodrow Wilson's Fourteen Points speech of January, 1918. But it also revealed his fear that the diplomacy of the war might be handled so ineptly as to cancel out the fruits of victory.

At the outset, Beard urged Americans to "strain every nerve to

15. James R. Mock and Cedric Larson, *Words that Won the War*, p. 173. First issued in January 1918, nearly 200,000 copies of *The War Cyclopedia* were distributed: George Creel, *How We Advertised America*, p. 455. Since the authors of particular passages are not identified, it is not possible to determine which items in *The War Cyclopedia* were written by Beard.

16. "A Call upon Every Citizen," p. 655.

the breaking point in the mobilization of our resources" and to "work for a smashing victory which will carry the soldiers of the Allies to the streets of Berlin." But poised, cold-blooded, Machiavellian-inspired diplomacy, he insisted, was just as indispensable to winning the war. The United States had to guard against a self-righteous posture. "A painful consciousness of the rectitude of our intentions and the purity of our purpose," he observed wryly, "is more likely to be a nuisance than a service."[17]

Beard conceded that there was some merit in the interpretation of the war as a struggle between ideological absolutes, such as "liberty against autocracy." But he hoped the Allied statesmen would avoid such characterizations, for he believed they would not contribute to effective negotiations. Instead, they should focus their attention on two immediate problems brought about by the war, the solution of which would have a bearing upon whether the peace could endure. First, Allied leaders would have to eliminate the political power of the Prussian military caste over the German masses. This would be done in order to place political authority in the hands of the "radical leaders" of the Social Democratic Party, which had been the principal voice of reform in prewar Germany. The second problem entailed appropriate Allied reassurances to the revolutionary regime of Alexander Kerensky that Russia's non-Czarist future would be guaranteed by Russia's remaining in the war. It was necessary, however, to convince the radical leaders of these countries "that this is not at bottom, or even potentially, a capitalist war for colonies, markets, and concessions."[18]

In this statement, Beard seemed to repudiate his earlier conclusions concerning the importance of imperialism as a cause for the war. Substantially, he was proposing the same principles of a nonpunitive, nonvictor's peace eventually espoused by Woodrow Wilson. He was not ruling out the possibility that the Allies were entertaining thoughts of imperialistic gains at that time. He was suggesting that they ought not to continue to embrace them as war aims. In short, they should not make one of the war's major causes its principal result. The United States, Beard declared, had a special obligation to make it unmistakably clear that it had no

17. "The Perils of Democracy," p. 136.
18. Ibid., p. 137.

intention of presiding over a distribution of German colonies among the victors or of haggling over indemnities, particularly if negotiations over these issues prolonged the duration and cost of the conflict. Foreshadowing a major theme of many disillusioned critics of the Treaty of Versailles, Beard warned, "Let us beware lest the diplomats make our burden a thousand times heavier than it need be."[19]

Beard elaborated upon these concerns in book reviews during the war. In Solomon Grumbach's *Das annexionistische Deutschland* (1917), for example, he found convincing evidence that the territorial expectations of Germany's leaders were so grandiose that they probably would regard any proposal for a restoration of the status quo ante bellum as a humiliating defeat. Compared to Germany's imperialist ambitions as detailed in this work, he wrote, "the loose-jointed, ramshackle British Empire is but a child's house of cards." Beard, nonetheless, believed that generous peace terms should be offered by the Allies to forestall the possibility that the German people would again be duped by imperialist-minded leaders, among whom were university professors as well as political, military, and business leaders.[20]

A year later Beard applauded the insights and conclusions found in *The End of the War* (1918), written by the progressive journalist Walter Weyl. In the course of the review, Beard itemized a number of instances when Germany's aggressive conduct was so flagrant as "to convince all but the unearthly of the justice of the cause for which America took up arms." Yet his most telling comments were reserved for Weyl's analysis of "the dread disease of capitalistic imperialism." In a passage which contained the essential thesis and the withering sarcasm of many of Beard's foreign policy writings of the 1930s, he wrote, "The old game of capitalistic exploitation, of interpenetration, of annexation, of economic rivalry for the main chance—which is little short of piracy—must cease. Governments must not be the servitors of capitalists searching in the out-of-the-way places of the earth for twenty-five per cent dividends and a guaranteed return of the original capital, plus betterments." In effect, Beard optimistically added his appeal to that of Weyl to strip diplomacy of its appearances, and to get down to the realities

19. Ibid.
20. "German Annexations and Indemnities."

which might bring about "a peace made in the open sunlight, with full knowledge of the nature of the imperialistic and capitalistic dynamic of industry as at present organized, shaped toward a future of internationalism, not of new coalitions, new balances of power —such is the peace for which Mr. Weyl pleads."[21]

In the summer of 1918, sixty internationalist-minded members of the League of Free Nations Association met in New York City. Charles and Mary Beard were two of the many distinguished academic and public figures who attended, including John Dewey, Herbert Croly, and Felix Frankfurter. The participants drafted a declaration of principles which they believed should guide the eventual peace negotiations. Together with the older League to Enforce Peace, the association issued, immediately after the armistice, a "Victory Program" that called for freedom of the seas, removal of trade barriers, and acceptance of limitations upon national sovereignty if such aims were to be realized.[22]

Since Beard did not permit his idealism to overwhelm his realism completely, he was reasonably forearmed against the profound bitterness and disillusionment experienced by many liberals after Woodrow Wilson's failure to implement significantly the principles and programs which the president and such organizations as the League of Free Nations Association had proclaimed. Like most liberals, however, Beard was troubled by the wartime infringement on civil liberties growing out of the mood of intolerance that gripped the nation.

Even during the period of American neutrality, Beard was personally involved in at least one episode which indicated how the war in Europe could discourage holding and expressing unpopular opinions. In 1916, Beard's name was publicly linked with *Official Documents Relating to the Outbreak of the World War*, a work edited by a scholar known to be sympathetic to the German cause, Dr. Edmund Von Mach. Beard had read the manuscript for the Macmillan Company, the publisher of many of his own works. Von Mach failed to make certain factual corrections recommended by Beard, and the publishers eventually took the book off the market because of its inaccuracies. Beard's scholarly integrity and his own pro-Allied sentiments were generally recognized. But this unfortu-

21. "The End of the War."
22. Ruhl J. Bartlett, *The League to Enforce Peace*, p. 111; Selig Adler, *The Isolationist Impulse: Its Twentieth-Century Reaction*, pp. 51–52.

nate incident briefly caused them to be called into question and probably gave him some inkling of the badgering he and other academics might expect in the event of American intervention in the war.[23]

Beard's controversial resignation from Columbia University in October 1917 had no direct bearing on his own views of the war at the time he departed. His major grievance was concerned indirectly with events that took place when many officials of the university, including President Nicholas Murray Butler, endorsed American neutrality. The decision to leave Columbia was precipitated by the dismissal of two professors, ostensibly for their noninterventionist sentiments prior to April 1917 and their alleged unwillingness to support the war effort once the United States became a belligerent.[24]

In the letter of resignation, Beard stressed his own vigorous support of the war and made it clear that he in no way endorsed what might have been the antiwar views of the two professors. But he insisted on the right of teachers to judge the actions of their colleagues in any case that seemed to warrant severe disciplinary action. Beard believed that "reactionary and visionless" trustees were not competent to make such important decisions. He was convinced that, under these circumstances, he could no longer maintain his association with Columbia, for he would not be able to effectively sustain "public opinion in support of the just war on the German Empire or take a position of independence in the days of reconstruction that are to follow."[25]

There would be rapprochements of sorts: Beard served twice as a visiting professor of government at Columbia, and he received an honorary degree from that institution in 1944.[26] But the controversy evoked occasional traces of bitterness after the war. With the passage of years, the circumstances surrounding his resignation became increasingly identified in his mind with the suppression of

23. *New York Times*, October 29, 1916, p. 14; ibid., December 31, 1916, p. 3.

24. George S. Counts, "Charles Beard, the Public Man," in *Beard Appraisal*, pp. 243–44.

25. "Letter of Resignation from Columbia University," p. 446. Twenty years later, Beard still regarded it as almost axiomatic that "no board of trustees is fitted to conduct a college or university without the assistance and participation of faculty representatives": *New Republic*, February 3, 1937, p. 413.

26. "Exile's Return," *New Republic*, October 4, 1939, p. 228; *New York Times*, April 29, 1941, p. 16, and June 7, 1944, p. 34.

civil liberties in wartime. The historian and friend Hubert Herring in 1939 quoted Beard as saying to him, "And then I slowly awoke to my abysmal ignorance . . . I saw Columbia use the war to suppress men. . . . I saw the freedom of the press trampled by spies, public and private."[27]

It was not until after World War I ended, however, that Beard publicly registered his private concern about such matters. In January 1918, he wrote to the *New Republic* to assert that it was now time for the federal government to free political prisoners "whose offense was to retain Mr. Wilson's pacifist views after he had abandoned them." The "blighting hand of the post office censor" should also be removed from political publications, and there should be a restoration of "the rights of press, speech and meeting which were curtailed during the war. . . . Is truth so frail and faith so slight," he asked indignantly, "that they must be handed over to the police?"[28]

That same week, Beard's name was included on a published list of "men and women who have been recorded as active in movements which did not help the United States when the country was fighting the Central Powers." This information was distributed by the Senate Judiciary Committee Investigating German Propaganda and was compiled from a roster furnished by the Military Intelligence Service. Beard was specifically cited for his allegedly "radical" connections with the Intercollegiate Socialist Society and the Rand School of Social Science, at which he had lectured after leaving Columbia. Understandably outraged by the falsity and ludicrousness of the insinuation that he had worked against the Allied cause, Beard wrote a biting letter of denial to the chairman of the Senate committee involved. In citing details which contradicted and refuted the charge, Beard used the occasion to take a swipe at Nicholas Murray Butler and others who, he claimed, were "manipulating the Carnegie peace millions," issuing pacifist pamphlets, organizing pacifist societies, and employing Columbia instructors to write pacifist tracts at a time when Beard himself was urging American involvement on the side of the Allies.[29]

These personal experiences undoubtedly contributed to the ardor

27. "Freelance among the Historians," p. 652.
28. "The Supreme Issue," *New Republic*, January 25, 1919, p. 343.
29. Quoted in *New York Times*, January 25, 1919, p. 1; ibid., January 26, 1919, p. 8.

found in Beard's repeated warnings after World War I that America's participation in another world conflict would signal the imminent and irretrievable loss of civil liberties in the United States. The very depth of feeling which he occasionally displayed in support of the war effort might also account, in part, for his equally fervent determination to oppose American involvement in the affairs of Europe and the Far East during the 1930s. As Max Lerner has suggested, Beard, looking back, must have felt that "after all he had been had. The sense of humiliation" in supporting an abortive, idealistic crusade "became a rankling resolve to be revenged on his own folly."[30] Beard's son-in-law, the historian Alfred Vagts, supports this judgment. But he also suggests that Beard was equally determined that the historical guild should never again be "had if he could help it."[31]

It was not until the 1930s that Beard thoroughly repudiated his thoughts and behavior in regard to America's role in World War I. Up to that time, he often made a distinction between the immediate need for the United States to aid in defeating Imperial Germany to safeguard its own national interest on the one hand, and to promote the long-range goal of establishing an enduring peace on the other. The failure to achieve the latter objective would become a matter of disappointment and concern to Beard. But his personal involvement in supporting the Allied war effort and American intervention did not, of itself, invalidate his many acute observations about the potential threats to the United States of a German victory in World War I.

30. "Charles Beard: Civilization and the Devils," p. 23.
31. Vagts to author, May 9, 1968.

4

The Peace Settlement to the Great Depression, 1919-1930

Dв URING the period from the peace settlement to the Great Depression,[1] Beard's thinking on world affairs was marked by alternating moods of optimism and pessimism that coincided, respectively, with many features of liberal internationalist and liberal isolationist thought in America during the 1920s.[2] Consistent with his conviction that it had been necessary and desirable for the United States to adopt a belligerent status in 1917–18, throughout the 1920s Beard frequently emphasized the responsible and active role which America would have to assume in foreign affairs. Immediately after the war and through 1930, he was generally sanguine in his appraisal of the prospects for international peace and stability.

[1]. The material in this chapter, with slight revisions, appeared in the author's "Charles A. Beard in Midpassage."

[2]. The terms "liberal internationalist" and "liberal isolationist" are derived from Eric F. Goldman's delineation of progressive-liberal opinion in regard to American foreign policy during and after World War I. The liberal internationalist was basically wedded to the notion of collective security in the promotion of world peace, which meant support of American intervention in World War I and extensive participation in world affairs, including membership in the League of Nations following the end of hostilities. The liberal isolationist, on the other hand, was distinguished by his attachment to an economic interpretation of war, a fear that war meant the end of domestic reform and compromised civil liberties, a skeptical attitude toward the league, and, by the 1930s, a "deep-seated disillusionment with Wilsonianism": *Rendezvous with Destiny*, pp. 223–61, 374–76.

At times, however, Beard despaired of the possibility of establishing a world that would be "safe for democracy" even if the United States embraced significant international commitments. On occasion, he feared that these commitments, particularly in foreign commercial ventures, might jeopardize the nation's security. His deliberations on the origins of World War I and the "war guilt" question also gave rise to doubts about the validity and wisdom of his vigorous support of the war effort. When his thoughts ran in these channels, he expressed views which clearly foreshadowed a number of the isolationist and revisionist themes found in his writings during the 1930s and after.

On the eve of the Paris Peace Conference of 1919, Beard, in *National Governments and the World War*, summarized the reasons for American intervention and reviewed the war aims of the United States. A German victory, he contended, "would imperil democracy in the United States in coming years." The defeat of Great Britain and Germany's annexation of her colonies would have led to a situation in which "America would not be spared by a power founded on the sword." Thus, the war was patently one of national self-defense, a case of "taking up arms to repel acts of violence and wrong already being committed against the United States" by the Imperial German Government. But in responding to this challenge, he added, President Wilson had made it clear that "the United States sought no new material gains from the war—no new territories, no forcibly won markets for American trade, no compensations in money for wrong done—but rather to overthrow militarism and imperialism, making way for peace and democratic governments throughout the earth."[3]

In a sympathetic fashion that implied acceptance of Wilson's program for a nonvindictive treaty, Beard outlined the major principles that were to guide American diplomacy in the forthcoming peace settlement. But optimism was tempered by words of caution. The worthy aims of Woodrow Wilson, he observed, probably would not be "universally accepted or lived up to by all nations in spirit as well as letter." He nevertheless concluded that "those who have faith will believe that a real change has come in the long

3. Beard and Frederick A. Ogg, *National Governments and the World War*, pp. 13–14, 556, 558. In the preface to this work (dated December 12, 1918), it is noted that Beard was responsible for writing the chapters from which these ideas were taken.

course of history and that the years 1917–18 . . . will mark the opening of a new epoch in the rise of government by the people and in the growth of a concert among the nations."[4]

In the final chapter of this book, America's membership in a League of Nations was strongly endorsed. Despite the "complete abandonment of her traditional policy of isolationism" implicit in such a course of action, the United States had already set aside this policy by participating in World War I. "The conditions obtaining in the modern world" would have made such a policy obsolete in any event.[5]

Before the formal signing of the Treaty of Versailles on June 28, 1919, however, many liberals who had enthusiastically embraced Wilson's war aims were disturbed by the prospect that the president would not be able to redeem his pledges. During the spring of 1919, editorials and articles in the *New Republic* chronicled the uncertain progress of the peace talks at Paris. Increasingly, many liberals came to doubt the fulfillment of the Fourteen Points, to question the integrity of America's recent comrades-in-arms, and to wonder whether Wilson himself had not lost sight of the noble aims for which the country had gone to war. By December 1919, when the *New Republic* began to serialize John Maynard Keynes' *Economic Consequences of the Peace*, a polemic against Wilson and the reparations clauses of the Treaty of Versailles, a considerable number of liberals were in virtual alliance with conservatives in opposition to the pact.[6]

Selig Adler has suggested that in 1919 Beard joined with Oswald Garrison Villard, Herbert Croly, and other liberals in the United States "who had turned against the League because of the 'imperialistic' parts of the Treaty of Versailles."[7] If so, Beard did not develop an implacable anti-league attitude, for he often praised the concept and certain activities of the league in the decade after Versailles. It is clear, however, that by mid-1919 Beard was becom-

4. Ibid., p. 570.
5. Ibid., p. 590. The political scientist Frederick A. Ogg assumed the responsibility for this passage. But the sentiments expressed in regard to the nonviability of isolationism and the membership of the United States in an international peace-keeping organization were consistent with Beard's own views before and during the war.
6. Goldman, *Rendezvous with Destiny*, pp. 263–70.
7. "The War Guilt Question and American Disillusionment, 1919–1928," p. 14n89.

ing impatient with what he regarded as distorted accounts of the origins and conduct of the war which gave the impression that members of the Triple Entente (Great Britain, France, and Russia) were impelled only by idealistic motives in waging war against the Central Powers. But he just as vigorously asserted that "America's part in the great war was just and needed no specious apology."[8]

Throughout the 1920s, Beard usually adhered to the belief that American intervention was warranted, regardless of any personal re-evaluations of the "war guilt" thesis and the Versailles treaty. Accordingly, he did not accept the views of those who argued, as did Harry Elmer Barnes in *The Genesis of the World War* (1926), that American participation was both unnecessary and unwise. In his review article of Barnes' work, Beard sustained the author's debunking of the victors' version of "war guilt," which Beard characterized as the "Sunday-school theory" of responsibility for the war. Barnes' analysis of the prime causes of the war, with "the bitter rivalry of the industrial powers for markets" at the head of the list, also met with Beard's approval. But he emphatically warned that "there is equal danger in the attempt to white-wash the German Kaiser, the Crown Prince, the war party and the super-patriots of the Fatherland."[9]

Beard pointedly refuted Barnes' contention that President Wilson had never been neutral and had deliberately promoted a war spirit throughout the country, observing that as late as February 1917, the President "looked rather coldly upon the pretensions of both parties to the European war." In view of Beard's extensive writings on the economic interpretation of war, it is perhaps noteworthy that this idea was not broached in the essay when he discussed the reasons for American involvement. Instead, the motive of national security appeared to be uppermost in his mind. Challenging the hypothesis that a German victory would have been of no consequence to the United States, Beard remarked, "Certainly Mr. Barnes could hardly say that the United States would be in a more favorable position with a triumphant German military party astride Europe than with the Entente Allies victorious and at one another's throats." He added, "It is decidedly to the interest of the United States to help prevent the rise of any single European

8. "Propaganda in the Schools," p. 598.
9. "Heroes and Villains of the World War," p. 733.

power to a dominant position." But in a conclusion that would find wide application in Beard's isolationist writings in the next decade, he stated that the American people "should not be bamboozled" by European statesmen and "should regard with cold blood all the quarrels of Europe."[10]

This interpretation of Wilson's restrained behavior and the national security motive with regard to America's involvement in World War I was substantially embodied in the highly acclaimed *The Rise of American Civilization,* published the following year. In this work, however, Beard and his wife Mary considered briefly the notion that Wilson had contemplated American entrance into the war in 1916. Moreover, the economic interpretation was introduced in a passage which implied that the pressures of interest groups—investors, munitions-makers, merchants, and manufacturers—were among the many forces "that helped to form the President's crucial decision" to ask for a declaration of war.[11]

By 1930, Beard's interpretation of presidential responsibility for American belligerency had become more critical. In a study written with his son, William, Woodrow Wilson's conduct of diplomacy after the sinking of the *Lusitania* in May 1915 was described as "a program destined to end in an open break." The impression conveyed was that the president's diplomacy might have been inept, but was without guile.[12] Such views stand in rather sharp contrast to Beard's position of the mid-1930s, when he joined the ranks of the revisionists who attacked Wilson's idealism and alleged guilt in dragging the nation into an unnecessary war at the instigation of economic interest groups.

If Beard was convinced during the 1920s of the power-political and ideological justification for American intervention in World War I, he was consistently critical of attempts to gloss over the complexities of the war's origins. An important impetus to Beard's revised estimate of the responsibilities for the war and pessimism over its consequences was a trip he made to Europe in 1919–20. While on the continent, he observed general breakdown of national economies combined with political unrest, including a riot in Italy associated with Benito Mussolini's subsequent rise to power.[13] It

10. Ibid., pp. 734–35.
11. 2:626–33.
12. *The American Leviathan: The Republic in the Machine Age,* p. 275.
13. W. Beard, comp., *Charles A. Beard,* p. xiii.

was at this time that Beard took the opportunity to examine some of the official documents then available in European archives. From these papers and published accounts, he gained insights into the operations of the alliance system before and after 1914 which caused him to view his earlier appraisals of "war guilt" with increasing skepticism.[14]

Also as a consequence of this postwar trip to Europe, Charles and Mary Beard came back to their homeland with the intention "to inquire what we can do here to create an American civilization, determined to center my efforts on the promise of America rather than upon the fifty century-old quarrels of Europe."[15] This remark to a friend might have been an instance of Beard projecting his feelings of the 1930s back to an earlier period. However disappointed he might have been with the new diplomatic revelations and with some of the results of the war, neither he nor his wife believed in 1921 that the imperfections of the Treaty of Versailles and the Senate's rejection of American membership in the League of Nations absolved the United States of international responsibilities. In the Beards' first joint effort in American history, the high school text *History of the United States* (1921), they clearly rejected isolationism: "By no conceivable process could America be disentangled from the web of world affairs. Isolationism, if desirable, had become impossible. . . . America, by virtue of its institutions, its population, its wealth, and its commerce, had become first among the nations of the earth. By moral obligations and by practical interests its fate was thus linked with the destiny of all mankind."[16] Within a year, however, Beard was recommending that the United States allow Europe "to set its own house in order under the stress of its own necessities and experiences. Its statesmen know little enough, perhaps, but they know Europe better than any agents sent out from Washington."[17]

This ambivalence seems to have stemmed, in large part, from Beard's troubled reflections—demonstrated in several book reviews

14. M. Beard, *The Making of Charles A. Beard*, pp. 30–31; Cushing Strout, *The Pragmatic Revolt in American History: Carl Becker and Charles Beard*, p. 138; Borning, *The Political and Social Thought of Charles A. Beard*, p. 107.

15. Quoted in Herring, "Freelance among the Historians," p. 646.

16. (New York: Macmillan Co., 1921), p. 620.

17. C. A. Beard, *Cross Currents in Europe Today*, p. 265, hereafter cited as *Cross Currents*.

by him—on the origins of the war, the gap between the idealistic and actual aftermath of World War I, economic imperialism, and war propaganda.[18] At this juncture in Beard's life, the most complete expression of his shifting attitudes toward the causes and results of World War I and the future course of American foreign policy in the light of this episode is contained in *Cross Currents in Europe Today*, based on eight lectures delivered at Dartmouth College in the fall of 1921.

The first three lectures dealt with the "war guilt" question, and in them Beard claimed he would "pass no judgments upon the motives and policies of the actors in the great drama that opened on August 1, 1914." Yet, he soon commented bitterly on the diplomats who secretly "exchanged pledges and created situations which drove Europe relentlessly into the abyss. Out of the millions that went forth to die, out of the millions that stayed home to suffer and bear the burdens, only a handful—a score or more—knew by what process the terrible *dénouement* had been brought to pass."[19] However inadvertently, Beard was blaming specific individuals for wrong choices freely made, not inexorable, abstract forces that presumably made war inevitable.

In his analysis of primary responsibility for the war, Russia and France were accorded special blame in view of an alleged Franco-Russian scheme, formulated as early as 1908, to destroy the Austro-Hungarian Empire in a general European war.[20] Beard's moderate-revisionist account received slight critical notice at the time. But one reviewer thought the presentation lacked balance and charged that Beard's entire "war guilt" thesis rested on the questionable assumption that the whole course of European events after 1908 turned on a vague promise by the Russian government to support Serbia in the future.[21]

18. "The Recent War"; "Transition in Politics"; "La Guerre Absolue."
19. *Cross Currents*, pp. 2, 6. A few years later, Beard confided in a letter to Harry Elmer Barnes, "I hesitate in measuring out the exact amount of damnation due to the liars and incompetents who got the world into the mess of 1914—but none of them can get too much": Beard to Barnes, July 14, 1926[?], Barnes Papers, Western History Research Center, University of Wyoming Library. From the context of the letter, it would appear that Beard wrote it just before his review of Barnes' book was published in *Current History*, August 1926.
20. *Cross Currents*, pp. 9–10, 26–27.
21. Joseph Fuller, review of *Cross Currents*, in *American Political Science*

It may be that Beard overstated his case at Dartmouth in his attempt to redress the balance of truth. Yet his views had not altered when he wrote three years later, "All must admit that one thing has been established beyond question, namely, that responsibility for the war must be distributed among all the participants with Russia and France bearing a Titan's share."[22] In 1930, however, Beard and James Harvey Robinson singled out for sympathetic discussion the revisionist work of Sidney B. Fay, *The Origins of the World War* (1928), which rejected the notion that one could fix ultimate or preponderant responsibility on any one of the powers and denied that the war resulted principally from a Franco-Russian conspiracy.[23]

The lecture-essay "America and the Balance of Power," in *Cross Currents in Europe Today*, reflected Beard's anxiety over the proper role which the United States should play in world affairs. His conclusions anticipated in remarkable detail some of his isolationist arguments in the 1930s, particularly the thesis of "continental Americanism." It is perhaps no exaggeration to suggest, therefore, that this lecture-essay presents the most revealing of Beard's statements on American foreign policy during the 1920s.

In the first of his Dartmouth lectures, Beard stressed the impact of world events and forces on the past, present, and future history of the United States, particularly in trade and finance, where there was "now a web of international relations . . . so fine in mesh and so tough in fibre that no sword can cut it. The East and West have met," he continued, "and they are one. The world is an economic unit and the United States is being woven into the very fabric of that unity."[24] This generalization was reminiscent of an idea first entertained in an important sense when he was in England and accepted almost as an article of faith during his first decade at Columbia University. In the final lecture on "America and the Balance of Power," however, Beard shifted his perspective to consider how American foreign policies affected world events and,

---

Review 17 (May 1923):332. Since Beard concluded elsewhere in his lectures (p. 81) that "circumstances rather than the form and language of the understandings" determined the extent to which commitments were fulfilled in 1914, the reviewer's fundamental criticism had some merit.

22. "Viscount Grey on War Guilt," p. 172.
23. *The Development of Modern Europe*, rev. ed., 2:319–20.
24. *Cross Currents*, pp. 1–2.

ultimately, American domestic policies. The conclusion of his analysis was that the United States should adopt a basic approach to diplomacy that would lead eventually to a severance from the aforementioned "web of international relations."

Beard observed in his introductory remarks to the last lecture that America's status as an industrial and trading nation was "the key to our domestic history and to our future foreign policies," with present signs indicating a continuing dependence upon foreign trade for national prosperity. Emerging from World War I as "first among the investing, industrial, commercial, maritime, and naval powers of the earth," the United States was in a favored position and thus appeared to be on the threshold of penetrating "the most inaccessible markets of the most distant lands."[25]

Since he had previously indicated his belief that the historic competition for overseas markets had led to imperialism, armaments races, and warfare, Beard regarded these new economic opportunities as being fraught with dangerous pitfalls, particularly in the Far East. He noted that the cornerstone of American diplomacy in that area of the world—the Open Door policy—appeared to have the dual advantage of satisfying pecuniary interests and ethical principles. But the fact that the recently concluded Washington Conference (1921–22) had been so involved with Pacific problems aroused his interest and concern. He was especially attracted to a remark in Warren G. Harding's Senate address in which he asked for approval of the major treaties concluded at the conference and in which the president had said that "the Pacific had its menaces and they deeply concerned us."[26]

To Beard, these "menaces" meant Japanese threats to American commercial interests in the Orient. He concluded that American diplomacy at the Washington Conference, owing to power vacuums created by the war, was essentially designed to isolate and check Japan by abrogating her twenty-year alliance with Great Britain, by keeping Japan in a position of naval inferiority, and by imposing a self-denying pledge on any possible expansionist ambitions Japan might have in East Asia. Although the fulfillment of these objectives presumably would carry out the principles of the Open

25. Ibid., pp. 240, 242, 251.
26. Ibid., pp. 253–54, 258–59.

Door policy, Beard wondered whether such a policy was in the national interest in view of the "intense and active rivalry" it would lead to with England and France, as well as Japan. "Shall the government," he asked, "follow trade and investments?"[27]

The answer to this question, he believed, would be determined by weighing the consequences of three policies open to the government and people of the United States. The first was "the policy of positive imperialism naked and unashamed." This policy, employing all the diplomatic and military instruments of the government, was dismissed by Beard because it entailed too many risks to national security and prosperity in behalf of special economic interests. The social consequences in the possible development of a "vaster aristocracy of wealth and a huger proletariat" also made it unacceptable.[28]

A second possible policy proposed by Beard was "that of no policy at all, save the policy of drift and muddle." In pursuit of overseas markets and investments, "it would follow in the paths of Alexander and Caesar but would be content with the philosophy of Buncombe County." Such a policy might achieve a number of things, Beard admitted, but he sarcastically stipulated only one possible accomplishment: "It might land the nation at the gates of destruction."[29]

The third policy received his most sympathetic consideration and, although proposed in 1922, embodied many features of his "continental Americanism" thesis of the 1930s. The devotees of imperialism, he remarked, referred to this policy disparagingly as "Little Americanism." As Beard described the policy, it would mean that the government of the United States would not use diplomatic or military means to encourage or protect the foreign trade or investments of American citizens; territorial annexations would cease, and spheres of influence would be discontinued; the Philippines would be granted independence, and Hawaii would become the farthest outpost of American interests and security in the Pacific; an army and navy would be established "by universal military service if necessary, and perhaps preferably"; and the American government might consider membership in the League

27. Ibid., pp. 259–62, 266.
28. Ibid., pp. 267–69.
29. Ibid., p. 270.

of Nations if other countries "were prepared to adopt a similar domestic policy." This diplomatic agenda, he declared, "would bend all national genius upon the creation of a civilization which, in power and glory and noble living, would rise above all the achievements of the past."[30]

During the two years which followed the Dartmouth lectures (1922–23), Charles and Mary Beard made two extensive trips to the Far East. About twenty-five years later, Beard could still recall that the first visit had such a profound impact upon him that he "became a changed person. I have never been the same again!"[31] These journeys, buttressed by his earlier speculations on American-Japanese rivalry and the furor caused by the discriminatory Immigration Act of 1924, led him, in 1925, to write an article analyzing the prospects of war between the United States and Japan. Once again, he set forth a number of opinions that were to be revived during the 1930s.

Beard did not discount the possibility of an armed clash between the United States and Japan arising out of economic competition for trade and investment opportunities in China. But he ridiculed the suggestion that the Japanese could "cross the Pacific Ocean, assail our Western coast and . . . seize all the territory as far east as Denver." Japan simply was not powerful or wealthy enough to contemplate such a scheme. At best, the Japanese might seize the Philippines. In that event, he observed with undisguised irony,

---

30. Ibid., pp. 269–70.
31. Beard to Curti, January 29, 1947, Curti Papers, Box 4, Folder 13. The first visit, in the winter and spring of 1922–23, was undertaken at the personal invitation of the mayor of Tokyo, Viscount Goto. In a nonofficial capacity, Beard was to advise the municipal authorities on administrative reforms. The results were recorded in Beard's *Administration and Politics of Tokyo: A Survey and Opinions.* The second trip was made after the Tokyo earthquake of September 1923, when Beard volunteered his services to help plan the rebuilding of the city: *New York Times,* September 5, 1923, p. 4; September 13, 1923, p. 5; September 17, 1923, p. 14; November 29, 1923, p. 35. Beard's modernization plan was not accepted, however, and he left discouraged because of the obstructionism of Tokyo real estate interests: A. Vagts to author, October 22, 1967. A fascinating postscript to this episode was a post-1945 conjecture in a Japanese newspaper: "Had [Beard's] plan been brought to reality, Tokyo would not have burned like a celluloid village even in [the] World War II bombings." Quoted in M. R. Beard, *The Making of C. A. Beard,* p. 26. During these visits to Tokyo, Beard presumably met Prince Konoye, later premier of Japan (1937–41): Beard to Morgenstern, October 20, 1947, Morgenstern Papers.

considerable effort would be required "to restore them to the position of liberty which they now so happily enjoy under American
sovereignty."[32]

The America that would emerge victorious from this hypothet-
ical war, he conjectured, probably would occupy Japanese-held
territories in the Far East (Formosa and Korea), as well as create
a few thousand millionaires. But he feared that the consequences
to life in the United States, notably in the violation of civil liberties, would more than offset the material gains of a war caused by
economic rivalry. This potential unpleasantness could be avoided,
Beard suggested, if Americans would pay more attention to the
statistics of trade and finance which demonstrated that our business dealings with Japan were far more profitable than with China.
In short, a proper understanding of where our economic interests
in the Far East really lay would enhance the prospects of peace
between the United States and Japan.[33]

The diplomatic record of the Harding and Coolidge admin-
istrations also influenced Beard's growing apprehension about the
direction in which American foreign policy was moving in the
mid-1920s. In their monumental study *The Rise of American
Civilization* (1927), the Beards made it clear that they found little
cause for optimism in contemporary foreign affairs. Specifically,
the husband and wife team detected what they regarded as a dis-
turbing tendency that was contradictory in nature. International
political entanglements such as the League of Nations, they noted,
may well have been anathema to both presidents. But the vigorous
pursuit of foreign commercial ventures saw the Harding administration take "all necessary and appropriate steps to protect and
advance the claims of business enterprise to goods of a ponderable
character."[34]

This policy reached its apogee under Calvin Coolidge, with
Secretary of the Navy Curtis Wilbur as one of its foremost official
spokesmen. In the summer of 1927, Beard publicly attacked Wilbur

32. C. A. Beard, "War with Japan: What Shall We Get Out of It?" p. 311.
33. Ibid. This idea of commercial rivalry in East Asia as the fundamental
reason for Japanese-American antagonisms was reiterated the following year in
an article Beard wrote with Mary Beard, "America and the Far East: The
Issues of Pacific Policy."
34. 2:680–81.

for his espousal of the notion that the government should protect private foreign investment anywhere in the world. Anticipating a prominent liberal isolationist theme in his *Open Door at Home* (1934), Beard maintained that every dollar in the "surplus of plutocracy" which was diverted from foreign investment to domestic use benefitted the nation as a whole. Put into effect on a large scale, he said, this program "would reduce our chances of becoming mixed-up in the next European adventure in Christian ballistics."[35]

In 1927–28, Charles and Mary Beard once again visited Europe. The trip was made at the request of the American-Yugoslav Society of New York and sponsored by the National Institute of Municipal Administration. In no sense, however, was it associated with activities in behalf of the government of Yugoslavia.[36] As a result of extensive travel throughout the country plus conversations with representatives of minority groups and some officials, Beard, in collaboration with George Radin, wrote *The Balkan Pivot, Yugoslavia: A Study in Government and Administration* (1929). Though the study dealt primarily with administrative conditions in that country, the authors pointed to the continuing political instability in the Balkans that could lead to a new flare-up. Were this to happen, they wondered, "do the peoples of Germany, France, England, and the United States wish to shed their blood and pour out their treasure in an effort to substitute new ways for old?"[37]

While in Yugoslavia, the Beards had an opportunity to visit with Stephen Raditch, leader of the Croatian Peasant Party, and also to attend a session of the Yugoslav Parliament. Prior to departing Belgrade for Greece, Mrs. Beard, in a letter to her daughter and son-in-law, wrote critically of the politics of Yugoslavia, observing that Raditch wanted the king to turn the country over to the army. About four months later, on June 20, 1928, Raditch was assassinated by a political rival, an episode which profoundly shocked Charles Beard.[38] According to a close friend, Beard returned to America in 1928 in a disillusioned frame of mind and often spoke

35. Ibid., 2:704–5; quoted in *New York Times*, August 3, 1927, p. 9.
36. M. R. Beard to Barnes, April 5, 1951, Barnes Papers.
37. Pages vi, 304, 321.
38. M. Vagts to author, February 16, 1971. Although Beard did not approve of all of Raditch's policies, he consented to write a memorial: "The Last Days of Stephen Raditch."

of the whole of Europe as just a "big Balkans" and a "madhouse."[39] Conceivably, it was about the time that Beard returned to the United States that he wrote a letter to Harry Elmer Barnes in which he complained about being "sick of the sniffling gang that runs Europe." The reluctance of European nations to pay "honest debts" also bothered him and led him to conclude, "But I am not going to have any more wool pulled over my eyes, if I can help it."[40]

Throughout 1928 and into early 1929, there were other signs that his recent trip had produced a profound skepticism of, if not outright contempt for, European civilization. On his visit he had met a number of German professors, whose obsession with the "war guilt" question disturbed the American historian.[41] Yet, in an article published in January 1929, Beard seemed sympathetically inclined toward those Germans who believed their country had been unjustly treated in the Treaty of Versailles with respect to such things as heavy indemnities and the loss of territory in which German nationals still resided.[42]

In the same essay, Beard presented a devastatingly ironic analysis of the practical effects which the Kellogg-Briand Pact (August 1928) might have in preventing carnage on the scale of World War I. The world, he noted, "is spending more money for preparedness in 1928 than in 1912." Thus, "at the very moment when war as an instrument of national policy (with reservations) is solemnly renounced, the civilized world, comparatively speaking, has ready for death and destruction bigger and better armaments than ever in its history."[43]

Shortly after this doleful commentary, Beard demonstrated a growing impatience with some of the smug criticisms of American civilization on the part of European intellectuals, some of whose

39. Quoted in Counts, "Charles Beard, the Public Man," in *Beard Appraisal*, p. 235. In later years, the memory of the time spent in Yugoslavia prompted Beard's allusion to a prominent internationalist-minded journalist in the following statement to Eric F. Goldman: "Let Dorothy Thompson settle the problems of Europe, I can't" (*Rendezvous with Destiny*, p. 235).

40. Beard to Barnes, June 24, 1928(?), Barnes Papers. Barnes placed the notation "late 1920's" on this letter.

41. A. Vagts to Cushing Strout, October 31, 1958, copy of letter in "The Charles A. Beard File," Microfilm No. 139.

42. "Bigger and Better Armaments," pp. 141–42.

43. Ibid., p. 135.

own notions of the good life in industrial societies struck him as archaic or irrelevant. But he also indicated his continuing disenchantment with the "ukases" of President Coolidge and Secretary of the Navy Wilbur for having asserted so often that "American citizens and American dollars are [to be] followed by the flag wherever they go on the broad surface of the earth."⁴⁴

Simultaneously, Mussolini's Italy was briefly regarded by Beard and some other prominent American liberals as one European country that ought to be looked at objectively for any universal lessons it might hold for the corporate organization of modern societies. In 1929, an American philosopher, Herbert W. Schneider, returned from research in Italy and was "enthusiastically questioned" by Beard about the nature of the Fascist state.⁴⁵ Beard then reviewed Schneider's book, *Making the Fascist State* (1928). He admitted that Italy under Mussolini repressed personal liberties and that the dictator might resort to foreign adventures to solve domestic problems. Beard insisted, nevertheless, that "an amazing experiment" was being undertaken in Italy. "It would be a mistake," he concluded, "to allow feelings aroused by contemplating the harsh deeds and extravagant assertions that have accompanied the Fascist process . . . to obscure the potentialities and the lessons of the adventure."⁴⁶

Despite the overall mood of discouragement reflected in many of Beard's writings in the year before the stock market crash, some of his mordant commentaries were paralleled by more hopeful views of world affairs. In August 1928, for example, Beard sounded an affirmative note in the preface to *Whither Mankind*, when he wrote that "for visions of despair," the contributors to the volume substituted "a more cheerful outlook upon the future of modern civilization, without at the same time resorting to the optimism of the real-estate agent." In the epilogue, he contended that "nations must associate themselves in understandings and guarantees" in order to avoid the devastation of war. "The magnitude and difficulties of this undertaking are immense," he readily conceded, "but

44. "The American Invasion of Europe," p. 472.
45. John P. Diggins, "Flirtation with Fascism: American Pragmatic Liberals and Mussolini's Italy," p. 493.
46. "Making the Fascist State," p. 278.

the League of Nations and treaties of renunciation already indicate
what the strategy of peace may be."[47]
Further evidence that Beard had partially returned to a liberal-
internationalist stance may be seen in an article published in
Harper's in February 1929, in which he went so far as to depict
the United States as a makeweight to any threat to the European
balance of power. "The almost dead certainty that the United
States will throw her sword into the scale if hostilities open again,"
he predicted, "gives pause to the boldest of warmakers." There
were also words of praise for the League of Nations, for, despite
some shortcomings, its very existence lessened the probabilities of
"such subterfuges, evasions, and double-dealing as those which
eventuated in the World War." Regardless of America's "myth of
isolation," he added, and in view of the nation's economic power
and stake in world peace, "the United States is in the League and
it matters little whether or not its adhesion is indicated by parch-
ment and seals."[48]

In the same *Harper's* essay and in words that are in dramatic
contrast to his later observations on the disclosures of the Nye
Committee in 1935 and 1936, Beard assigned to international
bankers an almost benevolent role as promoters of peace in the
world community—in contrast to national bankers whose activities
had often fostered economic rivalries between nations. The establishment of the Bank for International Settlement, a provision of
the Young Plan adopted in August 1929, gave Beard and James
Harvey Robinson additional reason to believe in 1930 that agencies of international finance could make positive contributions to
peace.[49]

Also in 1930, Beard and his son, William, forcefully underscored
the possible danger to the United States of blindly accepting isolationism. This doctrine was one of the "popular shibboleths approved by millions of citizens who could not give a ten-word
account" of its inner significance. It was, moreover, a "dogma"
formulated before technological developments had made the secur-

47. Beard, ed., *Whither Mankind: A Panorama of Modern Civilization*, pp. v,
407–8.
48. "Prospects for Peace," pp. 327, 330.
49. Ibid., pp. 327–28; *The Development of Modern Europe*, rev. ed., 2:546.

ity of formidable ocean barriers obsolete. "Hence the creed of isolationism which once seemed convincing," Charles and William Beard concluded, "may be employed to defeat its own purpose, namely, the maintenance of national security."[50]

Beard's former bitterness over "secret diplomacy" and the failure of statesmen to consult public opinion also seemed to be moderated in 1930. Father and son noted that there was substantial evidence that "clandestine negotiations" could be more productive of peace and good will between nations than the constant airing of diplomatic disputes in public. Further, the highly technical aspects of diplomacy and the uncertain passions of the general public did not justify the practice of constantly submitting important matters of foreign policy directly to the public for decisions. "The problem is one of intelligent discretion on the part of officials and watchfulness on the part of the public."[51]

Beard's ambivalent and shifting views on foreign affairs in the decade after World War I suggest the possible appropriateness of the phrase "Charles A. Beard in Midpassage" to describe this period in his life. One can almost sense, particularly in his writings that were affected by his personal experiences in Europe and Asia, his mental struggle as he weighed the merits of internationalism versus isolationism. He seemed torn between supporting what he often perceived to be the perilous necessity of extensive American participation in world affairs, or embracing a limited foreign policy in which future Americans would not have to feel guilt or responsibility for the devastating consequences of war such as those Beard had witnessed in Europe.[52]

Nevertheless, Beard appeared to face the decade of the 1930s with a relatively optimistic and qualified internationalist outlook. But even though he turned away from this outlook, Beard would continue, as he had in the 1920s, to shape his isolationist arguments within the general framework of the goals of national secur-

50. *The American Leviathan*, pp. 732–33, 736.
51. Ibid., pp. 730–32.
52. Professor C. Vann Woodward has suggested that a widespread attitude of this nature may explain, in part, the profound national isolationism of the 1930s. "The urge to return to a free security age of innocence and the flight from the guilt of wielding power," he wrote, "may be traced in elaborate efforts to maintain neutrality, in desperate struggles for isolationism and 'America First,' as well as in the idealistic plans of religious and secular pacifists": "The Age of Reinterpretation," p. 8.

ity and the extension of domestic liberal reform. Since the seeds of his intense reaction to an enlarged American involvement in world affairs—especially that of a commercial nature—had been sown and nurtured in the 1920s, Beard's advocacy of a policy of "continental Americanism," or isolationism, throughout the 1930s represented the fruition of previous convictions rather than a sharp departure from them or an entirely new thesis.

5

Formulating a Philosophy of
Isolationism, 1931-1935

Aᴀғᴛᴇʀ 1930, the deepening of the Great Depression, accompanied by world-wide economic, political, and military instability, was the major force influencing Beard's decision to devote the remainder of his life to advocating what he called a policy of "continental Americanism." His sweepingly revisionist interpretation of America's entrance into World War I fostered, to some degree, a radical departure from his internationalist views of previous decades. Finally, his reflections on the historiographical writings of European historians, begun in the late 1920s, continued to interest him and tended to make him more self-conscious about the relevance of frames of reference, causation, and objectivity in his approach to the study of American history during the 1930s and after. Some reservations might be expressed, however, as to whether Beard's speculations on historical relativism constituted a startling alteration of his earlier notions about the meliorist function of the historian. One may also question whether these reflections necessarily caused him to adopt an isolationist outlook. Carl L. Becker, for example, did not find his own attachment to relativism an impediment to his support of an interventionist role for the United States before 1941.[1]

1. Maurice Mandlebaum, "Causal Analysis in History," pp. 37–39; Harry J. Marks, "Ground under Our Feet: Beard's Relativism"; Whitaker T. Deininger,

During the first half of the decade of the 1930s, Beard formulated a major theory of foreign policy in which he was able to synthesize a number of previous ideas and attitudes, such as the economic interpretation of history, an antagonism toward laissez-faire economic theory, and a hostility toward militarism. The end result was *The Idea of National Interest: An Analytical Study in American Foreign Policy* and *The Open Door at Home: A Trial Philosophy of National Interest.* Taken together they constitute Beard's magnum opus on the theoretical and practical aspects of American diplomatic history.

Fundamental to Beard's thinking on foreign affairs in the early 1930s was his continuing belief in the Idea of Progress which, in the judgment of one historian, may account for Beard's passionate attachment to isolationism.[2] In the midst of the worst years of the Depression, he sought the ultimate fulfillment of this idea in the application of the rational techniques of technology to national planning to implement comprehensive economic and social reform. Thus, in mid-1931, Beard outlined his thoughts on national planning. He called for Congress to establish a National Economic Council that would coordinate the functions of finance, production, and distribution in a number of the nation's major industries. Other agencies under this council would be responsible for bringing about an efficient use and consumption of mineral and agricultural resources.[3]

Beard pointed out why the successful operation of such an ambitious domestic program probably would require significant revisions in the economic aspects of American foreign policy. Briefly, he suggested that the pursuit of foreign trade and investments on a substantial level would not solve, and might impede, domestic

---

"The Skepticism and Historical Faith of C. A. Beard"; Chester M. Destler, "Some Observations on Contemporary Historical Theory," p. 508; Lloyd R. Sorenson, "Charles A. Beard and German Historiographical Thought"; Harvey Wish, *The American Historian: A Social-Intellectual History of the Writing of the American Past,* pp. 147, 268, 289–90; Strout, *The Pragmatic Revolt,* pp. 128, 152; Hofstadter, *The Progressive Historians,* pp. 316–17.

2. Strout, *The Pragmatic Revolt,* p. 116. In 1932, Beard contributed a long introduction to a reprint of J. B. Bury's *Idea of Progress,* in which he wrote that it was an interpretation of history which, "as a faith in possibilities, [may] actually make history" (p. xxxviii).

3. C. A. Beard, ed., *America Faces the Future,* pp. 124–32. Beard's essay in this symposium on the Great Depression originally appeared as "A 'Five Year Plan' for America."

recovery. He also feared that war with economically competitive nations might result if the United States did not reduce significantly its commercial activities in a world increasingly beset by economic chaos and political instability. Accordingly, he recommended that a syndicate of the major export-import corporations be established to control America's foreign trade and investment. Beard hoped that such a syndicate would be able to bring about a more efficient and equitable distribution of the nation's products in the home market, thereby curtailing the necessity to export so-called surplus goods. He also envisioned a barter system whereby nations would exchange only those commodities not supplied by their own domestic enterprises, and thus remove wasteful competition and possible military conflict in the rivalry for world markets. Among his major proposals, he urged tighter controls over the issuance of foreign securities in the United States and the prevention of American loan extensions to "irresponsible governments."[4]

Still in effect at the time Beard presented this plan was President Herbert Hoover's moratorium on the payment of World War I debts. While he had earlier complained about the former Allies' nonpayment, Beard now was prepared to see the United States cancel these debts. But a hint of his growing commitment to economic nationalism and a minimum of diplomatic obligations is to be seen in the condition he attached to such cancellation—that all the debtor countries would have to reduce their armies to the level of national police forces. The United States itself would have to abandon what Beard puckishly called the "Coolidge theorem" of diplomacy, in which the army and navy were to be of sufficient strength "to protect any American citizen who wants to make ten per cent on the bonds of Weissnichtwo or sell cornflakes, shoehorns, and collar buttons to the world willy-nilly."[5]

Beard's analysis and proposals seemed to project the hard-headed realism often ascribed to him. But, in a sense, he was a utopian, or at least an idealist, in spite of himself. He was confident that the voluntary adoption of his plan would afford a golden opportunity to "lop off the deadwood of our futile plutocracy, so sinister in its influences on politics, culture and rational living."[6] Yet, as one reviewer could not resist commenting, he was surprised that

4. *America Faces the Future*, p. 136.
5. Ibid., p. 137.
6. Ibid., p. 124.

"the foremost historian of American class struggles" could assume that this plutocracy would accept, without a "bitter struggle," Beard's suggested restrictions on its economic and political activities.[7]

Additional evidence of Beard's willingness to endorse the notion of economic nationalism may be discerned in his response to the tariff issue in the campaign of 1932. In contrast to his many previous criticisms of the high protective tariff, he attacked the low-tariff advocates in both major parties for assuming that their programs would restore prosperity and rescue the free enterprise system. Reduction of existing tariff barriers, he insisted, would only flood the American market with cheaper foreign-made goods and would lead to further lay-offs of American workers.[8]

Beard was correct in noting that a significant removal of tariff barriers would not be a panacea for a desperately ailing economy. But he failed to consider the possible adverse impact of the Hawley-Smoot Tariff (1930) on America's relations with other countries and the potentially unfavorable consequences to the nation's domestic economy. In particular, he seemed to regard as unimportant the way in which the Hawley-Smoot legislation had already encouraged retaliatory tariffs that reflected, on an international scale, some of the "rugged individualism" in American life that Beard deplored.[9] These retaliatory tariffs, in turn, fostered the creed of every nation for itself and devil take the hindmost. The result of America's high tariff schedule was a partial intensification of those international frictions which Beard hoped to avoid by having the United States pursue what he regarded as a more rational trade policy.[10]

Paralleling Beard's search for ways to make the national economy free of extensive foreign commerce were his efforts to formulate a theory of national defense consistent with, and adequate to, the foreign policy goals and needs of the United States. In this quest, he was extremely critical of the American military establishment, particularly the United States Navy. He thus devoted considerable thought to the historical role of those he derisively

7. Carter Goodrich, review of America Faces the Future, in New Republic, March 9, 1932, p. 105.
8. Beard, "The Tariff Campaign: The Last Gasp."
9. Beard, "The Myth of Rugged American Individualism."
10. Joseph M. Jones, Jr., Tariff Retaliation: Repercussions of the Hawley-Smoot Bill.

labeled the "Big Navy Boys" in shaping American defense and diplomatic policies. His analysis sharply challenged the arguments, motives, and behavior of naval officers, of bureaucrats in the Department of the Navy, of politicians sympathetic to naval expansion, and of civilians who actively supported programs calling for increased naval expenditures.[11]

Beard had briefly considered these problems during the 1920s. But his most extensive and penetrating criticisms were presented in 1931 and 1932, with briefer elaborations throughout that decade.[12] Coincident with the early stages of the Great Depression, Beard had avidly read newspapers, periodicals, and published accounts of House and Senate hearings from 1929 to 1930, involving such matters as the failure of the Geneva Naval Disarmament Conference (1927), controversies in the Hoover administration over naval appropriations, debates over the approval of the London Naval Treaty (1930), and discussions over whether to grant independence to the Philippines. There was also a much publicized imbroglio in the fall of 1931 between President Hoover and some members of the Navy League of the United States. A year before, Beard privately had praised Hoover's secretary of state, Henry L. Stimson, for his public address in behalf of the London Treaty and for his "courageous action all along in connection with the negotiation and defense of the treaty, especially for telling so much wholesome truth in the radio address."[13] Perhaps the president knew of this praise and was encouraged enough, in the midst of the Navy League imbroglio, to place a phone call to Beard at his home in New Milford, Connecticut. The intent was to have Beard come to Washington to assist the president in his campaign against this nongovernmental agency which, for some time, had been a proponent of a "Big Navy." But the initial invitation was quickly withdrawn.[14]

11. For a detailed discussion of this theme covering the 1920s and 1930s, see Thomas C. Kennedy, "Charles A. Beard and the 'Big Navy Boys.'"
12. Beard, "Making a Bigger and Better Navy"; three articles entitled "Big Navy Boys"; "Confusion over National Defense: Shall We Listen to the Pacifists or the Admirals?" *Harper's*, February 1932, pp. 257–67. Most of the material in these articles was reprinted in C. A. Beard, *The Navy: Defense or Portent?*
13. Beard to Stimson, June 30, 1930, Stimson Papers, Yale University Library.
14. A. Vagts to author, October 22, 1967. The suspicion obtrudes that there may have been some advisors close to Hoover who, aware of Beard's criticisms of Coolidge's naval policy, feared they might be admitting a Trojan Horse within the gates and thus counseled the President to change his mind. Such a possible interpretation could be read into a letter Hoover's secretary of the

This episode may have had something to do with the timing of Beard's slashing indictment of American naval policy in 1931–32. But the most immediate stimulus was his reading of Eckart Kehr's *Schlachtflottenbau und Parteipolitik, 1894–1902* (1930), a work brought to his attention by his son-in-law, Alfred Vagts, a prominent military historian.[15] The study dealt with the political, economic, and ideological assumptions that underlay Germany's search, around the turn of the century, for "a place in the sun" of world politics, particularly through sea power. The "lessons of history" which Beard extrapolated from Kehr's work were clearly intended to be yardsticks for measuring recent naval policies of the United States, and a warning against the possible baneful domestic and foreign consequences should the "Big Navy Boys" be allowed to dictate comparable naval expansion for the United States. At this time, and throughout the 1930s, Beard regarded increased naval appropriations as a brake upon domestic economic recovery, as an instrument of economic expansion designed to benefit a few, as a threat to the principle of civilian supremacy over the military in formulating and executing defense policy, and as a grave provocation to other sea powers, especially Japan.[16]

A corollary of Beard's critical appraisal of extensive foreign commercial endeavors and increased naval expenditures during the early 1930s was his gradual acceptance of a large measure of diplomatic nonentanglement. Despite his own trenchant and perceptive remarks about the antidemocratic attitudes, militaristic behavior, and aggressively expansionist designs of Japan, Germany, and Italy,[17] he was reluctant to endorse significant diplomatic cooperation with nations which did not blatantly display these characteristics. In the second half of the decade, he occasionally embraced a rather cynical view of all European and Asian nations. When

navy, Charles F. Adams, wrote in rebuttal to Beard's *Harper's* article of February 1932. Secretary Adams vigorously protested what he thought to be Beard's insinuation that the Navy Department in the Hoover administration embraced, or was influenced by, the program of the Navy League. Beard denied any intention of conveying such an impression: *Harper's*, May 1932 [pp. 800–804?].

15. A. Vagts to author, October 18, 1967.

16. For an in-depth evaluation of his concerns and arguments along these lines, see Thomas C. Kennedy, "Beard vs. F.D.R. on National Defense and Rearmament."

17. See, for example, Beard, "Spooks: Made in Germany"; "Hitlerism and Our Liberties"; "Education under the Nazis"; "March and Countermarch."

he did so, he came uncomfortably close to fitting Albert K. Weinberg's witty description of American isolationists as persons who virtually maintained that "international society is a wanton, and that not even if the American marries the wench can he make an honest woman of her."[18]

In late 1931 and early 1932, however, Beard could still publicly recommend that the United States should adhere to the World Court and should abide by the tenets of the Kellogg-Briand Pact. He also contended that social science teachers were obligated "to create in the popular mind the conditions favorable to continuous realization" of the principles of the multilateral agreement renouncing war as an instrument of national policy.[19]

The concurrent Japanese invasion and conquest of Manchuria provided Beard with an important test of some of these internationalist-oriented ideas. In December 1931, soon after Japanese forces had become firmly entrenched in the Chinese province, Beard wrote a letter to the editor of the *New Republic* in which he discussed the influence of Japan's generals and admirals upon foreign policy. The army and navy in that country, he noted, were independent of civilian authority and were thus in a position to shape political and military decisions that could commit the government to an ambitious program of expansion. Of the Japanese militarists, he said, "Judging from the doings of their brethren in other countries, it [the Manchurian invasion] doubtless had some relation to 'strategic frontiers' which must be extended to the moon unless stopped by some immovable body."[20]

Approximately one week after Japan had established the puppet state of Manchukuo, Beard addressed a regional conference of professors held at the University of Southern California. In the speech, he lamented that "one more war fought with the latest instruments of technology will blast Western civilization from center to circumference." He referred to America's commitment to the principle of consulting with those powers, the signers of the Four Power Treaty of 1922, that had interests in the Pacific region, and of cooperating with the League of Nations for "specific pur-

18. "The Historical Meaning of the American Doctrine of Isolation," p. 545.
19. Beard, *America Faces the Future*, pp. 136–37; *A Charter for the Social Sciences in the Schools*, pp. 51–52.
20. Beard, "Who Runs the Japanese Government?"

poses." But Beard also implied that he rejected the notion of substantive American commitments to restrain Japan. He insisted that the United States ought to concern itself only with the defense of its "continental heritage." Moreover, such "cooperative under-takings" in which the United States might engage with other na-tions had to be supplemented by "reasoned policy at home with respect to commitments abroad in the form of foreign loans and trade rivalry supported by bounties, subsidies, and military force."[21] Thus, Beard's response to the first overt act of totalitarian aggres-sion in the 1930s was largely a commitment to ideals rather than action, and involved almost no sacrifices to the principle of abso-lute national sovereignty.

During the two years before Franklin D. Roosevelt was inaugu-rated, Beard recorded some of the arguments and attitudes that he would use as bench marks against which to measure the aims and accomplishments of a new president's diplomacy. This was partially achieved during the first year and a half of the New Deal—in Beard's mature reflections on the theoretical bases of American foreign policy, *The Idea of National Interest*, and in the program-matic sequel, *The Open Door at Home*.

Beard's scholarly concern about the meanings and uses of the phrase "national interest" was first demonstrated in a noteworthy fashion in an article written a few months before the convening of the Geneva Disarmament Conference in February 1932. In it, he posed a number of questions which he believed all the delegates should contemplate prior to the time of the conference: "What is the national interest? Who has the right to define it? What is ade-quate defense? Adequate to what and to whom? Why do armies and navies grow bigger and better? What is to be gained by war? Who gains it, when, as, and if? Do navalism and imperialism pay? Pay whom?"[22] Beard went on to indicate that he was distressed by the apparent failure of responsible officials to raise such questions and added that there was no study to which one could refer for guidance. Coincident with the writing of the essay, Beard ap-proached Frederick P. Keppel, an executive of the Carnegie Cor-poration, with the suggestion that such an inquiry into "national interest" be undertaken. In March 1932, it was reported that Beard

21. Quoted in *New York Times*, February 28, 1932, sec. 2, p. 4.
22. Beard, "Making a Bigger and Better Navy," p. 223.

had been asked by the Social Science Research Council to make this investigation.[23]

The opening chapter of *The Idea of National Interest* was devoted to a brief consideration of the historical background of the concept of "national interest." Its forerunners included the formulas of monarchical "reasons of state" and feudal notions of "national honor." Appeals to "national interest" were not only relatively recent, according to Beard, but were clearly related to the simultaneous developments of the "national commercial state" and "republican control over national affairs."[24]

In an intensive analysis of the American usages of the concept, from the Founding Fathers to FDR, Beard concluded that the term "national interest" had had ambiguous, and sometimes contradictory, meanings when it had been employed as an abstract formula in American diplomacy. When applied to concrete issues, however, American statesmen—in domestic as well as foreign policies—generally had been guided by the economic and political interests of the party and special groups they represented. The core of Beard's interpretation—which was first broached in his detailed study of the controversy over Jay's Treaty (1794), *The Economic Origins of Jeffersonian Democracy* (1915), and then applied to American political history in *The American Party Battle* (1928)—was that there had always been two rather clear-cut conceptions of the term national interest, which he often designated "Jeffersonian" and "Hamiltonian." Jefferson's political constituency and economic concerns were essentially agrarian; though expansionist, their primary goal was the acquisition of land within the continental domain for the purpose of enlarging a self-sufficient, independent civilization. Hamilton's followers and their economic activities were fundamentally commercial; thus, they consistently sought overseas markets as an outlet for manufactured goods and investment capital. By the late nineteenth century, the requirements of the latter conception of national interest demanded overseas terri-

23. *New York Times*, March 23, 1932, p. 23; George R. Leighton, "Beard and Foreign Policy," in *Beard Appraisal*, p. 169.
24. Beard and George H. E. Smith, *The Idea of National Interest*, p. 42. Smith was a professor of political science at Yale University, who, from 1933 to 1940, assisted Beard with his research and collaborated with him in writing this and five other studies.

tories in the Caribbean and Far East, in part for strategic reasons, but basically for further commercial expansion.[25]

The results of both conceptions, Beard thought, had often been contrary to the general welfare of the American people. But this was especially true of the Hamiltonian, or Federalist-Whig-Republican, application of national interest, for it had led to increasingly greater international commitments and naval expansion, both of which heightened rivalries with other nations in the competition for markets and territories. Such activities did not pay, and Beard sought to discredit the Hamiltonian stance by employing a balance sheet technique. This involved the calculation of the American stake in foreign trade and investment, as measured against the risk of political and military involvement that often accompanied these "outward thrusts of power," as Beard was fond of calling such activities.

Of special relevance to Beard's argument that the United States should no longer pursue what he considered a provocative Far Eastern policy were the tables which demonstrated that since 1910, the volume of America's import-export trade with Japan had been approximately twice that of her trade with China.[26] However, he did not press such statistics to one logical conclusion, that the United States should continue and enlarge this profitable trade relationship with Japan.

To suggest the economic desirability of granting outright independence to the Philippines, Beard noted that the United States had suffered an unfavorable balance of trade with these islands since 1906, in that American imports over the years had exceeded the value of exports. Even if one were to include other Pacific possessions, such as Hawaii, Guam, Samoa, and Alaska, there was still an excess of imports over exports. Further, the combined value of this trade interchange was minor in comparison to the total American stake in foreign trade. "To safeguard this stake, to strengthen and increase it," Beard concluded with obvious displeasure, "the whole weight of government activities had been brought into play, on the hypothesis, and no doubt conscientious belief, that the 'national interest' is truly advanced."[27]

25. Ibid., pp. 52–88, 548–51.
26. Ibid., p. 284.
27. Ibid., pp. 292–96.

68   Charles A. Beard and American Foreign Policy

The numerous pages of tables and statistics, plus the conclusions drawn from them, served to underscore the overarching economic interpretation of history that Beard was applying to his study. To be sure, he granted that the notion of "moral obligation" had been one aspect of the idea of national interest as proclaimed by American leaders, particularly since the Spanish-American War. He even agreed that it could operate as an independent psychological force in the conduct of foreign affairs. On balance, however, Beard did not seem to regard the notion of moral obligation as a very real, or as an especially desirable, factor in explaining or guiding American diplomacy. He described it as the embarking upon projects "for uplifting, civilizing, or Christianizing other peoples beyond the confines of the country." But it was essentially a "covering ideology" intended to serve materialistic, not idealistic, ends.[28]

Beard's own ideas about how America's national interest should be defined and carried out were subtly implied throughout the work. Carl L. Becker, with whom Beard exchanged a modest number of cordial letters during the 1930s and early 1940s, deftly made the following observation in his review of the work: "The pattern in which he arranges his facts in the present volume is revealing enough by itself, but the author is always at hand, for any reader who needs a little help, to run his pointer over the essential facts of the design."[29]

Beard's intention to assume the role of a frank advocate of a program of social, economic, and political nationalism was made crystal clear in his companion volume, *The Open Door at Home: A Trial Philosophy of National Interest.* The title of the work, he remarked in the preface, was borrowed in part from a "misleading formula of diplomacy" that ostensibly sought to promote the general welfare through the extensive pursuit of foreign commerce. As used in the book, however, the formula was "a direct antithesis of the historic policy which has eventuated in the present economic calamity."[30] The four areas in which his "trial philosophy of na-

28. Ibid., pp. 358, 388–89.
29. Carl L. Becker, review of *National Interest*, in *Yale Review* 23 (Summer 1934):816. Their correspondence, from 1932 to 1944, is in the Carl Becker Papers, John M. Olin Research Library, Cornell University.
30. Beard and George H. E. Smith, *The Open Door at Home: A Trial Philosophy of National Interest*, p. vii, hereafter cited as *Open Door*.

tional interest" was to be applied were nationality, national economy, national defense, and international relations.

Up to this point in his career, Beard's interest in preserving and promoting what he conceived of as distinctive qualities of American nationality, ethnically defined, did not represent a major theme in his writings. But by the early 1930s, for example, he was prepared to accept the quota system established by immigration legislation in the 1920s as a reasonable basis for maintaining what he called the "social cohesiveness and cooperative capacity" of American society. He felt this was essential in order that the existing racial mixtures, languages, and traditions of Americans from other countries would not be seriously altered by a tremendous wave of new immigration that could upset an already precarious balance. Though he repudiated the idea that race should be a determinant in establishing quotas, the "national origins" principle, which he tolerated, clearly discriminated against Orientals and persons of Latin and Slavic descent from Europe. He was most concerned, however, with the diplomatic implications of applying "universal ethics" to immigration policy. A thoroughly nondiscriminatory policy, he alleged, would mean acceptance of the principle that other nations not only had a right to dictate America's immigration legislation, but that their national interests took precedence over the national interests of the United States.[31]

In dealing with problems of the economy, Beard's principal recommendations included de-emphasizing foreign trade and investment and paying greater attention to production for domestic consumption. Policies in both areas would look to increasingly less dependence upon foreign economic relationships to bring about complete domestic recovery and security. He realized that the national planning measures necessary to maintain a satisfactory "national standard of life" would require the exercise of vigorous presidential authority. But he was confident this could be done without tampering with the Constitution.[32]

Beard's specific proposals for reducing foreign trade were more far-reaching than his export-import syndicate scheme of 1931. A Foreign Trade Authority would be set up in the State Department with substantial discretionary powers to control the nation's exports

31. Ibid., pp. 179–209.
32. Ibid., pp. 210–33, 308–11.

and imports. There could be some reciprocal trade agreements with certain countries, but they would have to be carried out under federal supervision in order to guarantee a flow of goods that would clearly contribute to the well-being of the American economy as a whole. As an alternative but possibly complementary plan, Beard proposed a scheme of tariff manipulation under which the Foreign Trade Authority would maintain up-to-date tariff schedules that could control the price and quantity of exports and imports.[33]

In one of the most vigorous and incisive summaries of the assumptions and aims of his trial philosophy, one which employed a favorite metaphor from Voltaire's *Candide*, Beard wrote that "by cultivating its own garden, by setting an example of national self-restraint . . . by making no commitments that cannot be readily enforced by arms, by adopting toward other nations a policy of fair and open commodity exchange, by refraining from giving them any moral advice on any subject, and by providing a military and naval machine as adequate as possible to the defense of this policy, the United States may realize maximum security, attain minimum dependence upon governments and conditions beyond its control, and develop its own resources to the utmost. Besides offering the most realistic approach to the dilemma and conforming to a high degree to the necessities presented by the posture of nations, it is a more promising way of life for the people of the United States."[34]

In both *The Idea of National Interest* and *The Open Door at Home*, Beard found opportunities to apply his analysis and philosophy to the early New Deal. His conclusions on the record of the first year were mixed; his hopes for the future were ambivalent. He was very encouraged by FDR's bold leadership in the domestic program for recovery, reform, and relief. But, despite earlier optimism in his treatment of the president's conduct of American diplomacy, Beard could not hide some of his disappointment over certain trends in the administration.[35] In contrast to his willing-

33. Ibid., pp. 287–94.
34. Ibid., pp. 273–74.
35. In a study completed in November 1933, Beard and Smith discussed the first few months of the New Deal. The authors thought the assumptions that guided FDR's recovery program included neither the notion that foreign trade was the only outlet for America's surplus goods nor the answer to America's economic problems. "Followed to its logical conclusions," they said, "this conception will lead to revolutionary adjustments in foreign trade and foreign

ness to accept a commanding role for the president in domestic matters, Beard began to lean toward the idea of severely limited presidential discretion in formulating and administering American foreign policy.

In *The Idea of National Interest*, it was noted that two major groups in the higher echelons of the Democratic Party were contending for leadership in guiding the foreign policy of the Roosevelt administration. The first, deriving inspiration from Woodrow Wilson and with Secretary of State Cordell Hull as its most prominent spokesman, embraced an internationalist outlook and was interested in ameliorating the current problems of world trade. "They look abroad," wrote Beard and George H. E. Smith, "for the escape from the dilemma presented by periodical crises, without offering any machinery for giving certain effect to their hopes or any policies guaranteed to work."[36]

The second group, though smaller, appeared to exercise greater influence in official circles and was led, Beard believed, by President Roosevelt himself. This group derived its inspiration from the principles of Jefferson, principles which Beard had already identified as including the desire to promote maximum national economic self-sufficiency and political independence in order to avoid foreign intrigues, entanglements, and war. These principles were part of a tradition in which "the old possibility of a distinct national life and character" continued to be "a living and vital force." For the group around Roosevelt which embraced this tradition, the fact that foreign trade accounted for less than 10 per cent of all American trade activity, whether foreign or domestic, demonstrated the importance of the strictly national market and the slight dependence of the United States upon foreign countries for economic prosperity.[37]

President Roosevelt's torpedoing of the London Economic Conference in July 1933 struck Beard as a proper application of the principles of Jefferson. In addition to defending FDR from charges that he was personally responsible for wrecking the conference,

---

relations": *The Future Comes: A Study of the New Deal*, p. 164, hereafter cited as *The Future Comes*.

36. *National Interest*, p. 533. Beard's collaborator blocked out this section on the New Deal, with Beard refining it. Smith to Beard, August 4, 1933, Smith Papers, Folder 2, Yale University Library.

37. *National Interest*, pp. 52–54, 85, 93, 534.

Beard claimed that since the conference and its agenda originally had been approved by President Hoover, Roosevelt was not bound to accept what Beard called the laissez-faire assumptions governing the deliberations. He further maintained that there had been no compelling reasons for believing that the other participating nations were prepared to make drastic changes in their own economic policies. He thus supported Roosevelt's contention that America's internal financial structure was of greater importance than the value of the dollar in relation to the currencies of other nations. Indeed, Beard lauded FDR's action as an example to other countries that foreign trade was not essential to a viable national economy. Under the new conception of national interest, he added, national security and prosperity were not to be achieved through international conferences or "outward thrusts of commercial power," but through an integrated domestic economy and a wider distribution of wealth.[38]

The wish seemed to be father to the latter thought, for Beard also saw some signs that portended a continuation of the "old nationalism" in the Hamiltonian tradition that would include the commercial imperialism of *Machtpolitik* (a German term for the idea of "power politics"). Specifically, President Roosevelt's shipbuilding program caused Beard to temper his optimism about the future of domestic "self-containment." His misgivings led him to speculate that a "grand diversion" in the Caribbean or the Pacific might be welcomed by the administration should the president's recovery program fail to solve the domestic economic crisis.[39] Beard did not explain what he meant by a "grand diversion," but he implied that FDR might resort to some kind of military action.

Similar reservations were expressed in *The Open Door at Home.* Beard was heartened by such measures as Roosevelt's recognition of the Soviet Union, his support of independence for the Philippines, and the abrogation of the Platt Amendment with regard to Cuba. But these actions were more than offset, in Beard's judgment, by the president's reassertion of the Open Door policy in the Far East, his expressed hope that foreign trade could be expanded, and his request for increased naval expenditures. If Roosevelt had a foreign policy that would not jeopardize his domestic program,

38. Ibid., pp. 542–45.
39. Ibid., pp. 548–49.

Beard thought he had yet to reveal it. In impassioned prose, Beard pleaded for the United States to "really make its diplomacy the diplomacy of 'the good neighbor,' as distinguished from the diplomacy of the dollar, the navy, and the marines," in order "to avoid costly and bloody entanglements in the historic quarrels of Europe and Asia."[40]

Beard's writing of *The Idea of National Interest* and *The Open Door at Home* when he did, and as he did, clearly constituted a personal "act of faith"; that is, he hoped his critical analysis of what he believed to be the controlling assumptions of American foreign policy would encourage the Roosevelt administration to formulate policies along the lines he proposed. Such policies, Beard was convinced, could be framed with a view to establishing in America a "collectivist democracy" or a "workers' republic," both of which he considered possible and desirable political-economic systems for the United States.[41] There is evidence that Beard was justified for a time in believing that these two volumes might carry weight in administration circles. For example, in the autumn of 1933, he and Mrs. Beard dined with the president and his wife in the White House where, Beard confided to George H. E. Smith, his collaborator on *The Idea of National Interest* and *The Open Door at Home*, he "got some first hand information on things." Later, he sent a copy of the book on national interest to the president.[42]

In January 1934, Ernest K. Lindley, one of FDR's favorite reporters, observed that Beard was "one of the intellectual parents of the New Deal." In part, this kinship was due to the presence of a number of Columbia University professors in the "Brain Trust," particularly Raymond Moley, a former student of "Uncle Charley." Lindley also thought the president's speeches "revealed that he understood the development of the United States very much as Mr. Beard saw it." In reviewing *The Open Door at Home*,

40. *Open Door*, pp. 316–19.
41. Beard, "Written History as an Act of Faith," p. 228; "The World as I Want It," p. 333.
42. Beard to Smith, October 28, 1934, Smith Papers, Folder 3; *National Interest*, edited with new material by A. Vagts and W. Beard (Chicago: Quadrangle Paperbacks, 1966), p. xvi. In February, 1934, the Beards attended an Army and Navy reception at the White House, where, according to their daughter, "Beard met several leading military men": M. Vagts to author, February 16, 1971.

Samuel Flagg Bemis found some shortcomings in the work. But he predicted that it might become "a classic of American political thought" nearly as influential as *The Federalist*. He added that it was generally understood that President Roosevelt had read the book, marked passages, and jotted down marginal comments.[43]

Beard learned from a friend that Bemis' remarks about FDR's reading the book were accurate and that he "kept it in his desk for callers to see for three weeks!"[44] But he also learned, eventually, that the president had described *The Open Door at Home* as "a bad dish" in one of his handwritten comments.[45] Thus, Beard was destined to be extremely disappointed and frustrated in his efforts to be an unofficial foreign policy advisor of sorts to the president, whose rhetoric and programs in the realm of domestic affairs often earned his respect and approbation. As the evidence became clearer that Roosevelt, in foreign affairs, apparently did not interpret the national interest as Beard had defined it, a note of personal betrayal crept into a number of Beard's publications and letters even before FDR's re-election in 1936. The mixed reception accorded *The Idea of National Interest* and *The Open Door at Home* foreshadowed, to some extent, the greater controversy Beard would arouse later in the decade when his warnings about Roosevelt's diplomacy became more strident and his commitment to a noninterventionist policy more profound.

Many contemporary reviewers, whether they agreed with him or not, were well aware that Beard, particularly in *The Open Door at Home*, was engaged in pleading a case and was not viewing the past with cold detachment. But some, like Professor Bemis, saw in these volumes ideas that were not ephemeral, and they, therefore, regarded the two volumes as more than just tracts for the times. The diplomatic historian Tyler Dennett believed the most valuable contribution made by Beard's study on national interest was the introduction of a much needed note of realism into the study of American diplomacy.[46] Beard was especially delighted by a letter he received from Walter Millis, "in which he says that the book is

43. Lindley, review of Beard and Smith, *The Future Comes*, in *New York Herald Tribune Books*, January 7, 1934, p. 5; Bemis, review of *Open Door*, in *American Historical Review* 40 (April 1935):543.

44. Beard to Smith, January 8, 1935, Smith Papers, Folder 7.

45. Beard to Curti, March 3, 1948, Curti Papers, Box 4, Folder 13.

46. Dennett, review of *National Interest*, in *American Historical Review* 39 (July 1934):744.

up to the level of the little boy who told the Prince that he had no clothes on—was stark naked in fact. Now that is a gem beyond price."[47]

There have been challenges both to Beard's interpretation of American foreign policy and his prescription for future policy. Some critics of *The Idea of National Interest*, for example, took exception to the heavy emphasis on economic forces and motives. Raymond L. Buell, who, at the time the volumes were written, was president of the Foreign Policy Association, was especially concerned about Beard's downgrading of nonmaterialistic factors, such as social psychology and power politics.[48] In a similar fashion, more recent critics have noted Beard's preoccupation with the economic motives of individuals and groups, to the near exclusion of the power-political implications of a nation's quest for security. While he was very astute in stressing the intimate connections between certain domestic and foreign policies, Beard, nevertheless, conveyed the impression that the latter were almost totally a function of internal necessity and were not apt to be reasoned and legitimate responses to the external actions of other nations.[49]

Whatever hopes Beard might have entertained about influencing Roosevelt must have been short-lived. A prominent member of the president's cabinet, Henry A. Wallace, penned a long and thoughtful, but critical, review of *The Open Door at Home* for the liberal periodical *New Republic*. The secretary of agriculture thought Beard unrealistic in his apparent assumption that America's foreign trade could be drastically curtailed and an enlarged domestic market created almost overnight. Wallace granted that Beard "dreams a great dream of a beautiful and peaceful future of our great land" to which "the heart thrills." He feared, however, that "even Beard has not seen the whole problem. He is not so good an economic technician as he is a historian."[50] Interestingly, the same month the review was published, Beard had an opportunity to speak with Wallace in Washington, at which time the secretary told him that "he was more in sympathy with the book than he indicated."[51]

47. Beard to Smith, March 8, 1934, Smith Papers, Folder 4.
48. Buell, review of *National Interest*, in *New York Herald Tribune Books*, March 4, 1934, p. 1.
49. Gerald Stourzh, "Charles A. Beard's Interpretations of American Foreign Policy," pp. 126–32; Hofstadter, *The Progressive Historians*, pp. 325, 328.
50. Wallace, review of *Open Door*, in *New Republic*, January 2, 1935, p. 227.
51. Beard to Smith, January 8, 1935, Smith Papers, Folder 7.

There were other responses to Beard's work, including one from Herbert Feis, at the time an economic advisor to the State Department. He suggested that Beard's comprehensive program of nationalism might very well lead to the type of belligerent American chauvinism that Beard deplored. In a similar vein, one reviewer expressed mild disbelief at what he characterized as "jingoistic phrases" in *The Open Door at Home*. Merle Curti, however, objected to those critics who accused Beard of adopting a narrow and selfish nationalism. He pointed out that Beard shared the major aspirations of the internationalists for an orderly and peaceful world, differing from them only in how these laudable aims were to be achieved.[52]

The question of the means to this desirable end was, of course, the essence of the matter. Most of those critics who disagreed with Beard did not impugn his motives or idealism, but his particular proposals. Until the Pearl Harbor attack, he continued to insist that a rejection of former policies of foreign trade and investment was a sine qua non for the success of domestic reform and avoidance of war. It should be observed that Beard was partially vindicated in his estimates of foreign trade, as borne out in his prediction that the expansion of foreign trade would not be the ultimate answer to America's economic malaise. In addition, world peace was not guaranteed by America's foreign commercial endeavors after FDR's election. On the other hand, the political ramifications of the reciprocal trade program were not detrimental to America's national interests. Nearly all the countries with which the United States had negotiated reciprocal trade agreements were lined up against the Axis Powers after December 7, 1941; however, none of them became belligerents against the United States.[53]

On the controversial subject of naval expansion, Beard did score a number of direct hits. This may be seen in his critical examination of long-accepted sea power doctrines; his skepticism about the competence of "naval experts"; his pointing out the frequent gaps between America's diplomatic aims and the inability or undesirability of the navy to fulfill them; and his suspicions about the

52. Herbert Feis, review of *Open Door*, in *Foreign Affairs* 13 (July 1935):611; Stewart Maxwell, review of ibid., in *Nation*, November 28, 1934, p. 625; Curti, review of ibid., *Mississippi Valley Historical Review* 22 (September 1935):323.
53. Power Yung-chao Chu, "A History of the Hull Trade Program, 1934–1939" (Ph.D. diss., Columbia University, 1957), pp. 401–2.

monetary motives of economic interest groups in supporting ship-building programs. In raising penetrating questions about these issues, Beard may have caused some "Big Navy" advocates to re-evaluate their own assumptions and to refine their arguments.

But a number of Beard's verbal salvos against the "Big Navy Boys" were wide of the mark, largely because of exaggeration or insufficient evidence. This was especially true of his slashing indict-ment of the Navy League of the United States for allegedly exer-cising an insidious influence on American naval policy.[54] His critique, therefore, failed to achieve the balance and temperate tone that might have made his views more acceptable in the coun-cils of the Roosevelt administration, in the Congress, and among the American people at large. More important, international events by the late 1930s had raised new anxieties about American security which would tend to overwhelm, and make less acceptable, Beard's implicit adherence to the efficacy of a "small navy."

With each act of the Roosevelt administration which further involved the nation in the world's political and economic prob-lems, and which was accompanied by an increase in defense ex-penditures, Beard became more and more convinced that Roosevelt was betraying his own program of domestic reform and recovery. Such policies were viewed by Beard as prima facie evidence that FDR was seeking war as a means of deflecting public attention from his failure to solve the obvious human suffering of the con-tinuing Great Depression.

54. The most judicious assessment of the role and influence of the Navy League is Armin Rappaport's *The Navy League of the United States*. Rappa-port found that, on balance, the Navy League was a relatively innocuous or-ganization insofar as the truly important determination of Navy policy was concerned. He concluded that "the conspiracy theory of history . . . when applied to the Navy League of the United States is sheer fantasy." It "was neither the tool nor the mouthpiece of special economic interest groups. The insinuations have often stemmed from too little investigation and too much preconception. They have gained credence not because they were rooted in fact, but from repetition by scholars, publicists, and legislators" (p. 205).

6

Waging the Cause of Neutrality, 1935-1941

THE Nye Committee's inquiry (1934–36) into the manufacturing of and traffic in arms, according to Robert E. Osgood, "provided the single most convincing argument in the whole arsenal of arguments that sustained the isolationism of the thirties." Hans J. Morgenthau, in characterizing "the official philosophy" of this committee as a "devil theory" of imperialism, concluded that it rested on the fallacious premise that, since such groups as bankers and munitions manufacturers profited from wars, they necessarily were primarily responsible for planning and starting wars. During the 1930s, many writers, with varying credentials for historical scholarship, promulgated this thesis in regard to America's involvement in World War I. But it was Charles A. Beard, in the opinion of Eric F. Goldman, who synthesized the revelations of the Nye Committee into "a widely imitated liberal economic interpretation."[1]

In the course of following these hearings, Beard not only concurred with the Nye Committee's recommendations for neutrality legislation; he also aligned himself with the "revisionist" interpretation of World War I in which Woodrow Wilson's reputation and

1. Robert E. Osgood, *Ideals and Self-Interest in America's Foreign Relations,* p. 366; Hans J. Morgenthau, *Politics among Nations: The Struggle for Power and Peace,* pp. 29–30; Goldman, *Rendezvous with Destiny,* p. 377.

idealism were attacked and discarded. Beard's interest in the enactment and enforcement of neutrality bills also led him to attach
ominous intentions to virtually every act or speech of President
Franklin D. Roosevelt that appeared to contradict the intent of
this congressional legislation.

Published findings of the Nye Committee in the first two months
of 1935 encouraged Beard's expectations for the passage of stringent
neutrality legislation which would "serve notice on future belligerents that they are to receive no aid or comfort from the United
States when they start on the headlong course of war, destruction,
and defeat."[2] It was also at this time that Beard made the first of
a number of public allegations that President Roosevelt might
seek a foreign war, particularly in the Pacific, either as a means of
diverting attention from, or solving, America's economic crisis.
Beard expressly denied that FDR would deliberately plunge the
country into an Asian war. His demur was not entirely convincing,
however, for he also intimated that the president might "stumble
into" a suitable "incident" or "provocation," magnifying it into a
"just cause for war." He then concluded, "The Jeffersonian party
gave the nation the War of 1812, the Mexican War, and its participation in the World War. The Pacific War awaits."[3]

Many students of Beard's life and thought have appreciated the
significance of these remarks in assessing his commitment to a noninterventionist stance many years before December 1941. Richard
Hofstadter perhaps stated the significance of this 1935 prediction
most succinctly: "It is a chilling note of prophecy that Beard
strikes here, and it is prophetic not only for the world but for himself: in this article he wrote the scenario for the rest of his career,
for the unrelenting battle he was to wage against an event which
he had forecast as all but inevitable."[4] What is generally not recognized, however, is that Beard's public prediction and anxiety, in
this instance, were the result of finally declaring private suspicions
he first entertained less than six months after Roosevelt's inaugura-
tion.

In the summer of 1933, George H. E. Smith wrote Beard about
the content of their forthcoming study, *The Idea of National*

2. Beard, "What Is This Sea Power?" See also Beard, "Our Foreign and
Domestic Policies."
3. Beard, "National Politics and the War," p. 70.
4. Hofstadter, *The Progressive Historians*, p. 328.

Interest, which was to include a treatment of New Deal diplomacy. Smith indicated that he did not feel that Roosevelt held anything like "the attitude of an international approach to national problems that Wilson held" and, in noting his uncertainty about FDR's political opportunism, wondered "how far he would permit strategy to take him on international lines." In reply, Beard expressed his agreement with Smith, adding, "I think he is a dangerous man in foreign affairs; he has no headlands for guidance and is moving as swiftly as he can, whatever his idea, into a war with Japan. Then to Ft. Leavenworth for me." Beard did concede that there was "something admirable about his [FDR's] freedom from old claptrap." But the nagging doubts persisted. Despite subsequent support for FDR's actions in regard to the London Economic Conference (1933) in *The Idea of National Interest*, in this letter Beard noted that the conference "showed-up his muddleheadedness from the start. What a mess. No policy, backing and filling, jumping and snorting."[5]

This early lack of confidence in Roosevelt's motives and statesmanship had the effect of heightening Beard's faith in Congress to restrict FDR's authority to conduct foreign policy. When the Senate rejected a treaty in the spring of 1935 that would have made the United States a member of the World Court, Beard hailed the action as one of the clearest signs that Congress was prepared to guard jealously its prerogatives in determining foreign policy.[6] When it was announced in June 1935 that the Nye Committee was planning to shift its examination of the munitions industry to the activities of American bankers, Beard claimed that the British and French ambassadors were supposed to have appealed to the State Department to halt such an inquiry. Beard alleged that a meeting between Roosevelt and some members of the committee was then held and that rumor had it that the president's attempt at personal dissuasion in the matter had not only failed, but had deepened the resolve of the committee to press on with its labors.[7]

Despite these actions of the Congress, and notwithstanding his realization that FDR was not following his blueprint for the "new

5. Smith to Beard, August 4, 1933; Beard to Smith, August 4[?], 1933, Smith Papers, Folder 2.
6. Beard, "The President Loses Prestige," pp. 64–65.
7. Beard, "America Debates War Plans," p. 293.

nationalism" in foreign affairs, Beard once again tried to influence the president in a personal way. In May 1935, Beard wrote to Raymond Moley, who still maintained contact with the White House. In the letter, Beard expressed deep concern about "the hazards of a futile and idiotic war in the Far Pacific," and he enclosed a copy of a recent article by a naval officer which, Beard emphasized, "contains more sound sense on sea power than all of [Alfred Thayer] Mahan's tomes." He hoped that Moley would comment on the article in *Today*, a magazine his former student edited. Beard also asked Moley to bring the heavily underlined article to the president's attention. Moley did ask Roosevelt's secretary to give Beard's letter and enclosure to the president.[8] Assuming FDR ever read the article, subsequent American diplomacy in the Far East, plus the continuing commitment to a program of naval expansion, indicated that Roosevelt did not heed Beard's implicit appeal to withdraw all diplomatic commitments and military forces from East Asia.

In the meantime, the Nye Committee's endeavors had led to the passage of the first of a series of Neutrality Acts in August 1935. The bill empowered the president to place an embargo on the sale and shipment of munitions to belligerent powers whenever he judged that a state of war existed. With an eye to the tragic experience of the *Lusitania* sinking in 1915, the bill also denied government protection to American citizens who chose to travel on the ships of belligerent nations. Although he still retained some discretionary powers, FDR signed the bill with reluctance because he thought it too inflexible, particularly in not distinguishing between an aggressor and the victim of aggression.[9] Henceforth, this legal and moral problem would be an important aspect of the

8. Beard to Moley, May 18, 1935; Moley to Marguerite Le Hand, May 25, 1935, Franklin D. Roosevelt Library, Hyde Park, N.Y. The article in question was Lt. Comdr. Melvin Talbot's prize essay, "Beyond the Naval Treaties." A number of Talbot's conclusions coincided with Beard's own ideas about the limited size and function of the U.S. Navy. Materials concerning Charles A. Beard in the Roosevelt Library, it might be added, are not extensive. Letters exchanged until August 1937, moreover, contain no direct criticisms of Roosevelt's diplomacy. On the other hand, in a few letters Beard was nearly effusive in his praise of the president's concern for education, the historic importance of his state papers, and his judiciary reform proposal. A presidential memo dated May 21, 1937, indicated FDR's desire to invite Charles and Mary Beard to spend "a weekend sometime on the Potomac."
9. Robert A. Divine, *The Illusion of Neutrality, 1935–1939*, pp. 115–17.

debate between the advocates of strict neutrality and the proponents of collective security who believed that the United States
should adopt selective embargoes and other measures short of war.
Following the Italian invasion of Ethiopia in October 1935,
Beard fervidly attacked this issue. He ridiculed the notion that one
could make precise distinctions between "good" and "bad" nations and was shocked by the idea that those who embraced the
principle of collective security would "employ the risk of war to
prevent war" on the strength of such distinctions.[10] Whatever questions might be raised about Beard's forcing the debate into absolutes rather than the more realistic and relative distinctions of
"less bad" or "more good," it is clear that by this time he was
emotionally and rationally dedicated to a hard-and-fast policy of
neutrality for the United States. Thus, it was fitting that his study
of *The Devil Theory of War* (1936) was subtitled *An Inquiry Into
the Nature of History and the Possibility of Keeping Out of War.*

The "devil theory," as Beard defined it, was essentially a scape-
goat-conspiracy thesis, in which "wicked politicians" and "wicked
bankers" were responsible for policies of self-aggrandizement that
caused wars between nations. "The people" were always assumed
to be peace-loving, desiring only to be left alone to follow their
daily routines. "If politicians would stop interfering at home and
stop making wars," the theory as delineated by Beard concluded,
"the whole world would be busy, employed and (almost) happy."[11]

Beard blasted this theory as an "old tune" that was "childish."
The nominally peaceful economic pursuits of "the people," particularly if they involved industrial and agricultural goods for sale
in foreign markets, had "a direct bearing on war." Politicians and
bankers also did not operate independently of their economic,
political, and social milieu. Accordingly, they did not "intrude
themselves upon the people from some magic world of their own."
The politician, he contended, "reflects the ideas and wishes of his
constituents," while the banker "lives right down in the middle of
things, amid the pushing and shoving of the marketplace."[12]

In the first half of his study, Beard persuasively and wittily

10. Beard, "Keeping America Out of War," p. 291.
11. Beard, *The Devil Theory of War*, pp. 18–20, hereafter cited as *Devil
Theory*. Most of the book was originally serialized as "Heat and Light on
Neutrality" and "Peace for America."
12. *Devil Theory*, pp. 21–23.

demonstrated that a nation's involvement in war could be a complex, collective responsibility of interaction between political and business leaders, the people, domestic needs, and external events. The implication was that an interpretation of this nature should be applied to America's involvement in World War I. But before he concluded his examination of how, by 1917, the United States found itself a belligerent in a war of European origins, Beard came full circle on the "devil theory of war," with his primary focus on economic motivation. Given Beard's well-known skill in the use of irony, one is tempted to wonder whether he may have intended the work as a masterful exercise in this particular literary style. In any event, he implicitly endorsed the very thesis which he had dismissed at the outset as "childish."

After a passage in which he pondered the problems of the historian in ever truly locating "cause" in history, Beard tentatively dealt with the issue of why the United States entered World War I. Rendering his own conclusions in an oblique fashion, Beard claimed that the "lesson" of World War I was to be found in the answers to the following questions, bearing on the policies of engaging in trade with, and extending loans to, belligerent nations: "Do we want, for the future, discussions and decisions of this character to be carried on secretly behind closed doors or openly in the Congress of the United States? In fine, are bans on loans, credits, and sales to belligerents to be raised clandestinely in huddled conferences of bankers and politicians or publicly by the representatives of the American people in Congress assembled?"[13]

Beard then presented his own sweeping proposals for neutrality legislation, which included an automatic arms embargo and restrictions on the sale of arms to neutral nations who might be engaged in the business of reselling munitions and other items of contraband to belligerent countries. He insisted that such legislation be mandatory—an obvious reflection of his distrust of President Roosevelt and the State Department. But it was also, in part, a case of Beard fearing that history would repeat itself, for he had become convinced that the unpublicized actions of some American bankers, Woodrow Wilson, Colonel Edward M. House, and Secretary of State Robert Lansing had been responsible for policies that were contrary to the national interest. He admitted there would be

13. Ibid., p. 103.

problems in carrying out such laws, but hoped that "perhaps enough of them can be enforced as to prevent the bankers and politicians from guiding the nation into calamity as in 1914–1917."[14]

What Beard desired, in essence, was the enactment of a legislative program that would severely curtail President Roosevelt's discretionary powers in shaping and conducting American foreign policy. In July 1937, for example, Beard decried the fact that the three neutrality bills passed since 1935 did not deny to FDR powers that he believed had been unwisely used in the past. As a consequence, Roosevelt was still in a position to take actions that would involve the nation in a full-scale war without asking Congress for a declaration of war, "a ceremony that is now apparently as obsolete as the dodo." Beard ruefully reflected, "The American people may well prepare themselves to see President Roosevelt plunge the country into the European war, when it comes, far more quickly than did President Wilson. Unless he is superhuman, the limelight of the world stage will be too great for his powers of restraint."[15]

This charge was repeated in September 1937, when Beard caustically remarked that Roosevelt, like Wilson, had made it clear that "he still follows the creed that the United States must do good all around the world." In another comparison with Wilson, Beard implied that FDR might not have as much difficulty as the former president in getting the country into war, since "in 1914 the American people had not yet been conditioned to the idea that the Government must favor one side or the other in every European quarrel." Under these circumstances, Beard wrote, "it took time for Woodrow Wilson to maneuver the nation into war."[16]

14. Ibid., pp. 118–23.
15. Beard, "Will Roosevelt Keep Us Out of War?" pp. 5–6. Recognizing the gravity of Beard's charge, the editors of *Events* wrote on the inside cover of this issue: "Dr. Beard's article is not only based upon his great knowledge as historian and social philosopher, but is also a result of the close study of the subject he is making from day to day. Some of his statements may appear to be startling, but just because they are put into print with the fullest sense of responsibility, they ought to receive the most careful attention."
16. " 'Will Roosevelt Keep Us Out of War?' Dr. Beard's Rejoinder," *Events*, September 1937, p. 164. The "rejoinder" in this instance was in answer to a White House reply to Beard's July 1937 accusation in *Events*. The official response, given Beard's stature and the nature of his charge, was incredibly inept. The secretary to the president, Stephen Early, merely sent to the periodical

During the summer and fall of 1937, Beard occasionally expressed views that seemed to contradict his tenacious attachment to strict neutrality and called into question the logical basis for his public animus toward Roosevelt and the advocates of collective security. For example, in July 1937, Beard took Roosevelt to task for his response to the Spanish Civil War, namely, his acquiescence when Congress applied neutrality legislation to this internal, not multinational, conflict. Beard correctly observed that this action "was a clear violation of the principles of international law as they then stood." But given his own statements about staying out of any European quarrels, his praise of Congress' initiative in trying to guarantee this, as well as his knowledge that most congressional supporters of this measure favored strict neutrality, one is apt to be puzzled by Beard's virtually snide criticism of FDR, and his assertion that *not* supplying either the Loyalists of Spain and the Franco rebels with munitions was "without any justification in terms of peril to American interests."[17]

The events of July 1937 were also critical as a prelude to Pearl Harbor; the start of the Sino-Japanese War demonstrated that Japan's territorial ambitions in East Asia involved much more than the one Chinese province of Manchuria. The following month, Beard's reflections on the aggressive mentality of what would soon become the Axis Powers appeared in print: "By their faith in force . . . Hitler and Mussolini are more or less beyond the reach of the old-fashioned calculations. Japanese militarists belong in the same emotional category. Having a philosophy of history in which 'anything can happen,' the directors of these three groups may fling prudence to the winds and make the experiment [of aggressive war], or without any deliberate intention or open declarations, the great powers may find themselves at war in the midst of a dissolving civilization."[18]

In August 1937, Beard also sent a telegram to the president,

---

copies of two addresses FDR had made, including the celebrated "I hate war" speech at Chautauqua, N.Y. (August 14, 1936). In effect, the administration chose not to engage Beard in a proper dialogue. One may never know how much this unsatisfactory reply might have further embittered Beard, or accentuated his distrust of the president. " 'Will Roosevelt Keep Us Out of War?'—A Reply from the White House," *Events*, September 1937, pp. 161–63.

17. Beard, "Will Roosevelt Keep Us Out of War?" p. 3.
18. Beard, "War—If, How, and When?" p. 86.

which read, in part, "By your action on the Far East, you open a grand epoch in American diplomacy. . . . Hearty Appreciation."[19] Since there was no mention of the particular action that Beard was praising, the communication seems enigmatic, not to mention apostatic, because Beard—as was true of most isolationists at the time—could not have been pleased with Roosevelt's failure to invoke immediately the relevant neutrality legislation once the Sino-Japanese War began. The seeming paradox may be explained by a presidential press conference held the day before Beard telegraphed his laudatory message. During this conference, Roosevelt told reporters that application of the provisions of the existing neutrality laws in regard to the Sino-Japanese War was on "a 24-hour basis."[20] Beard presumably learned of this and believed that it was a major departure in FDR's Far Eastern diplomacy. His hopes, of course, were soon dashed. Nonetheless, it is revealing of Beard's sincerely troubled outlook that he could pin such unrealistic expectations on this conditional statement by the president.

Beard's possible uncertainties about the validity of his own convictions were still partially evident in the early fall of 1937, about the time of Roosevelt's "quarantine" speech of October 5, 1937. When Beard reviewed Quincy Howe's anti-British polemic, *England Expects Every American to Do His Duty* (1937), he expressed substantial agreement with the author's argument that the United States should let England fight its own battles. Yet, in the same review, Beard acutely observed that the two countries were so intimately tied by such obvious bonds as geography, economics, and cultural traditions "that even blind isolationists must recognize the fact in all their thought about practice." Recalling his earlier justifications for American entry into World War I, Beard suggested that destruction of the British Empire and its navy, leaving Germany in control of the Atlantic, would create serious problems for the peace and security of the United States.[21]

But the quarantine speech probably constituted the greatest intellectual-emotional watershed in Beard's long-held suspicions about Roosevelt—it seemed to confirm beyond question that FDR was irrevocably committed to a belligerent course of action, regardless

19. Beard to FDR, August 18, 1937, FDR Library.
20. Quoted in Divine, *The Illusion of Neutrality*, p. 203.
21. Beard, "America's 'Duty' to England," p. 327.

of what other nations were doing throughout the world.[22] Immediately after Roosevelt's Chicago address, Beard construed the president's remark that "peace-loving nations" must join together to oppose violations of international treaties as evidence of "the overwhelming propensity of his will in the direction of involving the United States in the quarrels of Europe and the Orient, with all the fateful potentialities for war."[23]

During the first few months of 1938, Beard waged a thoroughgoing, and sometimes abusive, campaign against the principle of collective security and its adherents. Responding to the support given to Roosevelt's quarantine principle by Earl S. Browder, then general secretary of the Communist Party in America, Beard commented on the "curious array" of followers among those who were for and against collective security. On the side of collective action could be found American citizens of British birth and American Communists of the Stalinist persuasion. Among those who favored strict neutrality were Italian-Americans, German-Americans, and American Communists who owed allegiance to Leon Trotsky. "The contest," Beard concluded, was not "one of perfect truth against perfect error, knowledge against ignorance, wisdom against folly as many disputants would have it." These sardonic, well-informed commentaries were vintage Beard. He scorned the idea, however, that "another war for democracy" could have any beneficial results, and believed that American participation in such a conflict would likely result in universal fascism. Moreover, given the persistence of high unemployment in the United States, he pugnaciously asked, "how can we have the effrontery to assume that we can solve the problems of Asia and Europe, encrusted in the blood-rust of fifty centuries? Really, little boys and girls, how can we?"[24]

Beard's views at this time were still in general accord with the neutrality and antiwar sentiments of the nation as a whole. One

22. The revisionist critic of American participation in both world wars, Harry Elmer Barnes, who was a close friend of the Beards by the early 1940s, thought Beard generally approved of the domestic New Deal up to the "quarantine" speech. But Beard later told Barnes that "he felt that F.D.R. was a hypocrite about this and wished to detract attention from . . . the loss of the Supreme Court battle, and the sharp recession in the preceding months. He did not feel that F.D.R. had any really sincere fear of 'aggressors.' " Barnes to Charles M. Hepburn, December 16, 1961, Barnes Papers. Hepburn is the author of "Charles A. Beard and the Founding Fathers."
23. Beard, "Those Old-World Quarrels," p. 261.
24. Browder, "For Collective Security"; Beard, "A Reply to Mr. Browder."

of the more significant barometers of public opinion in this regard was the substantial public and congressional support of a constitutional amendment sponsored by Louis A. Ludlow (D., Ind.), which would require a nationwide referendum on war, except in the event of an enemy attack on the United States or its possessions. In January 1938, however, the amendment, which was strongly opposed by the Roosevelt administration, failed to gain House support by a vote of 209 to 108.[25] A few weeks after the defeat of this amendment, FDR asked Congress for a substantial increase in military and naval appropriations. This move, in conjunction with the quarantine speech, the administration's pressures against the Ludlow Amendment, and an invitation by some members of the House of Representatives,[26] prompted Beard to appear before the House Committee on Naval Affairs to register his strong opposition to the president's request for additional military expenditures.

In his prepared remarks before the House Committee on February 9, 1938, Beard alluded to the president's "policy of quarantine" as one that would require "big battleships to be used in aggressive warfare in the Far Pacific or the Far Atlantic." This charge was essential to sustaining his fundamental premise, that the continental United States was already suitably safe from foreign atttack. He ridiculed speculations in which "Fascist goblins of Europe are pictured as marching across the Atlantic to Brazil." This "simply fantastic" proposition was "the kind of nightmare which a holder of shipbuilding stocks had when ordinary business is bad." Such fears, Beard alleged, were part of "the new racket

25. Divine, *The Illusion of Neutrality*, pp. 219–21. In October 1937, 73 per cent of the persons polled by the American Institute of Public Opinion, under the direction of George Gallup, expressed approval of the Ludlow Amendment: *Public Opinion Quarterly* 2 (July 1938):387.

26. Beard, "The Supreme Issue for America," p. 268. In this article, Beard referred to these Congressmen only as "a group of men." Such an invitation could be extended because Beard was in the nation's capital at the time, a city that he flippantly regarded as a "burg" which was "a mad house." More important, as a clue to his attitude before he testified against the administration's proposed increase of naval funds, he also wrote to George H. E. Smith: "All social talk turns on the coming war and the administration is making a drive to stir war psychology. Nothing but the backfire from people who do not want to fight for our yellow brothers keeps the administration from lunging ahead—into another crusade for democracy or what have you": Beard to Smith, January 31, 1938, Smith Papers, Folder 8.

created to herd the American people into Roosevelt's quarantine camp."[27]

When he returned to testify the following day, Beard remarked that he was in general accord with the president's domestic policies, but believed that the proposed increase in armaments was another indication that Roosevelt had "set out on the road to collective action that leads to war." The president was faulted for not specifically informing Congress and the American people of the ways in which the security of the United States was endangered by any combination of powers planning to attack the country. He felt, therefore, that Roosevelt was not justified in asking for substantial sums of money in the name of national defense. The president's explanation that his request was based on the determination that the increasing armaments of "other nations" had made America's defensive posture inadequate was not acceptable to Beard.[28] In this instance, Beard seemed to imply that it was incumbent upon the executive branch to reveal any secret invasion plans of the totalitarian powers before it could legitimately request increased appropriations.

Beard's testimony attracted a good deal of favorable press commentary from prestigious and widely read newspapers and periodicals.[29] This may have encouraged Oswald Garrison Villard, editor of the liberal weekly *The Nation*, to ask Beard, on behalf of the National Peace Conference, to appear before the upcoming hearings of the Senate Naval Affairs Committee. Beard respectfully declined the invitation, observing that he had had his say. However, he did enthusiastically endorse Villard's suggestion that a

27. This statement was not included as part of the hearings published by the House Committee. The above remarks may be found in the *New York Times*, February 10, 1938, p. 14, or *Congressional Digest* 17 (March 1938):90–92.

28. *To Establish the Composition of the U.S. Navy: Hearings before the Committee on Naval Affairs, House of Representatives on House Resolution 9218*, 75th Cong., 3d sess., pp. 2134, 2136.

29. See, for example, *Christian Science Monitor*, March 9, 1938, p. 2; *New Republic*, February 16, 1938, pp. 32–33; *Time*, February 21, 1938, pp. 18–19. Despite the strong neutrality and antiwar sentiment throughout the nation, however, Beard was not necessarily in step with most of his countrymen on the question of increased expenditures for national defense. A poll published in July 1938 indicated these majorities in favor of expanding the military establishment: air force (80 per cent); navy (74 per cent); army (69 per cent): *Public Opinion Quarterly* 2 (July 1938):387.

commission of noteworthy citizens be formed to inquire into the problem of whether the United States actually could be invaded. Beard wrote that such an investigation "should cover not only invasion but the utility of battleships &c. in modern warfare of any kind, defensive or aggressive."[30]

Beard's reluctance to testify at the Senate hearings did not mean that he really had said all he was going to say on the matter of naval expansion. In *America in Midpassage*, completed soon after the fateful Munich Conference of September 1938, Beard—with his wife—discussed in detail the naval appropriations bill of 1938, including the hearings which preceded its approval, with amendments, by the House and Senate. The passage of time had neither moderated Beard's judgment of FDR's naval program nor diminished the vigor of his criticism.[31]

Of greater significance, however, was the section in which Beard definitively stated the isolationist position toward which he had been moving since the early 1930s. He essentially put old theory into new packaging, and the results were classified as major schools of thought about American foreign policy. The first was labeled the school of "isolationism pure and simple," which originated in the administration of George Washington. Though the expansion of foreign trade was one of its tenets, such trade was to be carried out free of entangling alliances and "the endless wars in Europe." This policy had been rather faithfully followed until 1898, when it was "destroyed" by such "war hawks" as Theodore Roosevelt, Alfred Thayer Mahan, Henry Cabot Lodge, John Hay, and Albert J. Beveridge. These men did not openly adopt the "imperialist dogma" of Great Britain, France, and Germany, but they sought "to combine the hazards of empire with continental security." Referring to this policy as "a bastard conception," the Beards designated it the school of "Imperial Isolationism."[32] It should be stressed that this view of American imperialism in 1898 as a radical departure in the history of American foreign policy represented a significant shift from Beard's previous interpretation of the for-

---

30. Villard to Beard, February 21, 1938; Beard to Villard, February 22, 1938, Villard Papers, Houghton Library, Harvard University.
31. 1:488–95, hereafter cited as *Midpassage*.
32. Ibid., pp. 442–43.

eign policy of this period as the culmination of even earlier ideas and policies.[33]

The Spanish-American War, followed by the annexation of territories in the Pacific and Caribbean, gave the followers of this school of policy an opportunity to test what Beard claimed was its fundamental theory: in a world of intense national rivalry, overseas possessions sustained by sea power were essential as outlets for manufactured goods and capital investments. As continued by the Republican heirs of this policy in the twentieth century, tariffs, subsidies, and diplomatic and naval power were employed in furthering "dollar diplomacy" throughout the world.[34]

The Beards' personal aversion to this school had been forecast much earlier in the work, where it was calculated that the net loss to the nation after thirty years of "empire building" was about $4 million a year. "Such was the outcome of all the blare, oratory, trumpeting, boasting, and plunging of the great adventure," they remarked caustically.[35] They also charged that the Philippines were a burden to American taxpayers, the Open Door policy "was in practice a cloak for imperialistic intrigues," and America's China trade was "relatively trivial, notwithstanding the huge volume of wild talk about four hundred million potential customers."[36]

The school of "Collective Internationalism" was also challenged because of its idealistic proposals to impose "permanent peace upon the world." Beard's primary objection was to the assumption that unrestricted world commerce would remove the economic causes of war and promote political harmony between nations. While he had often flirted with such a notion until the late 1920s, he now regarded those who continued to argue such a thesis as unrealistic "world imagists."[37]

The school of "International Communism" was dealt with in a summary fashion. This was appropriate, since it does not seem to warrant consideration as one of the *American* schools of foreign

33. Stourzh, "Charles A. Beard's Interpretations of American Foreign Policy," pp. 132–37.
34. *Midpassage*, 1:443–46.
35. Ibid., 1:84.
36. Ibid., 1:397–98, 441–42. The allusion in the last phrase undoubtedly was to Carl Crow's best seller on China, *Four Hundred Million Customers*, the seventh edition of which appeared in 1937.
37. *Midpassage*, 1:448, 450–51.

policy the Beards proposed to discuss. Their brief analysis might have been deemed relevant only to the extent that American Communists, taking their cues from Moscow, "supported Collective Internationalists in their campaign against the fascist foes of their world image."[38]

The basic tenets of the "American civilization," or "continental," school of foreign policy represented a compendium-synthesis of most of the views Beard had been expounding on American diplomacy since 1931, with a few echoes from the 1920s. At the core of this theory was his continuing dedication to the idea that the material and cultural standards of the United States could be vastly improved through comprehensive domestic reform legislation. Such a program would necessitate the defense only of the continental homeland, Hawaii, and the Canal Zone, with small but adequate military and naval establishments. The "theories and sentiments" of this school, the Beards wrote, "were enclosed in such phrases as: let us keep out of the next war; mind our own business; till our own garden; create the wealth; establish a sound and efficient domestic economy; make America a work of art."[39]

Charles and Mary Beard denied that this school was narrowly isolationist or chauvinistic. It was interested, they said, in avoiding competition for world markets in order to concentrate on the more efficient and equitable distribution of wealth at home. The American civilization school did not assume that its creed was universally applicable, and its adherents did not want "to force the faith upon other countries." In this way, the "continentalists" would avoid the "evangelism" of the Collective Internationalists and the aggressive commercialism of the Imperial Isolationists. War in defense of the continental domain was not ruled out by the continentalists, but under no circumstances would they accept the argument that war should be used as an instrument "of trade promotion, colonial expansion, or ideological world pacification." They eschewed any sort of collective action in which the power of the United States would be committed, in effect, to "old treaties of alliance in a new guise" that "would probably lead to war rather than peace."[40]

A major hope and premise in Beard's thinking at this time was

38. Ibid., 1:451–52.
39. Ibid.
40. Ibid., 1:453–55.

that the people of the United States were so desirous of peace that they might be able to compel the Roosevelt administration to adopt a course of action consistent with the American civilization school of foreign policy. He thus appeared to derive some encouragement from the public criticisms of FDR's "quarantine" address and armament program, which allegedly demonstrated "that a large part of the country was against the 'quarantine' doctrine and against all entanglements in foreign intrigues, quarrels, and wars to which it might lead."[41]

Shortly after *America in Midpassage* went to press, Roosevelt, in his annual message to Congress on January 4, 1939, briefly referred to the inadequacies of existing neutrality laws, thereby setting the stage for the hotly contested issue of neutrality revision. Less than two weeks later, Beard complained that the advocates of collective security were pressing for legislative changes that would enhance the president's authority "to discriminate among belligerents and to use the material resources of the country to implement whatever foreign policy he may choose to adopt in that connection." Authority of this nature, he charged, would be tantamount to transferring Congress' war-declaring power to the president. Such contemplated legislation, therefore, should be called "An Act for Allowing the President of the United States to Enter Any War that Begins Abroad." He further chastised those who attacked Roosevelt for seeking to establish a dictatorship through his domestic legislation, but who then contradicted themselves by supporting neutrality revisions that, according to Beard, would make him "a real dictator in a far more important matter—the power to maneuver the country into a position from which war is the only escape."[42]

The intensity and candor of Beard's criticisms may have been due to his perception of a possible drift in public opinion toward selective neutrality revision. From February to the summer of 1939, considerable sentiment had built up for applying a discriminatory embargo against Japan and for abrogating America's 1911 commer-

41. Ibid., 1:489.
42. "Neutrality: Shall We Have Revision?" Senator Gerald P. Nye asked to have this article reprinted in the *Congressional Record*, 76th Cong., 1st sess., vol. 84, pt. 11, pp. 259–60. During the next two years, a number of Congressmen affiliated with the isolationist bloc often made a similar request, or in the midst of debate cited Beard as an authority in support of their argument.

cial treaty with that country.[43] In the interim, and coincident with Germany's absorption of Czechoslovakia in March 1939, Beard wrote an especially vituperative article, castigating two major pressure groups which, he believed, made it "well-nigh impossible for the United States to follow any realistic foreign policy based upon its geographical position and its democratic ideals." One group was derisively branded "the missionaries," idealistic internationalists whose thinking on foreign affairs was no more realistic than "the apocalyptic visions of a backwoods camp meeting." The other group, flippantly referred to as "the boarders," consisted of ethnic groups and Communists in America "whose hopes and passions are linked with the fate of foreign governments and nationalities."[44]

Beard's principal grievance against these persons was their insistence that the United States should assist the democracies of Great Britain and France against the growing threats of totalitarian Germany and Italy. Beard countered with the argument that, in view of their greater combined population, wealth, resources, and control of the seas, the European democracies themselves should be able to stop the totalitarian powers if they were truly interested in bringing peace, stability, and prosperity to all of Europe. But, in Beard's opinion, they really had no such desire. He wrote of the Tory government of Neville Chamberlain, "I suspect that its primary aim is to let Hitler liquidate Soviet Russia." Accordingly, for the government and people of the United States "to operate on the ostensible fiction that a mere test of despotism and democracy is at hand would be nothing short of childish."[45]

Congressional attempts to revise neutrality legislation began as early as March 1939. But sufficient support for repeal of the arms embargo came only after the invasion of Poland in September 1939, and was not confirmed until November 4, 1939.[46] In the midst of the debate, which required a special session of Congress,

43. Donald F. Drummond, *The Passing of American Neutrality, 1937–1941*, pp. 93–94, 134.
44. "We're Blundering into War."
45. Ibid., pp. 392–93.
46. Divine, *The Illusion of Neutrality*, pp. 229–31. Beard was invited to testify against proposed neutrality revision in the hearings held by the House Committee on Foreign Affairs in April 1939, but he did not appear (p. 247).

Beard took note of the "unwonted unity" of the Republican opposition to the administration's proposals, and he wondered whether this portended a bitter election campaign in 1940, in which foreign policy would be made a partisan issue rather than one debated on its own merits.[47]

Simultaneously, Beard's brief polemic *Giddy Minds and Foreign Quarrels* was published.[48] The title was a slight paraphrasing of the passage in Shakespeare's *Henry IV*, where the dying king counsels his son and heir, Harry, "to busy giddy minds with foreign quarrels" in order to avert discontent within the kingdom. This, of course, was not the first time Beard had reflected on the phenomenon of national leaders resorting to war as a means of diverting public attention from domestic crises. In *Giddy Minds*, he was at least as blunt as previously in pressing his case that FDR was deliberately and deceitfully dragging the American people into war against their wishes and interests.[49]

The conclusion of Beard's argument was that "beyond this hemisphere, the United States should leave disputes over territory, over the ambitions of warriors, over the intrigues of hierarchies, over forms of government, over passing myths known as ideologies—all to the nations and peoples immediately and directly affected." The only "sincere undertakings" of a diplomatic nature in which the United States should participate were those problems directly affecting North and South America. "This much, nations of Europe," Beard concluded, "and may good fortune attend you."[50]

Beard's philippic was warmly greeted in some quarters. One of the Senate's more vocal isolationist spokesmen, William E. Borah (R., Idaho), wrote to Beard: "I do not know when I have read anything which pleased me so much. It is magnificent. I wish it might go into every home in our broad land."[51] One sympathetic reviewer characterized the work as a "tart little pamphlet" and

47. Beard, "Neutrality Deadlock," p. 164.
48. Hereafter cited as *Giddy Minds*. Excerpts, with the same title, appeared concurrently in *Harper's*, September 1939, pp. 337–51.
49. *Giddy Minds*, pp. 28–29.
50. Ibid., pp. 69–70, 77.
51. Quoted in letter from A. Vagts to author, August 8, 1960. More than a year and a half earlier, Beard and Borah had corresponded about the possibility of a Senate inquiry on responsibility for making American foreign policy: Orde S. Pinckney, "William E. Borah: Critic of American Foreign Policy," pp. 59–60.

said that it "comes to a nation very ready to receive its doctrine." The reviewer concluded that "the affirmative voice of the millions who want to keep out of a trouble which is none of our business will give a generous 'Yea' to his pamphlet, in spite of the criticism of the chief executive in whom they still believe."[52]

Giddy Minds was not well received by the professional community of scholars. Among the leading historical journals, the *Mississippi Valley Historical Review* was the only one which included a brief mention of "this fervent plea for isolationism."[53] An editor of *Harper's Magazine*, who supervised the makeup of the issue in which *Giddy Minds and Foreign Quarrels* appeared, later recalled that "its effect on liberal eastern seaboard aid-the-allies circles was instant. They could not bear it and their protests were vehement."[54]

It is true that the *New York Times*, then a supporter of a collective security policy, made Beard's work the subject of a critical editorial. But three weeks later, a lengthy letter to the same paper from four professors of Midwestern universities indicated that growing concern about Beard's role as a publicist was not confined to one region of the United States. Understandably, these academics took exception to those passages in *Giddy Minds* in which Beard imputed "both insincerity and incompetence" to professors of international relations. They pointed out that Beard offered no evidence to substantiate his allegations, and they criticized him for ignoring the arguments of the many reputable scholars who did not share his views on foreign policy.[55]

The passage of the fourth Neutrality Act in November 1939, with its repeal of the arms embargo, appeared to have made futile Beard's appeals for strict neutrality and noninvolvement. But during the military stalemate in Europe in the winter of 1939–40, isolationists in the United States were given a chance to recoup some of the prestige they had lost in the fight over neutrality revision. The Sitzkrieg, or "phony war," led many Americans to believe that Nazi Germany was not the formidable military threat

52. M. L. Elting, review of *Giddy Minds*, in *Forum* (November 1939), p. iv.
53. Review of *Giddy Minds*, in *Mississippi Valley Historical Review* 26 (March 1940):646.
54. Leighton, "Beard and Foreign Policy," in *Beard Appraisal*, p. 181.
55. *New York Times*, October 22, 1939, sec. 4, p. 8; ibid., November 12, 1939, sec. 4, p. 8. The four professors and their institutions were Clarence A. Berdahl (University of Illinois), Kenneth Colegrove (Northwestern University), Walter R. Sharp (University of Wisconsin), and Quincy Wright (University of Chicago).

collective security advocates had claimed. It also appeared as though Hitler's ambitions had been checked by the armies of Great Britain and France and that the United States had avoided the possibility of being drawn into World War II.[56]

After the spring thaw in April 1940, however, Germany's military juggernaut invaded and overran Denmark, Norway, Belgium, Holland, and Luxembourg, climaxing its drive with the capitulation of France on June 22, 1940, twelve days after Italy had declared war on Great Britain and France. Throughout this period, Beard's contributions to periodicals were curtailed because of his work on a book that represented his last major summation of the "continentalism" thesis prior to American entry into World War II—*A Foreign Policy for America*—which became available to the public in May 1940.

The policy of continentalism, Beard asserted, had been sanctioned by the Founding Fathers and was as relevant in 1940 as in 1776, when Thomas Paine wrote in *Common Sense* that "any submission to or dependence on Great Britain tends to involve this continent in European wars and quarrels." But the true fountainhead of the policy of continentalism, according to Beard, was to be found in the transcendental wisdom of George Washington's "Farewell Address," in which he warned the American people against entangling their "peace and prosperity in the toils of European ambition, rivalship, interest, humor, or caprice."[57] Until the 1890s, with the counsel and precept of the Founding Fathers as their guidelines, officials responsible for determining American foreign policy ignored or nullified popular appeals to extend aid to the oppressed of other nations. But the decade of the 1890s, Beard wrote, ushered in the era of "world interventionism and adventurism," buttressed by the policies of imperialism and internationalism, which he discredited and rejected as being provocative and impractical.[58]

In addition to Beard's national reputation as "dean of American historians," the fortuitous publication date (a month before the fall of France) guaranteed extensive comment on, and analysis of, his latest appeal for isolationism. Beard did have ardent sup-

56. Drummond, *The Passing of American Neutrality*, pp. 112–13.

57. Quoted in Beard, *A Foreign Policy for America*, pp. 14–15, hereafter cited as *Foreign Policy*.

58. Ibid., pp. 18–36, 54–64, 87–105.

porters for his argument. Nevertheless, the general response was critical, in part because it appeared at a time when, according to *Time* magazine, throughout the nation "signs multiplied that public sentiment had grown by leaps and bounds in favor of the President's policy . . . of giving the Allies every aid short of war."[59]

A notable aspect of the generally unfavorable reception accorded *A Foreign Policy for America* is to be seen in the number of scholars who had once acclaimed much of Beard's previous work, but who now departed from him on his interpretations of America's past and present foreign policies. Max Lerner, for example, deftly noted Beard's unique ability to achieve "the effects of a fierce polemicist by the methods of a detached historian" and his superb skill in making history serve his argument. But he was not convinced that Beard had proved the validity or desirability of "Continental Americanism," a term which Lerner thought to be only a semantic variation on the concept of isolationism.[60]

Walter Millis, a relatively recent convert to the notion of collective security, thought the book was another example of Beard's own "devil theory" thesis, in which "wicked imperialists and foolish international romantics are devils, to be exorcised by repeating the Founders' creed and going back to the true dogma."[61] Even Roosevelt, the primary object of Beard's foreign policy criticisms for a number of years, gave as good as he got when he disdainfully wrote on the inside cover of his copy, "40 years' hard and continuous study has brought forth an inbred mouse."[62]

Beard, an indefatigable book reviewer throughout his life, was not indifferent to the reception of his own writings. *A Foreign Policy for America* was scarcely the first (nor would it be the last) of his works that was subjected to attacks, ranging from moderate to vituperative. While he always tried to maintain a certain bemused detachment where his critics were concerned, scattered extant letters from 1940 until his death in 1948 betray a sensitivity to criticism, often relieved by self-deprecating humor, and a sense of perplexity over the nonacceptance of his interpretations and warnings.

59. May 20, 1940, p. 17.
60. Max Lerner, review of *Foreign Policy*, in *New Republic*, June 3, 1940, p. 765.
61. Walter Millis, review of *Foreign Policy*, in *New York Herald Tribune Books*, May 16, 1940, p. 3.
62. FDR Library.

In June 1940, Beard and George H. E. Smith corresponded in connection with a project amounting to a postmortem on their first joint venture, *The Future Comes* (1933), eventually published as *The Old Deal and the New* (1940). Early in the month, Smith heatedly wrote about how "the war whoop is on again" and predicted that there would be "an incident in Latin America or the Pacific and the Glorious Crusade will be on." Perhaps with some of the unsympathetic reviews of Beard's latest book in mind, he blurted out at one point, "And once more your proposed foreign policy will be damned by the din." Beard replied, "I fear that you are right about the cavalcade, but there's no way of stopping it. It has little to do with any foreign policy as reality. Someday we shall have to open the door here or go bust!"[63]

That same month, Beard was approached with a request to serve as the chairman of a proposed American Committee against Conscription. Beard declined, largely because of insufficient time, but partly because the suggested program was "merely negative." "Why don't you," he asked, "call for a congressional investigation of the whole defense business before we rush into anything?"[64] Following the presidential nominating conventions, Oswald Garrison Villard appealed to Beard to join in a public protest, "letting people know that we are through with the man in the White House," without necessarily endorsing the Republican candidate, Wendell Willkie.[65] There is no reply from Beard included in the Villard Papers. By mid-September, however, Beard felt that Willkie was "busted," and he did not want to make the forthcoming work on the New Deal "an election book."[66]

Shortly after FDR was re-elected to a third term, and when Beard was at Johns Hopkins University on a one-year appointment, he ruefully observed to Merle Curti, "I just keep plugging on the theory that the American world-savers and peace-through-the-joy-of-war-crowd will have to come home someday—I hope with

63. Smith to Beard, June 4, 1940; Beard to Smith, June 7, 1940; Smith Papers, Folder 9.
64. Beard to Edwin C. Johnson, June 20, 1940; copy of letter in Curti Papers, Box 4, Folder 13.
65. Villard to Beard, July 29, 1940, Villard Papers.
66. Beard to Smith, September 20, 1940, Smith Papers, Folder 9. When the book was published, the authors seemed disappointed that Willkie, during the campaign, had done little more than "say 'me too' to every step taken by President Roosevelt in foreign affairs": Beard and Smith, *The Old Deal and the New*, p. 275.

heads not too bloody and with domestic ruin not too widely spread. I suppose," he added passionately, "that I am just a damned patriot!"[67] About the same time, George Smith asked Beard's assistance in finding an academic post, for his position at Yale would expire the following June. Beard was anxious to help him but could not offer too much encouragement. "I fear," he said, "that the world-savers control most of all jobs in international affairs—and perhaps others. So you will have to watch your step." A few days later, Beard advised Smith, "I know of no job here or anywhere, and nobody asks my opinion on foreign affairs!"[68]

After the surrender of France and until the attack on Pearl Harbor, numerous groups competed for the support of American public opinion in order to influence governmental actions for or against an interventionist policy. The best known, and perhaps most influential, were the Committee to Defend America by Aiding the Allies and the America First Committee.[69] On two occasions, Beard was invited to join the national committee of America First, but he did not accept.[70] For a time, however, he publicly endorsed the aims of the committee and declared that this anti-interventionist group contained "no 'appeasers,' no 'ostrich isolationists,' no foreigners of any nationality in letter or spirit, and no pacifists."[71] The hero of the first transatlantic air flight, Charles A. Lindbergh, was one of the organization's most famous and effective speakers. Although the two men did not correspond with or meet each other until the spring of 1945, in 1940 Beard published a spirited defense of Lindbergh in the face of harsh criticisms directed against him for opposing a policy of American involvement in the European conflict.[72]

67. Beard to Curti, December 9, 1940, Curti Papers, Box 4, Folder 13.
68. Smith to Beard, December 17, 1940; Beard to Smith, December 20, 1940; Beard to Smith, December 25, 1940; Smith Papers, Folder 9.
69. John W. Masland, "Pressure Groups and American Foreign Policy." See also Walter Johnson, *The Battle against Isolationism,* and Wayne S. Cole, *America First: The Battle against Intervention.*
70. Cole, *America First,* p. 75.
71. Quoted in *New York Times,* September 7, 1940, p. 7.
72. Beard and Smith, *The Old Deal and the New,* p. 274. The personal association of Beard and Lindbergh is documented by Mrs. Miriam Beard Vagts, whose files indicate that they met only after the United States became a belligerent in World War II and "by the initiative of L." In March 1945, a Lindbergh letter, written from Westport, Connecticut, informed Beard that in the course of discussing national issues with friends, "your name has frequently arisen as the outstanding authority. I wonder if you would permit me to come

Nevertheless, Beard's unofficial association with the America First movement became a source of personal discomfort and poignant disappointment. Another Connecticut neighbor, Matthew Josephson, reported that some of Beard's friends persuaded him to cancel a speech to be delivered under the committee's auspices at Hartford, for he would find himself "in the company of leaders of the German-American Bund and other questionable characters." Disturbed by this affair, Beard told Josephson, "I wanted to speak out for peace. But I found that the wrong kind of people were in that camp, while those I like all seem to be on the other side."[73]

As public support grew for President Roosevelt's policy of aiding the Allies short of war, Beard and other isolationists became bolder in their accusations that FDR was scheming to take the nation into war. During the debate on the Selective Service Act, which passed by a one-vote margin in the House of Representatives on September 9, 1940, Representative George Bender (R., Ohio) made a charge that would be incorporated into many revisionist works after 1945: "Any device at all that suits the convenience of the President is used in order to get us into war *by the back door*."[74]

Whether Beard, an inveterate reader of congressional debates and hearings on foreign policy, knew of this particular allegation cannot be confirmed. But in November 1940, he suggested that, since public opinion was almost unanimous in its "condemnation and hatred" of Japan, a war with that country would meet with less opposition than open intervention on the side of Great Britain. "Authorities in Washington, eager to get into the war," he added, "could scarcely overlook this roundabout way of accomplishing their designs."[75]

Beard was equally candid in voicing his suspicions when he testified against the lend-lease bill in February 1941. At the outset of his prepared statement, he insisted that the real issues before the

---

to see you so that I might obtain the benefit of your advice." In a "Memorandum" to Mrs. Vagts' letter, her husband remembered that "there were two meetings in New Milford." All quotations from Mrs. Vagts to author, February 16, 1971.

73. Josephson, *Infidel in the Temple: A Memoir of the Nineteen-Thirties*, pp. 413–14.

74. *Congressional Record*, 76th Cong., 3d sess., vol. 86, pt. 10, p. 11394 (italics added). For the most extensive revisionist development of this idea, see Charles C. Tansill, *Back Door to War: The Roosevelt Foreign Policy*.

75. "War with Japan?" p. 321.

Senate committee had nothing to do with either sympathy for, or aid to, Great Britain. The positive declarations of the majority of Americans on both questions had settled these matters to his satisfaction. "Our immediate task," he declared, "is to analyze the meaning of the language in this bill, and to calculate as far as may be humanly possible the consequences for our country that are likely to flow from its enactment into law." Asserting that a number of its provisions were unconstitutional, Beard urged the Congress to disapprove the bill "with such force that no President of the United States will ever dare again, in all our history, to ask it to suspend the Constitution and the laws of this land and to confer upon him limitless dictatorial powers over life and death." Should Congress shirk this responsibility, the proposed legislation could as well be called "a bill for waging undeclared war."[76]

On the merits of extending aid to Great Britain, Beard seemed to have no objections at the beginning of his statement. But he soon expressed indignation at the "reasoning and morals" of those who sought to "buy peace" for America by letting others fight to preserve our security and democracy. If the conflict in Europe was truly a war bearing on the continuation of American democracy, "then it is shameful for us to be buying peace with gold, when we should be offering our bodies as living sacrifices. . . . Buying [peace] with money renders us contemptible in the eyes of the world and, if I understand the spirit of America, contemptible in our own eyes."[77]

The logic of this particular argument was airtight, and the statement was one worthy of the most ardent interventionist. Beard, of course, did not accept the fundamental premise. For many years he had rejected the ideas that the war in Europe was a struggle of democracy versus despotism and that American security was in jeopardy. His continuing attachment to these convictions was implied in his remark that Congress had to decide immediately whether it was prepared to take the country into a European and Asian war "and thus set the whole world on fire," or whether it was determined "to stay out of war to the last ditch," secure from

76. "Statement of Charles A. Beard," *To Promote the Defense of the U.S.: Hearings before the Committee on Foreign Relations, U.S. Senate, on Senate 275*, pp. 308–10.
77. Ibid., p. 310.

"the kind of conflict and terrorism in which the old worlds have indulged for such long ages of time."[78]

The thrust and tenor of Beard's argument should have led him to oppose any aid whatsoever. Yet he could not bring himself to make such a recommendation. Instead, he proposed that Congress draft its own legislation that would keep the administrative machinery of the bill in the hands of Congress only. It would also "authorize using the credit of the Government in aid of American industries engaged in supplying Great Britain with goods." It would, however, "put limits on the amount and terms of such credit."[79]

In effect, Beard appeared to accept the "contemptible" notion of "buying peace," as long as the Congress, not the executive branch, controlled the transaction. Presumably, he believed that in this way FDR's diplomatic initiatives would be considerably circumscribed. But since the administration's bill required congressional approval of lend-lease appropriations, it is difficult to see how Beard's proposal, if enacted, would have significantly reduced the risk of war. Adolf Hitler's reactions to the ways in which this aid was employed, not the branch of government administering the aid, ultimately would determine the risk to the United States. Thus, Beard's assumption that Congress would be able to perform the service of lend-lease with less provocation than the president was questionable and not capable of demonstration.

Within two months of congressional approval of the lend-lease bill in March 1941, Beard engaged in a brief, fascinating exchange of views with the Yale diplomatic historian Samuel Flagg Bemis. Bemis had asked George H. E. Smith whether Beard would consent to read his recently completed manuscript on American foreign policy. Beard agreed to do so. In commenting to Smith about Bemis' interpretations, Beard wrote that he respected Bemis' opinions, "but I do not accept them." He also wanted to know what Bemis thought the present policy of the United States should be, posing the following questions: "Declare war on Germany on the theory that we must have total victory or take our own downfall? If so, when and where do we begin to fight? And with what assurance of victory, judging the state of our arms?" Smith relayed these

78. Ibid., p. 312.
79. Ibid., p. 313.

sensible, if somewhat contentious, queries to Bemis. The latter responded that he "would continue the present policy of making war indirectly on Germany," but would not send American troops into combat. "If Germany loses, or is stalemated," Bemis added, "we get precious time for armament."[80]

It should not be supposed, however, that Beard's anti-interventionist stand was predicated upon a total indifference to the plight of the oppressed victims of totalitarian tyranny. Even before World War II began in September 1939, he discreetly offered his time and funds in assisting scholarly refugees from Nazi Germany.[81] As late as April 1941, he wrote the Yale librarian-historian Bernard Knollenberg, to thank him for a "generous gift to the fund for helping to get anti-fascists out of France." The head of the committee responsible for the fund was Dr. Spero, one of Beard's former students.[82]

Beard's testimony against the lend-lease bill was the last noteworthy public expression of his views on Roosevelt's diplomacy prior to Pearl Harbor. But, as Eric Goldman reports, when Japan attacked the American fleet, Beard was one of the few important liberals who received the news "unconvinced that it was not all a plot of Roosevelt's, but their statements were lost in the general acceptance of hostilities."[83] As Cushing Strout has suggested, Beard "must have nursed the corrosive confidence that, after all, he had six years before predicted the event."[84]

80. Smith to Beard, May 8, 1941; Beard to Smith, n.d. (but in chronological sequence); Bemis to Beard, May 27, 1941; Smith Papers, Folder 10.
81. Josephson, "Charles A. Beard: A Memoir," p. 592.
82. Beard to Knollenberg, April 24, 1941, Knollenberg Papers, Yale University Library.
83. Goldman, *Rendezvous with Destiny*, p. 385.
84. Strout, *The Pragmatic Revolt*, p. 146.

7

Beard during World War II,
1941-1945

O<small>N</small> S<small>UNDAY</small> afternoon, December 7, 1941, Beard recalled, upon learning of the events at Pearl Harbor, that he "was convinced that here was no mere accident or incident of war, but a culmination in more than a hundred years of American diplomatic negotiations and activities in respect of the Far East, and the opening of a new and dangerous age for the Republic."[1] But whatever suspicions he might have harbored about responsibilities immediately after the Japanese attack, he publicly set them aside during the next few years. Similarly repressed, for a time, were his misgivings about the necessity of American participation in World War II and about the nature of the postwar world. Indeed, there were occasions when Beard publicly and vigorously expressed support for the prosecution of the war against the Axis Powers, a support given added poignancy because his son, William, was serving in the United States Army.[2]

Comparable to his Liberty Bond appeals during World War I, Beard wrote a brief essay in the spring of 1942 to be used by the Treasury Department for the purpose of exhorting the public to purchase war bonds and stamps. He opened his appeal with a brief

1. *Roosevelt and the War,* p. 234n.
2. Beard to Curti, February 1, 1943, Curti Papers, Box 4, Folder 13.

review of aggressive Axis words and deeds which, he said, were statements of fact, "not the illusions of propaganda." He added that Americans had been aware of the "barbarism" of the Axis nations even though there had been differences of opinion over what policy the country should follow before we became a belligerent. American youth were now turning "their faces resolutely to the death-dealing storm of combat" to fight in a world conflict initiated by the Axis Powers. In asking Americans voluntarily to contribute the money to pay for the materials to sustain the men who were risking their lives, he observed, "In strict justice . . . Congress could require all Americans to dedicate fixed proportions of their incomes, remaining after taxes, to the purchase of bonds and stamps, but, in the tradition of liberty, it has left the discharge of that duty to the consciences of the people." Generous discharge of this duty, Beard concluded, would hasten "the triumph in arms and the possibility of advance into a better future for Americans and other peoples of the earth."[3]

In September 1942, Beard penned a remarkable introductory essay to *Voices of History*, a collection of diplomatic papers and speeches written and delivered by various public figures during the previous year. Some of his conclusions seemed to contradict views he had held on American foreign policy up to America's entry into World War II. In its moderate tone and cautious judgments, this particular essay revealed Beard not only as a patriot, but at his judicious best as a historian.

At the outset, Beard asserted that history never repeats itself. He then challenged the thesis of some prewar isolationist publicists, a thesis most forthrightly expressed in C. Hartley Grattan's *The Deadly Parallel* (1939) and implicitly espoused in Beard's own *Devil Theory of War* (1936). Rejecting the notion that World War II, in its origins or causes, was simply a replay of World War I, Beard argued that "this present war differs from every war that has ever

3. In cooperation with the Treasury Department, the Macmillan Company had requested some of their most famous authors to write such an essay. George P. Brett, Jr., president of the publishing house at the time, sent the original copy of Beard's appeal to President Roosevelt as an example of one of the more outstanding he had received. A copy of the essay was forwarded to the Treasury Department. The letter was acknowledged by FDR's secretary, Grace G. Tully, but there is no indication that the president ever read it: George P. Brett, Jr., to FDR, May 12, 1942; Grace G. Tully to G. P. Brett, Jr., May 18, 1942; FDR Library.

been waged" with respect to ideologies, scope, and possible results. "In this unique conflict," he added, "all the interests of the American people—moral, intellectual, and material—are at stake."[4]

In the course of his remarks, Beard also reflected upon the nature of leadership in history, dismissing as too extreme both Thomas Carlyle's "Great Man" theory and the determinism of Marxist historiography. Instead, he endorsed a compromise view in which "leaders and peoples alike are in some ways victims of history and some makers of it. The fortunes and actions of both are entangled in the same web of fate and subject to the same possibilities of creative action." Critical periods in the life of a society, he noted, may require vigorous and powerful leadership. The Constitution of the United States provided for emergency situations in which the president could be invested with "enormous war powers which are rightly his under the Constitution" and which could be augmented by congressional legislation. In the existing crisis, President Roosevelt was exercising such constitutional and "duly conferred" authority. Throughout 1941, FDR had not ignored public opinion in making declarations of policy. "Leaders in great affairs," wrote Beard, "must be followers as well, must give voice to the sentiments and aspirations of multitudes."[5]

Insofar as the "barbarous" doctrines and actions of the Axis Powers were concerned, Beard admitted that no American could claim "supermundane neutrality or objectivity." Neither he nor the editor of *Voices of History*, Franklin Watts, wished "to attain this unearthly indifference as to the merits of the issues involved in the conflict now raging." But he pointed out that he and the editor had tried to be as fair and as accurate as possible, even in the presentation of the Axis position, in the hope that this would produce a higher degree of knowledge and understanding of the policies and doctrines of the "insatiable and ferocious seekers after power over mankind."[6]

Of particular interest, for comparison with previous or later opinions, are Beard's comments in this introductory essay about the Lend-Lease Act and the reliability of such semiofficial accounts of prewar diplomacy as *How War Came: An American White*

4. Beard, introduction to *Voices of History: Great Speeches and Papers of the Year 1941*, ed. Franklin Watts, pp. ix–x.
5. Ibid., pp. xi–xiii.
6. Ibid., p. xv.

Paper; From the Fall of France to Pearl Harbor (1942), by the journalists Forrest Davis and Ernest K. Lindley. In the case of the bill against which he testified, Beard claimed that it would not be possible to include enough selections from the congressional hearings to give a balanced account of the opposing views, nor would it be desirable, for it would "foster an indulgence in recrimination, still all too common, though futile for political purposes and a menace to national unity." As for the Davis and Lindley book, Beard speculated that these journalists probably had been selected by the government as a channel to communicate to the public information about negotiations ordinarily kept secret for many years. *How War Came*, he believed at the time, "may be safely used in interpreting many documents in the collection which follows."[7]

In conclusion, Beard noted that a number of the documents outlined the objectives of peace, as well as the aims of the war. No one could safely predict the details of the settlement, but "it is certain that the responsibilities of the United States will be heavy. On that there can be no disagreement," he added, "although there may be differences of opinion over the degree and nature of these obligations." If preparations for peace were to accompany the prosecution of the war, Beard concluded, a study of such documents as those included in *Voices of History* would contribute to realistic thinking about postwar peace and stability.[8]

In the fall of 1942, and on the occasion of the dedication of a war memorial in his hometown of New Milford, Connecticut, Beard spoke movingly of the need to "prove to the men whose names are here inscribed, that out of their courage and sacrifice will come better homes, better fathers, mothers, sisters, wives, and friends—a better Republic, one and indivisible, than they left behind on their journey into the veiled unknown."[9]

Shortly after this, Beard's self-imposed moratorium on public criticism of the prevailing assumptions of American foreign policy came to an end. One sign of the opening of old wounds was his strident defense, on the eve of the congressional elections of 1942, of the powers and wisdom of Congress against the attacks of critics

7. Ibid., pp. xv–xvii.
8. Ibid., p. xix.
9. Text of address, October 25, 1942, in "The Charles A. Beard File," Microfilm No. 139.

and the pressures of public opinion. In a magazine article, Beard complained of "the wholesale indictment of Congress," and he berated the Gallup polls, which he believed were partly responsible for the generally low opinion of Congress. He did not specify the reasons for, or issues behind, this development. But he feared that "the promulgation and reiteration of such criticisms, so unqualified in nature, shake public confidence in constitutional government— one thing certainly worth fighting for in this age of self-imposed slavery and tyranny by conquest."[10]

About this time, Beard and his wife Mary completed *The American Spirit: A Study of the Idea of Civilization in the United States,* a work in which he partially renewed his debate with those Americans who had departed from the policy of continentalism.[11] With the publication of this book, Beard's wartime writings focused less on the war effort and more on the postwar policies of the United States. Although one reviewer suggested that the bitterness of Beard's recent prewar isolationism seemed behind him,[12] in the brief passages on foreign affairs, a number of Beard's isolationist assumptions could be discerned. This was particularly true of the criticisms of those Americans who believed that the United States should be engaged in "imposing civilization on other peoples in distant parts of the earth or underwriting civilization throughout the world."[13] In a chapter entitled "World Mission under Arms," the Beards analyzed the writings of a number of men—such as Josiah Strong and Alfred Thayer Mahan—who, they alleged, had weakened the idea of civilization in America by preaching the gospel that American civilization was for export. Included among the contemporary "advocates of a militant world mission" was Henry R. Luce, publisher of *Time, Life,* and *Fortune,* who, the Beards derisively noted, had "summoned to his aid the genie of [Western] civilization" (p. 574).

In *The American Century* (1941), Luce had indeed displayed a conspicuously righteous zeal in exhorting Americans to "accept wholeheartedly our duty and our opportunity as the most powerful and vital nation in the world and in consequence to exert upon

10. "In Defense of Congress," pp. 530, 533.
11. Hereafter cited as *American Spirit.*
12. Review of *American Spirit,* in *Time,* December 14, 1942, p. 122.
13. *American Spirit,* p. 550.

the world the full impact of our influence, for such purposes as we see fit and by such means as we see fit."[14] Since one of these means included world trade, Beard seized upon this proposal to discredit the programs of internationalists. "Luce dangled prizes of profits in world trade more enormous than any which the short-sighted imperialists of other years had ever conjured up in their wildest fantasies. . . . It remained," Beard added with heavy sarcasm, "for Luce to offer American traders prospects of gain so glittering as to make Marco Polo's lures look like Stygian murk."[15]

In contrast, a basic thesis of *The American Spirit* was that the idea of American civilization was unique in its "origins, substance, and development." For at least a century, the nation had derived its unity and strength from the ability to work out its destiny in relative freedom from outside pressures. Beard thus admonished that any attempts to extend American civilization by force of arms or through international organizations would result not only in a weakening of the vigor of American civilization, but in a decrease of the eventual contribution the United States could make to world civilization by the power of independent example.[16]

A measure of Beard's growing concern about the possibility of the United States assuming a major role in postwar world affairs was reflected in a Memorial Day address he delivered in 1943. "All about us," he told his audience, "are men and women who speak glibly of 'one world,' of 'the new world,' that is to be made at the end of this war." These individuals gave the impression that the problems of the world would "be suddenly solved by uttering words, by changing our laws, and signing pieces of paper at peace tables." Such expectations were more than illusory; they were "sheer madness, perilous to our safety and well-being, and deceptive to the nations of the earth." He shrewdly noted that, after the war, there would be "great and powerful governments besides our own" which would, "if there are any lessons for us in history, pursue their interests, as they have in centuries past."[17]

14. Page 23.
15. *American Spirit*, pp. 576–77.
16. Ibid., pp. 535–52, 672.
17. Quoted in *New Milford* (Conn.) *Times*, June 3, 1943, p. 1. Clipping in "Beard File," Microfilm No. 139. One of the specific objects of Beard's criticism was Wendell L. Willkie, the defeated Republican candidate for president in 1940 and author of *One World* (New York: Simon and Schuster, 1943).

A few months after this address, Beard praised Harry Elmer
Barnes for an article in *The Progressive* that dealt critically with
some American proposals for the postwar world. He called it "just
about the finest and most penetrating thing I have yet read on the
prospects at hand." The magazine, edited by Oswald Garrison
Villard and critical of FDR's diplomacy, was, in Beard's opinion,
"about the only civilized sheet in the country." He hoped to sub-
mit something to it one day, but was then "slaving on a job."[18]

The project in question probably was *The Republic: Conversations on Fundamentals*. The first of five printings appeared in
October 1943, and, despite Beard's cutting remarks about Henry R.
Luce in *The American Spirit*, was serialized in *Life* magazine from
January to March 1944. The work was a unique and significant
milestone in Beard's long career. It was certainly unique in its
literary construction, in which Beard engaged in a series of invented
conversations about American history with various fictitious individuals—principally a Dr. and Mrs. Smyth—of differing viewpoints.
It was perhaps most significant in the clear revision of his earlier
emphasis on economic motivation in the framing and adoption of
the Constitution. "The Founding Fathers" in *The Republic*, as
one student of Beard has suggested, "are no longer the Funding
Fathers; they are proponents of national unity and constitutional
government."[19]

While Beard now downgraded the force of economic motivation
in explaining the behavior of the Constitution-makers, he had not
thoroughly abandoned the economic factor in history. Soon after the
publication of *The Republic*, Beard wrote to the historian Merle
Curti, "There certainly is something in economic determinism,
more than most people suspect." In the same letter, however,
he intimated that he was going through another major reassess-
ment of the nature of history, for he added, "There is a lot of
sheer damned folly in the world, that is, no-sense or chaos."[20] These
ruminations may have been a partial reflection of what one historian has described as Beard's search for a general theory of causation during the last decade of his life. One of the major stimulants
in this quest was Brooks Adams' study *The Law of Civilization*

18. Beard to Barnes, September 2, 1943, Barnes Papers.
19. Strout, *The Pragmatic Revolt*, p. 99.
20. Beard to Curti, November 6, 1943, Curti Papers, Box 4, Folder 13.

and Decay, initially published in the United States in 1896, and for which Beard wrote a lengthy introduction in the 1943 reprint.[21] Beard was struck by what he discerned to be the timeliness of this volume's "protests against plutocratic tendencies in American development" which have "recently found livid expression in the New Deal." He was also impressed with the timeless qualities of the work, which, "whatever its shortcomings, is entitled to rank among the permanent classics of American thought relative to the nature and history of humanity's experience." Possibly the most challengeable aspect of the work to Beard was Brooks Adams' cyclic view of history. Beard did not accept the idea that history repeats itself. The determinism implicit in such a theory left "out of account acts of creative intelligence and the cumulative force of such acts." Beard was pleased, however, with Adams' provocative description of the process of civilization in which the "imaginative" mind and man (e.g., priests, artists, soldiers) had been replaced by the "economic" mind and man as the dominant force and role in society. Yet, Beard did not think that Adams, in a truly comprehensive sense, had presented either an economic or Marxian interpretation; rather, "in one respect Brooks offered a psychological interpretation of history, with fear and greed as the two great instincts of mankind which gave direction to human energies."[22]

Beard's continuing interest in some of the ideas of Brooks Adams was shown in *The Republic*, most notably in a discussion of the cyclic theory of history. The writings of Oswald Spengler, the German philosopher-historian, received the most attention, although Brooks Adams' theory was mentioned. As he had done the year before, Beard rejected the determinism, pessimism, and arguments from analogies found in such theories.[23] Other scattered comments suggest how Adams' work may have influenced a recasting of Beard's historiographical priorities. At one point, in response to a thesis set forth in James Burnham's *Managerial Revolution* (1941), Beard challenged the idea "that economic managers have guts enough to make a revolution and could make good

21. William A. Williams, "A Note on Charles Austin Beard's Search for a General Theory of Causation."

22. Beard, introduction to Brooks Adams, *The Law of Civilization and Decay: An Essay on History*, pp. vii–viii.

23. Beard, *The Republic: Conversations on Fundamentals*, pp. 331–41, hereafter cited as *The Republic*.

afterward, as against the warrior, the statesman, the saint, or the popular hero. . . . the economic man, as such, is not cast in a heroic mold." Later, he bluntly remarked, "I sometimes think that politics is more of a determining force in history than economics."[24]

A more tenuous, but nonetheless possible, impact of Brooks Adams on Beard involved a re-inforcement of his earlier concerns about the nature of centralized political power and leadership. For Adams, modern political centralization had been brought about principally by finance capitalists who appeared to be incapable of resolving socioeconomic conflicts, a failure which would result in the decline of Western civilization.[25] In contrast, by 1945 Beard thought that "political man" had replaced "economic man" as the dominant force in American life.

In *The Republic*, Beard tentatively moved in this direction in his discussion of the relative powers of the Congress and the president, which, in the case of foreign affairs, would find more pointed analysis in his two volumes on Roosevelt's diplomacy. In 1943, he was particularly disturbed by one view of Congress as a mechanistic institution in which individual members had "no free will to shape their own conduct and procedure." Such a conception "drives them into supine dependence on executive will," Beard argued, thereby paralyzing "their own capacity for constructive thinking and action" and precluding their ability to develop "leadership in national affairs." The Founding Fathers, he insisted, had expected "that Congress should be the dominant branch of the Federal Government." Conceding that the president had been allowed "to assume a dominant position, the fault," he said, "lies with Congress, not with the Constitution."[26]

In the brief conversation about the office of the president, Beard pointed out that the power which any particular president exercised was not dependent solely upon the text of the Constitution. His personality and the historical circumstances were also important. "Times of crisis" created situations in which "executive power is about as great as the President can make or cares to make it, within physical limits and subject to the restraints imposed by Congress, the Supreme Court, and the temper of the people."[27]

24. Ibid., pp. 284, 316.
25. *The Law of Civilization and Decay*, p. 7.
26. *The Republic*, pp. 199–200.
27. Ibid., p. 208.

Beard then turned to a detailed consideration of the Senate's rejection of the Versailles Treaty and American membership in the League of Nations after World War I. In selecting this episode, Beard intended to challenge a widely held view of the president as always being the symbol of national unity and as *the* spokesman for the United States in foreign affairs. He also wanted to illustrate his contention that the president was not omnipotent in the conduct of American diplomacy. Suggesting that the framers of the Constitution had intended it this way, he noted the many instances in which that document requires congressional initiative or approval in matters bearing on America's relations with other countries. This was followed by quotations from *The Federalist*, including one from Alexander Hamilton, who, according to Beard, "said that an ambitious executive of a republic, *unless restrained in power over foreign affairs as our Constitution provides,* might come under foreign influences and betray his country. He was arguing against conferring upon the President unlimited power over foreign affairs."[28]

In a chapter entitled "The Republic in the World of Nations," Beard had his day in court as a prosecuting attorney against the various postwar proposals of those he characterized as "world-planners." But he was able to have it both ways, for he was also the star witness in defense of a more limited view of America's diplomatic responsibilities and actions once the war ended. It could be argued that Beard's statement of some of the internationalist schemes was so overdrawn as to depict "straw men," whose ideas could be readily knocked down—a technique which one reviewer aptly suggested made Beard appear to be "a tiger among lesser cats," who clawed all his enemies to death.[29] There were, however, much sense and sensibility in Beard's relentless questioning, even if devastating at times, of the unstated assumptions, cloudy rhetoric, and naïve expectations of the "world-planners."

Before these advocates could spell out their positions, Beard wanted to clarify the issue of what "the supreme object of American foreign policy should be." It was not, in his judgment, "to bring permanent peace to the nations of the world." Indeed, he had already deftly disposed of the word "permanent"—meaning, in

28. Ibid., pp. 208–17. Hamilton's *Federalist Number 75* was Beard's source for these conclusions.
29. Review of *The Republic*, in *Time*, October 18, 1943, p. 100.

Beard's definition, "forever"—as being inadequate to any realistic postwar expectations. He preferred the idea of an enduring peace which might last anywhere from thirty to fifty years. More positively, he believed that "the supreme object of American foreign policy should be to protect and promote the interests, spiritual and material, of the American people, and, subject to that mandate, to conduct foreign affairs in such a manner as to contribute to the peace and civilization of mankind."[30]

One of the participants in this particular conversation in *The Republic* was a Protestant minister who almost seemed to apologize for the idea that World War II was "a righteous war against war." He desired a plan for world peace that would be guided by Christian principles. Most Americans, according to recent Gallup polls, he asserted, were now ready to make great sacrifices and would participate in a new form of world organization, which they would have joined in 1919 but for the "tricky and ambitious Republicans" who defeated the League of Nations (p. 309).

In response, Beard said that he favored waging a successful military campaign against the Axis Powers, but he was prepared to leave the question of righteousness to "our theologian." He did agree that there had been "a decline in the sheer love of war among many nations," but he could not resist the sardonic comment that "the great nations seem to like a war every generation or two." On the failure of the United States to become a member of the League of Nations in 1919, Beard would not condone Republican tactics. At the same time, however, he stressed Woodrow Wilson's uncompromising behavior as a contributing factor to the episode. More important, perhaps, he did not believe the majority of the American people ever favored the league intensely enough to "force ratification by the Senate." Nor did he think World War II could have been prevented even if the United States had been a member of the league. This was largely because such nations as Britain, France, and Russia, which had the power to resist Axis encroachments upon league principles in the 1930s, did not do so (pp. 309–14).

Without denying the importance or relevance of morality and ethics between nations, Beard raised some awkward questions about

---

30. *The Republic*, p. 307. Page numbers in the paragraphs that follow refer to this book.

the Christian and moralistic emphases in the minister's hopes for the postwar peace settlement. The concept of the United States as a "Christian nation" was an exaggeration, Beard claimed, since "more than half of the population does not belong to any Christian denomination." In addition, he wondered whether Christians really "have obligations to help, without limits," persons of other world religions, or even pagans, especially when so many of them "are doing their best to beat back the tide of Christian missionaries." The paradoxes, or potential inconsistencies, of the moralist's position were also underscored in *The Republic*. Beard was able to demonstrate, for example, that most of these persons—though embracing the "brotherhood of man" as an ideal—would not accept, or did not believe practicable, a wholesale repeal of immigration laws which might result in millions of immigrants from Europe or Asia pouring into the United States immediately after the war. "The issue," Beard concluded, "is one of our having morality without going to such extremes of sentimental sympathy that morality is destroyed in the United States" (pp. 324–27).

Somewhat less tendentious criticism was applied to the projects for world federation on the American model and an Economic Union. The questionable efficacy of the former was brusquely rejected by Beard as "a far-fetched analogy." The nature of the American federation formed in the eighteenth century, compared to "the basic conditions of the fifty or more independent nations of the earth" in the 1940s, was "utterly diverse in race, history, sentiments, and economy" (pp. 314–15).

The Economic Union was to be composed of major democratic nations that had no extensive government control of the economy. This proposal provided Beard with an opportunity to return to some cherished arguments of the 1930s. It appeared, though only momentarily, that Beard might be caught in a rejection of his own previous emphasis on the war-producing aspects of international trade rivalries—something the proponents of an Economic Union believed their program would eliminate. Since he quickly indicated his lack of enthusiasm for this program, Beard was confronted with the angry question "So you want wars over commerce and raw materials to go on forever?" Beard replied by noting that the free trade environment of the United States had not prevented a Civil War. Implicitly, he was backing off from his traditional emphasis on economic factors as the principal causes of wars. He almost tacitly admitted as much when he said with exaggerated self-deprecation, "As to what you call the chief cause of wars, or the decisive cause, I confess I do not know the cause of anything" (p. 321).

Beard's more substantive and convincing objections to the idea of internationalized free trade included his skeptical inquiry concerning the number of nations, regardless of political ideology, that could or would enter into such an arrangement. He also asked if the Economic Union's plan for guaranteeing all countries equal access to raw materials meant that the United States would have to allow "capitalists and laborers" from countries without certain raw materials "to enter the United States and exploit our resources for themselves?" How would prices for these resources be determined and enforced? Moreover, would not this access, as in the past, always be greater for the wealthier nations? "The have-nots with little or nothing to exchange for our raw materials," he added, "will be able to get little or nothing here. Their equality of access is thus a mere fiction." Beard also observed that the proposal for "unshackling trade throughout the world" held no automatic guarantee of eliminating mass unemployment or raising standards of living. The United States in the early 1930s had, in effect, a free trade system throughout the nation. Yet, "millions were suffering in the four sections of the country" (pp. 319–24).

In *The Republic*'s passages dealing with the postwar world, Beard demonstrated commendable prescience in predicting the possible breakup of the Allied war coalition, internal strife in seemingly stable nations, and the appearance of "new combinations of power." Because of these future uncertainties, he would not support "an elaborate world constitution, full of vague phrases that could, and probably would, be twisted and turned by governments competing for power." Hoping the Allied statesmen would think in terms of a "durable rather than a permanent peace," he favored "a brief and simple treaty," limited to about ten years' duration and "subject to renewal." The document would "bind the signatory powers to refrain from resorting to violence during that period, and to abide by stipulated methods of arbitration and conciliation in case controversies arise under the terms of the treaty." Despite the absence of any enforcement powers or authority, Beard believed that his modest program would be far more successful "than grandiose plans for settling everything and everybody all at once and for all time and for trying to hold millions of people down by police and propaganda" (pp. 328–30).

About a year after the publication of the widely read[31] and generally acclaimed *The Republic*, Charles and Mary Beard's *Basic History of the United States* appeared.[32] In terms of sales (about 650,000 copies), it was their most successful joint effort. But this last cooperative undertaking was also their most controversial work as a team, as Beard, for the first time since Pearl Harbor, publicly returned to his personal campaign against FDR's diplomacy. The reactions to the highly interpretive sections on foreign affairs amply forecast the bitter controversies that would be stirred up by Beard's two-volume study of Roosevelt's foreign policy.

The Beards characterized American diplomacy from 1898 to 1917 as "The Breach with Historic Continentalism." As in Charles Beard's previous works in the decade of the 1930s, America's overseas expansion was interpreted as the handiwork of a small group of agitators who seized upon the crusading zeal of Americans to maneuver the country into a war with Spain. The war not only allayed domestic discontent, but, through territorial acquisition, served the interests of traders, manufacturers, bankers, and the naval bureaucracy. The result was that the United States was "thrust into the eternal wars of the Orient and into the endless intrigues of the great Powers of Europe." Theodore Roosevelt, "loving power for its own sake," guided the nation through nearly eight years of a " 'vigorous' foreign policy," followed by William Howard Taft's "dollar diplomacy," or "imperialist activity" with a different name. Despite Woodrow Wilson's renunciation of imperialism in theory, "as practice it was by no means discounted." The chapter concluded on this melancholy note: "Certainly it could be said with truth that the adventure of the United States in world-power politics had not brightened the outlook for world peace" (pp. 337–55).

In their account of World War I, the Beards mentioned American sympathy for the Allies from 1914 to 1917, and they alluded to the

31. *The Republic* may well have been the *most* widely read of Beard's works. Regular sales ran to more than 183,000; the *Life* edition sold more than 40 million copies; postwar Japanese editions totaled more than 30,000. Beale compiled the sales figures for most of Beard's works in *Beard Appraisal*, pp. 310–12.

32. Hereafter cited as *A Basic History*. Page numbers in the paragraphs that follow refer to this book.

activities of "hordes" of propagandists from both sides. But whether this propaganda created or simply augmented existing sympathy was not clarified. Sufficient emphasis was placed upon the issues of German violations of the rights of neutrals and the unrestricted submarine campaign as important reasons for American intervention (pp. 428–31). Also in their discussion of the war, the "devil theory" or "merchants of death" thesis was recapitulated: "Although this spurt of prosperity before the United States entered the war was largely due to the purchases made by the Entente Allies, Wilson's partisans attributed it in some measure to the New Freedom. But leading Democrats, including the president himself, knew that it was mainly artificial and that the defeat of the Allies or the ending of the war would bring in its train an economic crash in the United States. In fact, to some members of the administration this was an argument for enlarging the borrowing facilities of the Allies and, finally, for entering the war directly" (p. 439).

The military aspects of America's participation received only passing notice. Though brief, there were pointed passages critical of violations of civil liberties and freedom of the press. The authors also described continuing domestic struggles, such as those between capital and labor, and concluded that the war had "magnified the problems and sharpened the issues." In spite of the fact that such struggles were expected to continue after the war, "President Wilson proposed remedies couched primarily in international terms" (pp. 432, 434, 439–40).

In the evaluation of Wilson's role as a peacemaker, the disparity between the president's war aims and the terms imposed upon Germany were duly noted. Nevertheless, the Beards conceded that the Versailles Treaty probably would have been more vindictive without Wilson's "moderating influence" at the peace conference. But the defeat of the treaty in America and the election of Warren G. Harding in 1920 were seen as evidence that the American people had probably rejected Wilsonian idealism (pp. 435–38, 440, 442).

Charles and Mary Beard's denial of any justification for the war and American intervention in it was implied in a passage on the revision of "war guilt," inspired by revelations stemming from archival research soon after the war. By consulting the documents or revisionist studies grounded on them, "literate Americans in large numbers learned something of the innumerable lies, deceptions, and frauds perpetrated by the governments of Czarist Russia, Great

Britain, and France, as well as of the Central Powers, at the expense of their own peoples and other nations. The gleaming mirage that pictured the World War as purely or even mainly a war for democracy and civilization dissolved beyond recognition. Countless Americans who in 1914–18 had yearned for a 'brave new world' at the conclusion of the war were disheartened by the proofs of sinister purposes running against their dreams" (p. 442).

In *A Basic History*, the interpretation of Franklin Roosevelt's foreign policy before December 1941 was comparable to that found in most of Beard's writings from the mid-1930s to Pearl Harbor. After FDR showed early signs of committing the nation to a policy of nonentanglement, he soon began to make statements and take actions which combined some of the worst features of imperialism and internationalism. The growing unrest in Europe, the Beards maintained, did not blind the American people to the nature of fascist aggression. The successive neutrality acts, however, indicated an unshakable national resolve to stay out of the next world war. But Roosevelt, who seemed to be in accord with this sentiment, dramatically changed his position in the "quarantine" address in October 1937. This was followed by his request for increased naval appropriations in January 1938 (pp. 462–65).

To further demonstrate the apparent contradictions in FDR's diplomacy—or the "appearances vs. realities" theme that figured prominently in Beard's two postwar works—the Beards observed that the president had given assurances that repeal of the arms embargo in 1939 would aid in keeping the country out of the European conflict. But they added, "In vain opponents of repeal or alteration insisted that the changes were steps toward entry into another war along the very road Woodrow Wilson had traveled from 1915 to 1917." Quoted without comment was the "solemn pledge" from Roosevelt's campaign speech in Boston on October 30, 1940, in which he had declared, "Your boys are not going to be sent into any foreign wars." Although the administration claimed that the lend-lease bill was designed to promote the defense of the United States, it was "an act of war" (pp. 465–67).

Charles Beard's private suspicions about the Pearl Harbor disaster were publicly aired for the first time in *A Basic History*. He cited the January 1941 prophecy of Joseph C. Grew, the American ambassador in Tokyo, that Japan was planning a surprise attack on Pearl Harbor in the event of impending hostilities with the

United States. Given this advance warning, an explanation of the debacle had to be found in one of two possibilities: either President Roosevelt and his secretaries of war and navy had failed to advise the Pacific commanders of the possibility of such an attack, or the officers in question had been "inexcusably negligent in the performance of duty. Wherever the responsibility lay, the United States had been assaulted by Japan and was severely crippled for quick counterblows by the disaster at Pearl Harbor" (p. 469).

Following a one-page summary of the military campaigns of the war, a lengthy section was devoted to the impact of the war on American society. Charles and Mary Beard painted a rather grim picture of "revolutionary" dislocations in "every branch of economy, . . . all the relations of men, women, and children, every phase of education, every medium of expression and communications, all processes of government, [and] all aspects of civil and military government." In seeming vindication of their repeated predictions between the world wars about the disastrous consequences to life in America if the United States participated in another world war, the Beards catalogued some "regimenting and disruptive effects" of World War II: "menaces to health, education, welfare, and every other human value reached frightening proportions"; "juvenile delinquency and crimes increased to an extent that threatened the moral basis of American society"; "families were undergoing disintegration"; public education showed tendencies "savoring of militarism"; the enforcement of much social and welfare legislation "was relaxed or openly disregarded amid the rush of war mobilization"; civil liberties were in jeopardy; controls over thought were expanded; and a bill like the Alien Registration Act of 1940 was compared to the "European state-police system" (pp. 472–77). It should be observed in passing that many of these descriptions of wartime life did have some substance in fact. But a number of contemporary observers, as well as a number of scholars since World War II, have regarded accounts like those found in *A Basic History* as overdrawn.[33]

As for postwar concerns, the Beards did not challenge the fact

33. See, for example, Edmund Fuller, "What's in a Name?" [Letter to Editor], *Saturday.Review of Literature*, November 11, 1944, p. 13; Dixon Wecter, review of *A Basic History*, ibid., p. 8; Jack Goodman, ed., *While You Were Gone: A Report on Wartime Life in the United States*; Richard Polenberg, ed., *America at War: The Home Front, 1941–1945.*

that Americans by 1944 were virtually unanimous in their agreement that the United States would have to assume a very active role in shaping and guaranteeing world peace. But the question as to how this peace was to be achieved by American participation had not been definitively answered. Schemes for some type of world organization had widespread support; an alliance among the United States, Great Britain, Russia, and China was viewed as a possibility by some. But "no simple or intricate plan that was set forth commanded wholesale approval." The Beards implied, however, that power-political disputes among the Allies might reduce the prospects for postwar international conciliation. Further, there were signs which pointed to continuing postwar confrontations between the executive and legislative branches over foreign, as well as domestic, policies.[34]

Given some of these problems, Charles and Mary Beard wondered whether the plans submitted for a durable peace could be carried out with the expectation of much success. They wondered also whether the American people were really prepared to make the substantial sacrifices necessary if the nation was to assume a role of world leadership and responsibility. Of particular concern was the ability of the American people to put their own domestic affairs in order. If they could not, how could they reasonably expect to solve the world's problems? The New Deal, the Beards argued, needed a war boom to solve the problem of unemployment. However, there was no evidence to suggest that a postwar version of the New Deal could cope with the anticipated greater social and economic problems. Nor did they think that one could place much faith in a return to the system of "freer" enterprise of the 1920s.[35]

The Beards offered no alternatives to these policies, but they observed somewhat ominously that the alien theories of fascism and communism had "entered into the discussion of destiny and opportunity ahead in the United States." Supporters of such theories regarded as virtues the ability of these systems to solve unemployment and to maintain social order. But the common vices of these systems were anathema to the Beards: "suppression of civil liberties, representative government, and intellectual freedom," accompanied by "the regimentation of the people under a despotic ruler." Slight consolation was found in the fact that leaders in

34. *A Basic History*, pp. 479–84.
35. Ibid., pp. 485–88.

American business, industry, labor, and agriculture, hoping to avert the adoption of either system in the United States, were studying anticipated problems and making plans to deal with them.[36]

A Basic History of the United States was praised and damned in the book review columns of newspapers, magazines, and professional journals throughout the country. The most bitter comments about the work and Beard's stature as a historian, however, probably appeared in the editorial and letters pages of the *Saturday Review of Literature*. A Beard partisan once described these critics as a "lynching mob" and the weekly as "the leading publicity organ for war mongers."[37] The so-called lynching mob was led by Henry Seidel Canby, a contributing editor to the *Saturday Review*. Confining his remarks to the Beards' discussion of FDR's diplomacy, he charged that this section of the book was "unhistorical in method, violently biased in opinion, and, worst of all, unfair and untrue" in the insinuation that what President Roosevelt said and did, rather than the acts of Germany and Japan, were solely responsible for America's belligerent status.[38]

A few weeks later, Lewis Mumford—who once lavishly praised the Beards' *Rise of American Civilization* as "the high-water mark of modern historic presentation in America"[39]—wrote an impassioned letter about *A Basic History* to the *Saturday Review*. Mumford made no effort to conceal the fact that he was personally distraught by what he believed to be the "tragedy of a good man gone wrong." He paid tribute to the "friendly interest" and "kindly help" that Beard had given him in earlier years. He also called attention to the historian's "good reputation, earned by a life-time of devoted scholarship." But Beard's prestige, Mumford alleged, "increases the menace of what he has written during the last dozen years: our pro-Nazis, our so-called nationalists, will use Beard as their respectable front." Mumford then called for a critical examination of all of Beard's recent writings on foreign policy in order

36. Ibid., pp. 488–89.
37. Porter Sargent, *Between Two Wars: The Failure of Education, 1920–1940*, p. 41*n*2. From at least 1939 to 1941, Sargent published a monthly "bulletin" espousing isolationism. Copies were sent to Beard, who often wrote Sargent about their contents: Sargent, *Getting Us into War* (Boston: Porter Sargent, 1941), pp. 186, 333.
38. "History by Innuendo," *Saturday Review of Literature*, November 11, 1944, p. 12.
39. Mumford, review of *The Rise of American Civilization*, in *New Republic*, May 11, 1927, pp. 338–39 (Literary Supplement).

to "save another generation from Beard's studied misguidance."[40] Beard did not publicly respond to the more vituperative charges of his detractors. Privately, however, he confided to friends his concern about attacks such as Mumford's. It was not criticism, as such, that disturbed him; rather, it was personal abuse, which he did not think appropriate for a literary journal.[41]

In the spring of 1945, Beard completed the third revision of *The Economic Basis of Politics*. For this revision, he added a chapter that indicated the impact upon him of totalitarian movements and World War II, as well as the continuing influence of Brooks Adams' study on *Civilization and Decay*. These influences did not, however, result in a wholesale repudiation of economic forces or motives in explaining political behavior. There was, nonetheless, a more explicit recognition on his part of noneconomic "aspects of human behavior," including "the ambitions and force of unique personalities." But it was Fascist ideology in particular, with its racial doctrine and glorification of "irrationality and violence," that made the idea of rational economic behavior in the political realm a less satisfying or comprehensive tool of analysis for Beard. "Economic forces undoubtedly entered into the rise of Fascism," he concluded, "but they do not wholly account for its appearance and course" (p. 91).

Shortly after, in a similar but more exasperated vein, Beard confessed to Oswald Garrison Villard, "I was foolish in laying such emphasis on economic aspects of the business. Man hasn't sense enough to pursue economic interests consistently. . . . Man seems bound to have a berserk rage ever so often—a senseless berserk rage, and I regard it as a mistake to gloss that fact over. Look at Hitler. He had control over Europe, but cut his own throat by attacking Russia (as Napoleon did)."[42]

In the 1945 revision of *The Economic Basis of Politics*, Beard also observed how, in many societies, "the military man" seemed to be gaining in authority over both "the political man" and "the

40. "Mr. Beard and His 'Basic History,'" *Saturday Review of Literature*, December 2, 1944, p. 27. So intense was Mumford's disappointment with Beard that he publicly resigned his membership in the prestigious National Institute of Arts and Letters when Beard was designated the recipient of the Institute's Gold Medal for History in 1948: *New York Times*, February 4, 1948, p. 25; February 7, 1948, p. 1.

41. Beard to Curti, December 24, 1944; January 31, April 15, 1945; Curti Papers, Box 4, Folder 13.

42. Beard to Villard, July 18, 1945, Villard Papers.

economic man." This development, he predicted, "leads to the expectation that *'the military man' and 'military force' will play an increasing role in the public affairs of the United States* as well as in the affairs of other countries." As partial support for this forecast, he noted that President Roosevelt had declared himself in favor of "making universal military training a regular feature of American military policy after peace was restored" (pp. 101–2).

Fortuitously, perhaps, in the spring of 1945, Secretary of the Navy James Forrestal appointed Ferdinand Eberstadt, a prominent Washington lawyer, to undertake a study of the postwar security requirements of the United States. Beard was among more than fifty distinguished Americans Eberstadt canvassed for their ideas on the subject. On August 25, 1945, Beard submitted a memorandum entitled "Propositions for Consideration." At one point, Beard stressed the necessity for "the coordination of foreign policy and the conduct of foreign affairs with military policy means, and management," for "the lack of such coordination was tragically demonstrated at Pearl Harbor, December 7, 1941."[43]

Some months previous to making this suggestion, Beard had written the well-known advertising executive Bruce Barton that he had resolved "to write a history of the past ten years. . . . Only a Lucian or a Swift or a Voltaire (Candide) could do them justice but I intend to do my best at the job." The next month, Beard asked Barton's assistance in compiling Wendell Willkie's 1940 campaign statements about keeping America out of war. The request was fulfilled a few weeks later.[44]

A month after Germany's surrender in May 1945, Beard also informed Merle Curti of his current project on FDR, writing that he was gathering "neglected and unpublished materials"—with a hint that some might contain startling revelations. He also indicated his annoyance that many peoples of Eastern Europe had been, or would be, betrayed by Roosevelt's diplomacy.[45] Soon after

43. Quoted in Calvin L. Christman, "Charles A. Beard, Ferdinand Eberstadt, and America's Postwar Security," p. 192. Most of Beard's other comments and proposals in this memorandum were consistent with his earlier endorsement of a foreign policy of "continentalism."

44. Beard to Barton, March 6, April 15, May 12, 1945; Barton Papers, State Historical Society of Wisconsin. Bruce Barton, for many years the leading member of a famous advertising agency, is perhaps best known for his commercially rewarding effort of converting Jesus Christ into a successful businessman in *The Man Nobody Knows* (1925).

45. Beard to Curti, June 12, 1945, Curti Papers, Box 4, Folder 13.

the capitulation of Japan, however, Beard wrote a letter to Charles G. Ross, press secretary to President Harry S Truman. In a "Memorandum for the President," Ross quoted an extremely laudatory passage from the letter: "President Truman has handled the Japanese problem with rare skill and insight and now has a splendid opportunity to aid powerfully in finishing off the Japanese warlords for good, and setting the Japanese people on the road to self-government and decent membership in the family of nations."[46]

Despite the surprising implication that the United States should adopt something like a policeman-preacher role toward Japan, and despite the allusion to probable Japanese "war guilt," Beard had not set aside his apparent desire to vindicate his previous suspicions and prophecies concerning FDR's diplomacy.[47] In the same month, he submitted an article to *The Progressive* magazine, in which he observed that with the "murderous Japanese war lords . . . brought to doom," the American people must now devote themselves to the "problems of peace." Of the pressing problems, Beard contended that "none is more important than the determination of the responsibility for the American catastrophe at Pearl Harbor on December 7, 1941."[48]

Anticipating criticism that his claim might be called "extravagant" or a case of "raising academic curiosities that had better be left to dust-sifting historians of coming generations," Beard cited eight issues of vital importance to the nation that would be subject for review during such an investigation. Among these were the roles of the president and Congress in shaping and conducting foreign policy, the need to inform public opinion of the possible consequences of diplomatic decisions, and the relationship of the military to the civil branches of government. The issue which attracted Beard's greatest attention, however, was the question of the guilt of the Pearl Harbor commanders, Admiral Husband E. Kimmel and General Walter C. Short. Congress, he insisted, should give these men an opportunity to disprove any assumptions that they had been derelict in their duty. This was all the more impera-

46. Copy of memorandum dated August 24, 1945, in files of Harry S Truman Library.
47. In 1944, according to Richard Hofstadter, Beard "had two long talks with Henry Luce, preparatory to writing a sharp article on Pearl Harbor for *Life*, which, to his disappointment, Luce decided not to use": *The Progressive Historians*, pp. 342–43.
48. "Pearl Harbor: Challenge to the Republic," p. 1.

tive, he added, because there were rumors that "high authorities" in Washington knew in advance about the surprise attack. Therefore, Congress had to initiate such an investigation, "for such an inquiry will be forced upon that honorable body if it delays too long in meeting a challenge surging up from the people."[49]

By the end of World War II, Beard seemed to be lacking only an authoritative congressional report to confirm his prewar thesis of Roosevelt's alleged duplicity in taking the nation into war, a war that presumably would jeopardize American civilization through the loss of American freedoms and the establishment of a militaristic, totalitarian state.

49. Ibid., pp. 1–2. On September 5, 1945, Henry Luce's wife, then Congresswoman Clare Boothe Luce, requested the printing of this article in the *Congressional Record*, 79th Cong., 1st sess., Appendix, pp. 3759–61.

8

The Efforts to Confirm a Thesis, 1945-1948

ON SEPTEMBER 6, 1945, shortly after Beard's appeal for a Pearl Harbor investigation appeared in print, a joint congressional resolution called for the establishment of a bipartisan committee to conduct an inquiry into the circumstances surrounding the Japanese attack. Though pleased with this development, Beard, as noted in the previous chapter, had resolved by the spring of 1945 to pursue such an inquiry independently. In this quest, he had occasion to correspond and converse with elected and appointed officials of the Republican Party. These associations were instrumental in securing for Beard access to a number of published and unpublished documents which aided him not only in the writing of his last two works on Franklin D. Roosevelt, but also in counseling the minority leader of the Committee on the Pearl Harbor Inquiry, Senator Homer C. Ferguson (R., Mich.).[1]

Beard's most valuable contact in this venture, however, was George H. E. Smith, his erstwhile collaborator on six books, who by 1945 had become secretary of the Steering Committee of the Senate Minority. Following the Republican congressional victories

1. A. Vagts to author, August 8, 1960. In a letter to the author (January 18, 1961), Homer C. Ferguson wrote that he "consulted with a number of people on various aspects of the case but such consultations are always considered confidential. . . . Dr. Beard was a personal friend of mine and I saw him on a number of occasions and always enjoyed his friendship and my talks with him."

in November 1946, Smith became staff director of the Senate Majority Policy Committee.

In July 1945, Beard wrote to Smith to request copies of various documents, including the navy report on Admiral Husband E. Kimmel and the War Department report on General Walter C. Short, both issued on December 1, 1944. Smith complied with the request, but was unable to furnish an official text of the cabinet officers' statements about the reports. Smith also expressed the hope that the Republicans would soon be able to open all the archives and that "we shall find the proper documents still there." Beard, in reply, mentioned that he had already read certain State Department volumes, observing caustically, "What wonders in fact and fancy!"[2]

After World War II, Beard's correspondence and meetings with the revisionist Harry Elmer Barnes increased notably, as they shared opinions on the progress of challenges to the "official" view of how the United States entered World War II. About mid-September 1945, Beard confessed to Barnes that he did not know "the secret of the mystery" surrounding Pearl Harbor, but he did not believe that the president "was surprised. That explanation seems to me to be too 'rational.' " Slightly more than a week later, he referred to the army and navy reports on Pearl Harbor as "astounding documents," adding, "White-washing is now out of the question, no matter what is done by the new committee."[3] The next month, he informed George Smith that these same reports "are alone almost enough to convict high parties of torts if not misdemeanors!"[4]

Concurrently, Beard was laboring on his own study. By December 1945, however, he had decided to divide it into two volumes in order to get the first to the publisher by February 1946 for publication that summer.[5] He was still receiving material from Smith, including some that was "non-quotable, and for background only." In December 1945, Smith was very optimistic that someone like Senator Ferguson eventually would be able to "force every document, scrap of paper, and the last piece of evidence into the

2. Beard to Smith, July 13, 1945; Smith to Beard, July 17, 1945; Beard to Smith, July 30, 1945; Smith Papers, Folder 11.
3. Beard to Barnes, September 15, September 26, 1945; Barnes Papers.
4. Beard to Smith, October 22, 1945, Smith Papers, Folder 11.
5. Beard to Barnes, December 13, 1945, Barnes Papers.

record before they get through." Beard hailed Ferguson as "a gentleman and a genius" who "alone has saved the day" and hoped that he would drive "ahead with deadly and effective precision." In particular, Beard wanted him to probe deeply into the question of why Secretary of State Cordell Hull had rejected what Beard believed was a reasonable Japanese modus vivendi on November 20, 1941. However, Beard implicitly took the cutting edge off his theme of Roosevelt's alleged desire for war when he remarked, "Apparently he [Hull] did it without F.D.'s knowledge and advance approval. F.D.'s pencil memo in the fotostats I have was a sensible proposal for a real settlement with Japan."[6]

During the winter of 1945–46, as signs of U.S.-Soviet tensions became more evident, Beard's private despair over some of the consequences of World War II were increasingly shown in his letters, consequences which undoubtedly enhanced his prior conviction that the United States should have remained out of the war. Some of his correspondents, moreover, were not apt to reverse or temper this departure from Beard's usual optimistic outlook. Oswald Garrison Villard, for example, blasted Harry S Truman as "a highly militaristic, lower middle class, back-slapping American legionnaire" and bitterly complained to Beard that the United States was being turned "into a tremendous military imperialistic Power—exactly what we went to war with Germany to prevent their becoming! . . . It is very hard, dear friend, to keep one's spirit up in the face of all this utter destruction of the finest American traditions and ideals."[7] A similar mordant pessimism was evident in Beard's letter to Harry Elmer Barnes about two weeks later. Labeling a recent article by Walter Lippmann a "declaration of war on Russia," Beard mused, "The grand farce roars ahead to its thunderous denouement."[8]

In the interim, George Smith had tried to get Beard to cooperate in the drafting of a report that "could be used officially" by some members of the Pearl Harbor Inquiry Committee. Beard, however, emphasized his nonpartisanship in the matter and his desire to draw careful conclusions from the evidence. Thus, he expressed

6. Smith to Beard, December 7, December 16, 1945; Beard to Smith, December 18, December 27, 1945; Smith Papers, Folder 11. For the text of the note to which Beard probably was alluding, see James MacGregor Burns, *Roosevelt: The Soldier of Freedom*, p. 156.
7. Villard to Beard, February 6, 1946, Villard Papers.
8. Beard to Barnes, February 18, 1946, Barnes Papers.

his willingness to draft the report for the entire committee. By March 11, 1946, he had compiled a series of "fundamental questions as to responsibility for Pearl Harbor which the Committee must answer." But since he felt that he was still working in the dark, he wanted to talk to someone about it at his home in New Milford.[9]

The latter request set the stage for an exchange of letters which resulted in a meeting between Beard and Senator Ferguson. As a result of this meeting, Beard did send a memorandum to George Smith which contained all his "fundamental conclusions as to the affair, put in the form of questions, with indications as to how they are answered in the testimony and other documents." Beard briefly feared that perhaps even Ferguson's "outlook and view on the subject" might lead to a "milk and water report." But Smith reassured him that the senator "will give P.H. the works for all that the evidence will show."[10]

Despite his memorandum and face-to-face encounter with Senator Ferguson, Beard was disappointed with the Minority Report on Pearl Harbor, the rough draft of which he received in July 1946. The report, he insisted, "evades the supreme issue" of whether Admiral Kimmel and General Short were "guilty of derelictions of duty . . . as charged by the Roberts Commission [1942]." Although Beard had proposed that these commanders be cleared of such a charge, he did not mean they had to be absolved of "errors of judgment, and lack of efficiency and alertness. . . ." He believed that "they were befuddled by the kind of orders they received." Thus, if the draft report was left as it was, it would be "utterly inadequate as a historical document on the subject of responsibility for the disaster at Pearl Harbor."[11]

9. Beard to Smith, March 2, March 11, March 12, 1946; Smith Papers, Folder 12.
10. Smith to Homer C. Ferguson, March 12, 1946; Smith to Beard, March 13, 1946; Beard to Smith, March 18, April 3, 1946; Ferguson to Beard, April 9, 1946; Smith to Beard, April 10, June 19, 1946; Smith Papers, Folder 12.
11. Smith to Beard, July 8, 1946; Beard to Smith, July 10, 1946; Smith Papers, Folder 12. The Minority Report, unlike the Majority Report, did place a large measure of responsibility upon officials in Washington for failing to notify the Pearl Harbor commanders sufficiently of the possibility of an imminent Japanese attack. Beard would emphasize this in his second volume on FDR, but he was still disturbed that the Minority Report "left General Short and Admiral Kimmel under the stigma put upon them by the Roberts Report and the subsequent action of the President": *Roosevelt and the War*, pp. 353, 362–64.

132   *Charles A. Beard and American Foreign Policy*

In a lengthy and judiciously worded response, Smith pointed out that all members of the joint committee had been sympathetic to the plight of the Pearl Harbor commanders. Nevertheless, "not a single one would say that they did not bear responsibility on the Hawaiian end for the disaster." Admitting the disagreement between them, Smith affirmed his own belief that what these commanders "did and failed to do, given the facts they did have and the facts that they did not have, constitutes something more than errors of judgment." Notwithstanding mitigating or extenuating circumstances, the joint committee could not "override the blindness and inaction these two commanders displayed in the face of plenty of warning both from Washington and directly on the scene —in their own front yard."[12]

In the midst of researching and writing his first volume on Roosevelt's diplomacy, Beard was involved in a project for the Social Science Research Council dealing with the problems encountered in the writing of history. His own major contribution was an essay, "Grounds for a Reconsideration of Historiography," in which he suggested some of the basic principles that should guide historical writing, principles to which most historians could subscribe. But he was especially concerned that the historian become master in his own house, for Beard believed that too many men who were engaged in public affairs, such as politicians and journalists, were displaying what the general public assumed to be sound arguments in " 'proving' the validity of their propositions, dogmas, and assertions." In order that such "instructors of the public" not usurp the function of the historian, he urged historians to make their work socially significant.[13]

Beard undoubtedly felt that he was fulfilling this role in his study of FDR's diplomacy. But as the publication date neared for *American Foreign Policy in the Making, 1932–1940: A Study in*

12. Smith to Beard, July 17, 1946, Smith Papers, Folder 12. It should be noted that this first truly significant difference of opinion between the two men on a substantive issue did not end a cordial correspondence. Smith continued to aid Beard in gathering documentary material for his second volume on FDR, and Beard asked Smith to extend his gratitude to Senator Ferguson, especially for his "acumen" in forcing many documents "out and into the record." Beard to Smith, September 10, 1946; Smith to Beard, October 3, 1946; Beard to Smith, November 5, 1946; ibid.
13. Beard, "Grounds for a Reconsideration of Historiography," in Merle Curti, ed., *Theory and Practice in Historical Study: A Report on the Committee on Historiography*. pp. 3–4.

Responsibilities,[14] he confided to some friends that he thought some reviewers already had their axes sharpened in anticipation.[15] Overlooking his occasional use of the pejorative term "hatchet men" to cover most of his critics, Beard's suspicions, as we shall see, were largely borne out.

In keeping with the subtitle of the volume, Beard devoted the first two chapters to challenging the hypothesis that the Congress (especially the Senate) and the American people, by pursuing an isolationist policy in the two decades after the defeat of the Treaty of Versailles, were responsible for World War II (pp. 1–39). One effective argument Beard used to undermine the more exaggerated versions of this charge was that some of the same critics had charged that the aggressive acts of the Axis Powers were responsible for the war. Underscoring their logical inconsistency, Beard aptly remarked that "the whole responsibility for the second World War can scarcely be placed on or in the United States" (pp. 41–42).

This did not mean, however, that Beard was prepared to concede that all, or even most, of the responsibility for the war lay with the Axis Powers. To fix blame on Germany, Italy, and Japan, he said, would involve "perplexing questions of historical interpretation, including the issues connected with 'causation' and 'free will' in the making of history, national and universal." He insisted that the scope of such an investigation in the case of Japan alone "would call for a mastery of languages, documentation, and philosophic thinking which few, if any, students of history or political science can command" (p. 42).

In approaching the admittedly complex problem of "guilt" in this fashion, Beard made no distinction, semantic or moral, between passive and active responsibilities for World War II. For example, one could contrast the failure of the United States to join the League of Nations, the "sin of omission" which *might* have contributed to the prevention of another world war, with the German invasion of Poland in 1939, a "sin of commission" that unquestionably marked the beginning of World War II. Whether American membership in the league actually could have or would have forestalled World War II is still a debatable, and ultimately unprovable, hypothesis. Beard was quite within scholarly bounds

14. Hereafter cited as *Foreign Policy in the Making*.
15. Beard to Barton, June 20, 1946, Barton Papers; Beard to Barnes, June 24, August 7, 1946; Barnes Papers.

when he classified the affirmative argument as "a mere matter of opinion" (p. 43n5). It may be suggested, however, that perhaps Beard accepted this hypothesis too literally, rather than viewing it as an emotional expression of chagrin on the part of many Americans for failing to assume more diplomatic responsibilities after World War I that *might* have made a difference.

But by challenging certain monolithic interpretations and by considering the actions of the Axis Powers only in a marginal way, Beard was able to limit the scope of his inquiry largely to the foreign policy statements of American leaders from 1932 to 1940, principally to those of Roosevelt. The result of this approach was to transfer any possible responsibility for the eventual belligerent status of the United States from the Congress and public to the executive branch. In the process, Beard was thus led, as Cushing Strout suggested with slight hyperbole, "to propound an even simpler version of history which featured the villainy of the wicked Roosevelt and his unscrupulous entourage."[16]

In effect, Beard was laying the foundation for the "appearances versus realities" motif of his companion volume, published two years later. In *American Foreign Policy in the Making*, Beard repeatedly claimed that an examination of the public record from 1932 to 1940 showed, with few exceptions, that President Roosevelt did not depart radically from the sentiments of most Congressmen and Americans in his frequent professions in favor of neutrality and peace, that is, American noninvolvement in a foreign war.[17] But since by early 1941 the United States had become more unneutral toward the war raging in Europe and a formal belligerent by the end of the year, Beard implied that Roosevelt all along had been speaking publicly of neutrality and peace while clandestinely preparing to take the United States into war against the Axis Powers.

In this and the subsequent volume, Beard was on solid ground in noting that Roosevelt was less than candid in some of his public utterances on foreign affairs prior to December 7, 1941. A number of the supporters of the president's foreign policies at the time and since have conceded this point. In granting the dissembling charge,

16. *The Pragmatic Revolt*, p. 151.
17. *Foreign Policy in the Making*, pp. 155, 173–74, 207, 219–20, 222, 263–64, 268, 294, 321–23.

however, those who still supported the general aims of FDR departed from Beard on at least these points: (1) the extent or degree of deliberate deception involved was not as great as Beard intimated; (2) the president's move toward an unneutral posture was not as circumspect as Beard depicted; (3) FDR had more public support for this move by 1941 than Beard conceded; (4) the president's principal motive in committing the United States to the Allied cause was concern for our national security, a motive Beard did not regard as valid.[18]

Paradoxically, by portraying Roosevelt as consistently espousing noninterventionist principles throughout the 1930s, Beard, inadvertently perhaps, was repudiating a good deal of his own critical analysis of FDR's diplomatic words and deeds during the decade. It has been shown that, privately as early as August 1933, and publicly as early as February 1935, Beard suspected that the president's words and deeds amounted to an internationalist-interventionist policy that would lead to war. During the 1930s, a number of national journals or periodicals prominently featured Beard's views. Many of them were also critical of Roosevelt's departures from strict neutrality, particularly after the "quarantine" speech of 1937 and through the "great foreign policy debate" of 1940–41, when it was widely known that the president's most vocal supporters, including persons of national reputation and influence, were associated with the Committee to Defend America by Aiding the Allies.

After the war, Beard was annoyed that a State Department document did not furnish the names of those isolationist congressmen, "journals of opinion," or "makers of opinion" who did not believe the security of the United States could be adversely affected by the

18. The journalists, scholars, and public officials who probably would accept most, if not all, of the points in this paragraph would constitute a formidable list of names and publications. A sampling of the contemporary reviews for both of Beard's books should suffice to support the points. *Foreign Policy in the Making*: Blair Bolles in *New Republic*, September 2, 1946, pp. 268–69; Thomas K. Finletter in *Saturday Review of Literature*, August 17, 1946, p. 9; Edward Skillin, Jr., in *Commonweal*, September 6, 1946, pp. 505–6; Adolph A. Berle, Jr., in *Tomorrow* 6 (November 1946):52–53; John M. Mathews in *American Political Science Review* 40 (December 1946):1189–91. *Roosevelt and the War*: Walter Millis in *New York Herald Tribune Weekly Book Review*, April 11, 1948, p. 5; Henry F. Pringle in *Saturday Review of Literature*, April 24, 1948, p. 15; Gordon A. Craig in *Yale Review* 37 (Summer 1948):764–65; Charles C. Griffin in *American Historical Review* 54 (January 1949):382–86.

outcome of the war in Europe.[19] His questions in this segment of the book tended to imply that readers of the State Department volume—for the most part public officials, journalists, and scholars —would not immediately free-associate, as it were, and recall the *Chicago Tribune*, the America First organization, Senators Borah and Vandenberg, Charles A. Lindbergh, and, of course, Charles A. Beard.

Beard's vigorous protest against the State Department's contention that "much public opinion" was opposed to the collective security views of the Roosevelt administration, bore within it a massive contradiction of his own conviction that the Axis Powers posed no genuine physical threat to the United States from 1939 through 1941. By casting so much doubt on the veracity or validity of this official account, Beard gave the impression that "much public opinion" was indeed aware of the Axis threat even when the war was still geographically confined to Europe and Asia.[20]

More to the point, Roosevelt did, on occasion, publicly warn of existing foreign threats to the security of the United States. In these speeches, according to one of the more tenacious critics of Beard's interpretation of Roosevelt's diplomacy, the president plainly indicated that he and other members of his administration had "rejected the isolationist strategic conception of waiting to fight in America's back yard."[21] But since the thrust of Beard's analysis was that Roosevelt had not openly advised the American people of the noncontinental threat to American security, the motives behind the president's behavior seemed to be obscure, if not sinister. Not surprisingly, most critics of both of Beard's vol-

19. *Foreign Policy in the Making*, pp. 31–32. Beard in this segment was taking issue with the introductory comments to the volume *Peace and War: United States Foreign Policy, 1931–1941* (Washington: U.S. Government Printing Office, 1943).

20. The possibility that Beard's method of argumentation in this work could convey this ambivalence was recognized by Professor Edwin M. Borchard of Yale University's School of Law. A critical revisionist on America's entry into World War I, Borchard read Beard's manuscript for *Foreign Policy in the Making*. After the book was in print, Borchard made clear his low opinion of Franklin Roosevelt in a letter to Beard. But he also wrote, with more than a touch of irony, "This reviewer admits the deception of FDR but says you quoted him only in part. This is unfair since it gives the impression that he also stated the opposite of your quotations": Borchard to Beard, August 31, 1946, Smith Papers, Folder 12.

21. Basil Rauch, *Roosevelt from Munich to Pearl Harbor*, p. 205.

umes have focused on the almost total absence of a rigorous consideration of certain actions of Japan, Germany, and Italy as contrary to the interests of the United States.

But Beard and his first book on FDR's diplomacy were not without defenders. *Newsweek*'s reviewer, for example, described him as "a historian rather than a pamphleteer" who had presented his case "with his usual scholarly objectivity." The speeches and documents quoted by Beard, the reviewer continued, "show the shifting, often shifty, trend of thought on the part of men entrusted with leadership in a war-torn world." The diplomatic historian Louis Martin Sears claimed that "no more objective treatment could readily be conceived. The author nowhere injects a personal opinion about where the war responsibility actually lies."[22]

Oswald Garrison Villard was also prepared to break a lance for his friend. Publishing his review many months after most newspapers and periodicals, Villard expressed indignation at the extreme criticisms or indifference with which such revisionist works had been greeted by "the daily upholders of the nobility and necessity of World War II and the supreme infallibility of Mr. Roosevelt." Villard believed that Beard had indulged neither in personal attacks nor personal opinion, but had "let the facts speak for themselves." Possibly expecting a similar critical response to Beard's next volume, Villard concluded, "Someday, I hope, a book will appear composed solely of Mr. Roosevelt's direct falsifications."[23]

Whatever the mixed reception given the book, *American Foreign Policy in the Making* hinted at one of Beard's concerns that would soon provoke a major public controversy over scholars' access to unpublished, official records. As we have seen, during his research on Roosevelt's diplomacy, Beard was able to secure a substantial amount of material, some of it confidential in nature, through the auspices of his friend George H. E. Smith. But in *American Foreign Policy in the Making*, he suggested that some published accounts of America's prewar diplomacy were official in character owing to the authors' privileged access to government documents.

22. Review of *Foreign Policy in the Making*, in *Newsweek*, August 19, 1946, p. 92; Louis Martin Sears, review of ibid., in *American Historical Review* 52 (April 1947):532–33.
23. "Book Burning—U.S. Style," *The Progressive*, April 28, 1947, p. 8.

138   *Charles A. Beard and American Foreign Policy*

Singled out for special consideration was *How War Came: An American White Paper* (1942) by Forrest Davis and Ernest K. Lindley. Beard observed that "various circumstances connected with the preparation and publication demonstrated that the volume was more than an 'unofficial' report by two journalists who had at their command only the ordinary information available to all their colleagues in the profession."[24]

In September 1946, Beard's suspicions were further aroused when he was informed by the director of the Franklin D. Roosevelt Library that copies of the president's press conferences were not yet available to any scholars.[25] His concern was soon expressed in letters to friends. Recounting this experience to George Smith, he hoped that Republican control of Congress after the November elections might "force the Roosevelt papers open for examination."[26] In response to Bruce Barton's query about the differences between the post–World War I and post–World War II periods, Beard said that he "thought the plight of the world is far worse [now] in terms of debts, devastations, demoralization, and broken hopes." The one major similarity he found was the unearthing "of secret diplomatic and other documents," which furnished the materials for "reconstructing the story of how war came to Europe and the United States."[27]

Beard's most dramatic airing of this grievance about access to government papers was not made public until October 1947. In a guest editorial-essay for the *Saturday Evening Post*, Beard charged that the Rockefeller Foundation, the Council on Foreign Relations, and Professor William L. Langer of Harvard University were in the process of "preparing the 'right kind' of history of World War II for the American people." The desire to avoid "the debunking journalistic campaign following World War I" was construed by Beard to mean that the foundation and the council did not want any persons "to examine too closely and criticize too freely" Roosevelt's foreign policies. He further charged that the intent was to

24. *Foreign Policy in the Making*, pp. 25–26.
25. Beard to Fred W. Shipman, September 11, 1946; Shipman to Beard, September 16, 1946; Administrative Files, FDR Library.
26. Beard to Smith, November 5, 1946, Smith Papers, Folder 12.
27. Barton to Beard, December 24, 1946; Beard to Barton, December 30, 1946; Barton Papers.

guarantee that FDR's policies would escape the revisionist fate of Woodrow Wilson's policies.[28]

The selection of Professor Langer disturbed Beard, ostensibly because of his study, *Our Vichy Gamble* (1947), a defense of the Roosevelt administration's cooperation with the Vichy regime in North Africa in 1942. Interestingly, however, Beard wrote Harry Elmer Barnes that he agreed with Langer "entirely on the wisdom of our relations with Vichy" and was "glad he did his book."[29] What Beard really objected to was the passage in Langer's preface in which the historian acknowledged that he had been granted access to confidential government sources for his study. This apparently convinced Beard that Langer's participation in the writing of a history of American diplomacy before World War II would be "unfortunate for the cause of truth about the war and the judicious discussion of the great issues that have ensued from the war." Beard asked if the history of World War II was to be written only by "some person or persons well-subsidized and enjoying access, under Government patronage, to secret archives? Or is the opportunity of inquiring and writing the story of this critical period to be open to all talents on the same terms, without official interference or favoritism?"[30]

Beard's provocative essay prompted widespread commentary, most of it sympathetic, from newspaper editors and journalists of both conservative and liberal political persuasion.[31] It also led to an exchange of bitter letters between Langer and Beard in the *Washington Post*.[32] In a speech before the American Political Science Association in December 1947, Beard renewed his attack against "approved writers" and "subsidized . . . institutions of learning." The indictment was now broadened, however, to include government officials who "carried off official papers or digests of official papers containing vital secrets; and for their own satis-

28. "Who's to Write the History of the War?"; *Annual Report of the Rockefeller Foundation for 1946* (New York, 1946), pp. 188–89. For a more detailed discussion of Beard's charges, see Thomas C. Kennedy, "Charles A. Beard and the 'Court Historians.'"
29. Beard to Barnes, December 10, 1947, Barnes Papers.
30. "Who's to Write the History of the War?"
31. Many newspaper clippings on this matter from around the nation are included in "The Charles A. Beard File," Microfilm No. 139.
32. *Washington Post*, November 9, 1947, p. 4B; November 15, 1947, p. 8.

faction if not glory, they have published such parts as they, in their own wisdom, have deemed fitting for the public to buy and read."[33]

Clearly, Beard's desire to see the fullest possible publication of, and accessibility to, official records was not, in principle, a debatable proposition. Indeed, it is a matter of continuing concern to all historians and other scholars, regardless of their personal political preferences.[34] Nevertheless, there were some deficiencies in Beard's statement of the case.

For one thing, he virtually implied that scholars, regardless of possible adverse consequences to the national interest, had an inherent right to see every confidential or secret government document almost immediately after the event. But the British historian Herbert Butterfield, while critical of the even greater restrictions of the British government in allowing scholars to examine official records, persuasively observed that "academic students would be over-arrogant if they were to think that governments exist only in order that historians should be able to write about them afterwards."[35]

Beard's allegations about the difficulties encountered in gaining access to official documents were overly speculative; he gratuitously impugned the integrity of some historians and custodians of official papers, and erroneously led some of his friends to believe that he was being singled out for discriminatory treatment. With respect to the latter, for example, Harry Elmer Barnes made the vigorous assertion that Beard could not get the manuscript for his last two books accepted by any of his former publishers because of a so-called blackout on revisionist historians critical of FDR.[36] It should

33. Beard, "Some Neglected Aspects of Political Science." In the context of his remarks, Beard apparently was referring to officials who had published, or were in the process of writing, their memoirs, such as Secretaries of State Cordell Hull and James F. Byrnes, and Undersecretary of State Sumner Welles.

34. Herbert Feis, a historian who had considerable access to unpublished government materials, noted in 1961 that President Truman retained "records of various sorts" in his own custody about episodes which he apparently thought best not to reveal. Feis also observed that "outsiders" had not been given permission to examine the papers of the Joint Chiefs of Staff: "Concerning World War II, Many Facts Are Still Missing in Action," *New York Times Book Review*, February 5, 1961, p. 6. The complaint of unnecessary restrictions on access to certain government records was renewed by Feis some years later in "The Shackled Historian."

35. *History and Human Relations*, p. 191.

36. Barnes, "Revisionism and the Historical Blackout," in Barnes, ed., *Perpetual War for Perpetual Peace: A Critical Examination of the Foreign Policy*

be pointed out, however, that Barnes made the charge even though Charles Beard, more than a year before his death, and Mary Beard, shortly after the death of her husband, advised Barnes that they were not certain his manuscripts on Roosevelt would have been turned down by his former publishers, because he sent them only to the Yale University Press.[37] Beard, nonetheless, was convinced that "revisionist" manuscripts would not be well received by many publishers, particularly those in the East. In the summer of 1947, for example, he contended in a letter to the *Chicago Tribune* editor, George Morgenstern, "You know there is a kind of conspiracy among publishers against anything that touches, even gently, the hem of the garments of FDR. What I think of most publishers isn't fit to print!"[38]

Barnes also contended that Beard's attacks "on State Department favorites" were partially responsible for the fact that the revisionist historian Charles C. Tansill was able to see official records.[39] Tansill's *America Goes to War* (1938) was so critical of the Wilson administration and its intervention in World War I that it virtually guaranteed an unfavorable treatment of Franklin Roosevelt's diplomacy. Nevertheless, in August 1947, more than a month *before* Beard's protest appeared in the *Saturday Evening Post*,[40] Tansill was granted permission to consult State Department files.

---

of Franklin Delano Roosevelt and Its Aftermath, p. 18. Barnes noted in the preface (p. viii) to this work (which was dedicated to Charles A. Beard) that the book's title came from a remark Beard made to him during their last conversation.

37. Beard to Barnes, May 23, 1947; M. R. Beard to Barnes, November 19, 1948; Barnes Papers.

38. Beard to Morgenstern, July 11, 1947, Morgenstern Papers. Morgenstern was the author of the revisionist work *Pearl Harbor: The Story of the Secret War*, which Beard read in proof. Although he accepted the general thesis of the book, he told Morgenstern that he had gone "too far in some of his conclusions. . . . " Beard found no evidence to challenge Morgenstern's conclusions "based on circumstantial evidence," but thought that Morgenstern did not realize "how utterly senseless Roosevelt could be at times": Beard to Barnes, January 16, 1948, Barnes Papers.

39. Barnes, *Perpetual War for Perpetual Peace*, p. 47.

40. Dr. G. Bernard Noble (Director of the Historical Office of the Department of State) to author, February 9, 1961. Tansill subsequently published a book based on these researches, *Back Door to War*, a bitter indictment of Roosevelt and his diplomacy. When he favorably reviewed Beard's last book on FDR, Tansill alluded to the fact that he personally had examined unpublished State Department files and referred to Beard's work as "an extended study in presidential mendacity" which demonstrated that President Roosevelt and

In 1953, the historian Howard K. Beale had occasion to praise both the "exemplary" attitude of the historians in charge of the State Department papers and the "enlightened" approach of the Director of the Roosevelt Library in permitting scholars to examine unpublished materials. But he went on to say that "on occasion one historian has been excluded from papers another had been permitted to see."[41] Beale did not cite a particular instance of such exclusion, but he might have had his friend Beard in mind. Elsewhere Beale wrote that Beard's *American Foreign Policy in the Making* "was handicapped by the fact that the sources were mostly controlled by a government unwilling to make them available to any but the military and such scholars as were willing to write official history on government pay for government purposes." The book thus reflected the limitations "imposed by Beard's exclusion from more revealing sources."[42]

It is true that until the spring of 1947, there was no official policy governing the use of unpublished State Department records by *all* scholars.[43] It is also true that in the wake of Beard's critical essay, the question of Beard's access to government records was favorably discussed by the Committee on the Use of Departmental Files. Beard, however, neither asked for nor submitted the appropriate application. Indeed, the State Department's Central Files from 1910 through 1947 do not reveal a single instance of Beard's requesting access to unpublished documents.[44]

Perhaps the mistaken impression Beard conveyed as to who could or could not see official records was somewhat academic in his own case. The manuscript of his second volume on Roosevelt had been completed in the spring of 1947, and he was reading page proofs in the fall of 1947.[45] After this, declining health may have ruled out any sustained research in State Department files. In any event, before his death, Beard was planning to write a book on the wartime conferences, had assembled a substantial body of notes, and

---

Phineas T. Barnum "had much in common": *Mississippi Valley Historical Review* 35 (December 1948):532–34.

41. "The Professional Historian: His Theory and His Practice," p. 239*n*.
42. Beale, "Charles Beard: Historian," in *Beard Appraisal*, pp. 259–60.
43. U.S. Department of State, Bulletin 16, May 25, 1947, pp. 1048–49.
44. Noble to author, February 9, 1961.
45. Beard to Barnes, May 23, November 27, 1947; Barnes Papers.

claimed that he was receiving "help on my 3rd vol. from insiders who had secret info."[46]

Beard's correspondence with some friends in the midst of this access-to-documents controversy dramatically reveals his pessimism about the warlike propensities even of democratic nations and his growing fear that America was becoming a militaristic nation with the prospect of engaging in what he called "perpetual war for perpetual peace."[47] It was also during this period that George H. E. Smith—still staff director of the Senate Majority Policy Committee—asked for Beard's cooperation in writing a statement that Republicans might be able to use in challenging President Truman's proposed universal military training bill. Beard eventually agreed to personally testify against the bill. Because of ill health at the time, however, Charles C. Tansill had to read Beard's prepared statement before a Senate committee.[48]

Universal military training, Beard contended, was an attempt to introduce into the United States a system of peacetime conscription that was "a well-known curse of the Old World" which had ruined and enslaved countries in Europe. If adopted by the United States, the consequences would be the same: the violation of civil liberties, the creation of a "monstrous military bureaucracy drawn from the upper and middle classes," the enslavement of the "sons of the plain people," and the abolishment of the constitutional principle of civilian supremacy over the military.[49] Although Beard had once cited the successful operation of such a program in countries with a history of democratic institutions and practices

46. Beard to Morgenstern, June 11, 1948, Morgenstern Papers. For a time, Beard's son, William, seemed prepared to complete the work his father had started. W. Beard to Barnes, October 5, 1948, Barnes Papers.

47. Beard to Curti, January 19, February 6, April 4, 1948; Curti Papers, Box 4, Folder 13.

48. Beard to Smith, October 27, 1947; Smith to Beard, November 7, 1947; March 29, 1948 (telegram); Beard to Smith, March 30, 1948 (telegram); Smith to Beard, April 2, 1948 (telegram); Beard to Smith (undated, but before April 3, 1948, when Beard's statement was read by Tansill); Smith Papers, Folder 13. In November 1947, Beard also exchanged letters with Bruce Barton, who wanted Beard to suggest names of persons who might testify against the Marshall Plan bill: Barton to Beard, November 18, 1947; Beard to Barton, November 21, 1947; Barton to Beard, November 24, 1947; Beard to Barton, November 26, 1947; Barton Papers.

49. "Statement of Dr. Charles A. Beard," *Universal Military Training: Hearings before the Committee on Armed Services, U.S. Senate*, p. 1053.

and thought it might be necessary for the United States to adopt it in the early 1930s,[50] in 1948 he described only the German conscript system before World War I to buttress his appeal. "To imagine that the American people would escape the major effects of this 'militarism,' if universal military training were permanently established in the United States," he warned, "is to indulge in day dreaming and self-deception."[51]

Unlike his congressional testimony against increased naval appropriations in 1938 and against lend-lease in 1941, in this instance Beard could feel that his efforts had been at least partially rewarded. The Truman administration could not get its universal military training program approved and had to settle for a new Selective Service Act passed in June 1948, under which men between the ages of nineteen and twenty-five could be inducted for twenty-one months of service.[52]

Shortly after Beard's anti-UMT statement was read to the Senate Armed Services Committee, his second volume on FDR's diplomacy was placed on sale. Both in organization and historical method, *President Roosevelt and the Coming of the War, 1941: A Study in Appearances and Realities* was in many respects a more detailed version of *American Foreign Policy in the Making*. Extensive quotations from the published statements of leading political figures, from congressional debates and hearings, and from the press give the impression of a thoroughly documented appraisal devoid of value judgments. In the companion volume, however, Beard contrasted what he called the "appearances" of Roosevelt's commitment to a policy of neutrality and peace and what he regarded as the "realities" of secret deeds and utterances, which involved a policy deliberately aimed at dragging the United States into the war in Europe. When a series of unneutral acts failed to incite Hitler into declaring war against the United States, the administration provoked Japan into attacking the Pacific Fleet at Pearl Harbor and thus provided a pretext for waging war against Germany.

50. C. A. and W. Beard, *The American Leviathan*, pp. 766–67; C. A. Beard, *America Faces the Future*, p. 137.
51. "Statement of Dr. Charles A. Beard," *Universal Military Training*, p. 1056.
52. Eric F. Goldman, *The Crucial Decade: America, 1945–1955*, pp. 36–37.

Perhaps the most vigorous summary statement of this thesis was
set forth in what Beard described as the "position taken by opponents of President Roosevelt's conduct of foreign affairs during
the months preceding Pearl Harbor": "The supplying of munitions to belligerents, using the American Navy to convoy ships to
belligerents, and shooting at German subs, are acts of war in purpose and reality. They will and are intended to carry the United
States into full and open war. It is hypocrisy to maintain otherwise. It is flagrant deception to tell the American people that they
can keep out of war and avoid sending their boys to fight outside
the Americas while committing these acts of hostility with increasing abandon. It is mockery to assert that this 'shooting war' is
waged only for the defense of the United States, to keep war away
from American shores. It is chicanery to pretend that the United
States is neutral and that retaliations of German ships of war
against American vessels are unprovoked and unwarranted 'attacks'
on the United States. It is a fraud of the deepest dye to insist that
the aggressive measures taken under color of the Lend-Lease Act
are not 'warlike acts'—are merely in defense of the United States.
It is make-believe to protest that the Administration does not in
fact want to engage the United States in the war, is not deliberately
maneuvering the country into war."[53]

In this section, as in others throughout the work, Beard once
again touched upon the issue of Roosevelt's penchant for indulg-
ing in what a later generation of Americans would call a "credibility gap." He also was alluding to specific actions of the Roosevelt administration which were regarded as tacitly belligerent even
by pro-Roosevelt historians of whom Beard did not approve.[54] But
there was a corollary assumption to Beard's charge: a majority of
the American people in 1941 who supported the actions alluded
to in Beard's summary statement were unaware of the possibility
that the United States *might* become directly involved in World
War II. This assumption, however, was at odds with contemporary
public opinion polls, whatever their shortcomings may be in terms
of intensity of conviction.[55]

53. *Roosevelt and the War*, p. 173.
54. Most notably, William L. Langer and S. Everett Gleason, *The Undeclared War, 1940–1941*.
55. In monthly polls from January to April 1941, for example, the percent-

Beard's allegation that the Roosevelt administration deliberately sought war throughout 1941 failed to account for the existence of conflicting views between the president and some of his advisors. On more than one occasion, for example, Secretary of War Henry L. Stimson advised FDR to ask the Congress for a declaration of war. Roosevelt's reluctance to do so, which irritated Stimson somewhat, does not suggest the straightforward pursuit of war that Beard implied.[56] Beard himself briefly noted how anxious the president was to effect a truce or modus vivendi with Japan in November 1941. Without questioning Roosevelt's sincerity, he further described the hectic negotiations and pressures impinging upon Roosevelt and Hull at the time.[57]

To underscore his emphasis on Roosevelt's powers of initiative in foreign affairs, quite apart from what the leaders of other nations might have been doing, Beard on one occasion engaged in something of a philosophic aside. "At what point in time, if any," he asked, "did President Roosevelt decide that the United States would, deliberately or of necessity, enter or become involved in the war and begin to make plans with this issue in view?" In an extensive footnote to this question, Beard reflected on the semantic inadequacy of certain phrases, such as "war was inevitable," "forced into war," and "drawn into war." Such phrases, he said, "connote a determinism of events for the United States, as if President Roosevelt was a mere agent of 'forces' beyond his control, not an active agent in a conjuncture of circumstances which he had helped to create by deliberate actions on his own part."[58] But the tone of this aside and the theme of the work as a whole imply that the president alone had the freedom to choose to stay out of any war, regardless of the changing circumstances of the chaotic international scene in which his decisions had to be made.[59]

----

age of those who answered yes to the question of whether the United States would be involved in the European war before it was over rose from 72 per cent to 82 per cent: Phillips Bradley, ed., *American Isolation Reconsidered*, pp. 103–4. By the summer of 1941, according to one poll, only 15 per cent thought the United States could remain out of the war: William A. Lydgate, *What Our People Think*, p. 35.

56. Richard N. Current, *Secretary Stimson: A Study in Statecraft*, pp. 148–54.
57. *Roosevelt and the War*, pp. 510, 517.
58. Ibid., p. 407n1.
59. Hofstadter, *The Progressive Historians*, pp. 335–36.

The notion that FDR's diplomacy may have been fundamentally motivated by a concern for American interests, particularly national security, was greeted with much the same skepticism Beard had displayed when he criticized the naval appropriations bill of 1938. Summarily, Beard's case against President Roosevelt rested, to a large degree, on the assumption that the Axis Powers did not constitute either an immediate or long-range danger to the United States. In Beard's account, the assumption gained a large measure of plausibility owing to the slight attention he paid to the aggressive moves of the Axis nations that prompted most of FDR's actions.[60] Accordingly, the president's motives in presumably goading the Axis Powers into war with the United States remain rather obscure.

Partially to bolster his contention that Roosevelt was not really motivated by considerations of national security, Beard appealed to the Constitution. That document, he noted, obligates the president to ask Congress for a declaration of war if he thinks the threat to American security is so great as to warrant this action before the United States is attacked. Since FDR failed to comply with this obligation, the implication was that he did not truly entertain such a belief. Yet, Beard later remarked, "A call from the President for a declaration of war at any time near the middle of November would precipitate a prolonged conflict in the House and Senate and . . . even if the appeal was successful, it would fail to achieve national solidarity—to silence the large antiwar party."[61] It is somewhat difficult to square this astute appraisal of the problems confronting Roosevelt with Beard's suggestion, on the one hand, that the president had great freedom of action. On the other hand, Beard insisted that FDR should have abided by the Constitution and asked a divided Congress for the sanction to take a divided nation into war. On the strength of Beard's own estimate of the situation, Roosevelt would have committed a monumental political and diplomatic blunder had he followed this course.

Beard also tried to discredit the threat-to-American-security thesis, not only by suggesting that Roosevelt had provoked the Japanese and Germans, but also by contrasting the results of the

60. Ibid., pp. 337–38.
61. *Roosevelt and the War*, pp. 134–35, 175.

war with the stated reasons for committing the nation to the defeat of the Axis Powers, i.e., ridding the world of major threats to America's security and to international peace and security. "But judging by results of participation in the war, and the prospects of evident tendencies," he asked, "were these dreadful evils obviated by the victory at arms?" Beard then painted a gloomy landscape of the postwar United States as a nation which, as a consequence of cold war tensions, was militarily insecure and had assumed vast economic burdens and worldwide commitments that might weaken and destroy the constitutional structure of American government in the near future.[62]

Certainly at the time Beard wrote and published this work, the prospects for economic and political stability in Europe were not promising (the Marshall Plan's success was in the future and NATO was yet to be organized). The outcome of programs for reforming the Axis Powers was still in doubt. Nor could one deny that, within a few years after the conclusion of World War II, the United States and many former allies were confronted by new, complex, and dangerous problems posed by the Soviet Union. But to cite such consequences of wartime decisions and certain unforeseen postwar developments as a vindication of the wisdom of American isolationism in 1941 involved, at the least, the post hoc ergo propter hoc fallacy in logic. Such a vindication depends upon a hypothesis that cannot be demonstrated: if the United States had not been a belligerent in the war, the nation and the world would have been no worse off than if the Axis countries had been victorious.[63]

These considerations aside, Beard's indictment of FDR was based largely on particular decisions, the wisdom or value of which have been questioned even by historians who have not discerned sinister motives behind Roosevelt's diplomacy. These would include the July 25, 1941, order to "freeze" Japanese funds in the United States following the movement of Japanese troops into southern Indochina; the decision in early September 1941 not to hold a proposed summit conference between FDR and Premier Konoye; and the rejection of Japan's last proposal of November 20, 1941. But it was the words and actions of high civilian and military officials of the United States from November 25 to December 7, and

62. Ibid., pp. 578–81.
63. Dexter Perkins, "Was Roosevelt Wrong?" pp. 355–57.

the conspiratorial overtones Beard perceived in them, that were most central to his suggestion that Japan's attack at Pearl Harbor not only was provoked but was expected.

Possibly the most potentially damning item of evidence that Beard used to give this charge the appearance of credibility came from an entry that Secretary of War Henry L. Stimson made in his diary for November 25, 1941. In a White House conference of high-level advisors that day, the possibility of an imminent Japanese attack in Southeast Asia and the Pacific was broached. "The question," Stimson wrote of the discussion, "was how we should maneuver them into the position of firing the first shot without allowing too much danger to ourselves. It was a difficult position." Beard's reaction to this remark, which he quoted, apparently was that it constituted irrefutable evidence of provocative intent. It should also be recalled that before December 1941, Beard often employed the word "maneuver" in his predictions about FDR's desire to take the United States into war. As a result, he entitled a fifty-two page chapter "Maneuvering the Japanese into Firing the First Shot."[64]

Even Roosevelt supporters have conceded that if peace could not be maintained in the Pacific, the president and his advisors wanted Japan to initiate aggressive action. Some have pointed to FDR's reluctance to have a democratic nation "strike the first blow."[65] Others have examined Stimson's comment in the larger context of the political and strategic problems confronting the nation's leaders at this time and have rejected both the literal and sinister connotations that Beard read into the diary entry.[66]

Secretary of State Hull's note to Japan on November 26, 1941, seemed to bolster Beard's contention that the Roosevelt administration did not sincerely desire peace with Japan. Since, among other things, the document called upon Japan to withdraw all troops from China and Indochina, Beard repeatedly referred to it

64. *Roosevelt and the War*, pp. 517–69.
65. Burns, *Roosevelt: The Soldier of Freedom*, p. 161.
66. For the most thorough, persuasive explanation of Stimson's comment, see Richard N. Current, "How Stimson Meant to 'Maneuver' the Japanese." In addition to noting the political-ethical dilemmas posed for a democracy to initiate war through an aggressive act, Current describes how Washington officials assumed the impending Japanese attacks would be confined to British and Dutch possessions in Southeast Asia. The "maneuver," then, entailed the problem of convincing the American people that such attacks were sufficiently threatening to American interests to warrant a formal declaration of war.

150   *Charles A. Beard and American Foreign Policy*

as an "ultimative note," "ultimative action," or "ultimative memo-randum." In addition to challenging the wisdom of its terms, Beard implied that the United States intended to sever diplomatic rela-tions immediately if Japan did not quickly comply with all the terms of the memorandum.[67]

Beard was correct in suggesting that Hull's note did not meet Japan's minimal demands and that officials of the Japanese govern-ment chose to regard it as an ultimatum—an interpretation that many nonrevisionists would not challenge. But, as his own fre-quent use of the word "ultimative" implies, Beard himself seemed aware that the memorandum was not an "ultimatum" in the usual diplomatic sense: there was no definite time limit for compliance; there was no explicit statement that further discussions would be foreclosed; and it did not threaten Japan with any overt or veiled suggestion that the United States would resort to force in the event of noncompliance with the terms.[68] Many scholars have long be-lieved, with Richard Hofstadter, that FDR's acquiescence in Ja-pan's minimum demands "would have sapped the Allied cause everywhere, and [he] would have laid himself open to domestic critics for having been a feeble custodian of American security."[69]

Beard and other revisionists, however, argued that Japan, faced with America's November 26 proposal, had no alternative but to destroy the Pacific Fleet in order to remove a potential threat to her expansionist activities in East Asia. The Japanese belief that this was the case cannot be gainsaid, for at least two Japanese officials cited Beard's study in their postwar memoirs to "prove" the valid-ity of this conviction.[70] To argue that Japan did have the alterna-tive of sidestepping America's possessions in the Pacific, or that the consequences of the decision taken scarcely justified it, may be academic and is certainly hindsight. But some Japanese and Ameri-cans at that time and since have pointed out that the Pearl Harbor attack was a major political blunder because of the way in which it immediately unified a divided America and was not militarily

67. *Roosevelt and the War*, pp. 246, 506, 516, 517, 559, 561, 564.
68. Robert H. Ferrell, "Pearl Harbor and the Revisionists," p. 231.
69. *The Progressive Historians*, pp. 338–39.
70. Toshikazu Kase, *Journey to the Missouri*, pp. 253–56; Shigenori Togo, *The Cause of Japan*, pp. 163–64, 173. The first official was present at the signing of Japan's formal surrender on the battleship *Missouri* in September 1945. The other was Japan's foreign minister at the time of the Pearl Harbor attack.

decisive enough to enable Japan to consolidate her far-flung empire by the late spring of 1942.[71]

Nevertheless, the element of surprise at Pearl Harbor, as well as the magnitude of the losses in lives, ships, and planes, amply justified Beard's search for responsibility in the greatest military disaster in American history. As noted earlier, Beard was disappointed even with the Minority Report on Pearl Harbor, for it did not absolve Admiral Kimmel and General Short of blame, although it placed greater blame upon Washington officials than did the Majority Report.[72] Some nonrevisionist contributors to the voluminous literature on the subject have thought an excessive burden of guilt may have been placed upon the Pearl Harbor commanders, who were, in effect, scapegoats.[73] Equally unsatisfactory, however, has been the thesis that the entire responsibility can be laid at the feet of President Roosevelt and a few of his advisors, who allegedly willfully aided and abetted the tragedy. The assumption of many civilian and military authorities that Japan would not attack the Hawaiian Islands was certainly a calamitous error in human judgment. The blunders, miscalculations, and confusion of many of these authorities, in both Washington and the Pacific, raise legitimate questions about administrative inefficiency and the inadequacies of our intelligence apparatus at the time. Taken as a whole, however, they do not sustain the idea of a Washington cabal, with sinister intent, plotting to induce a Japanese attack on Pearl Harbor or other American possessions in the Pacific.[74]

The degree to which Beard's writings on foreign policy from about 1943 until his death represented a conscious attempt to vindicate himself will always be debatable. It is clear, however, that he was aware of the generally adverse criticism of his last two

71. Sherman Miles, "Pearl Harbor in Retrospect," pp. 65–66; Ferrell, "Pearl Harbor and the Revisionists," p. 221; Joseph C. Grew, *Ten Years in Japan* (New York: Simon and Schuster, 1944), pp. 472–73; Samuel E. Morison, *Strategy and Compromise* (Boston: Little, Brown and Company, 1958), pp. 68–69; Burns, *Roosevelt: The Soldier of Freedom*, pp. 137–39.

72. Louis Morton, "Pearl Harbor in Perspective: A Bibliographic Survey," p. 463.

73. Ferrell, "Pearl Harbor and the Revisionists," pp. 224–26.

74. Miles, "Pearl Harbor in Retrospect," pp. 65, 68; Morton, "Pearl Harbor in Perspective," pp. 465–66; Harry H. Ransom, *Central Intelligence and National Security*, p. 56. The most exhaustive, scholarly analysis of the intelligence aspect is Roberta Wohlstetter's *Pearl Harbor: Warning and Decision.*

volumes on Roosevelt. At times, as his surviving correspondence reveals, he could shrug off his critics and detractors in an Olympian and almost bemused fashion. But beneath the bravado, there seemed to be a sense of disappointment and possibly a feeling of betrayal by his former constituency, the many liberal-progressive historians and journalists who had often sung Beard's praises but who seemed to him to be captives of "the Roosevelt myth."[75]

During the last few months of his life, there were instances when Beard was extremely depressed about national and world affairs. "I do not see," he wrote Merle Curti in April 1948, "any signs of a reversal in the headlong trend in the direction of war and national collapse." On this occasion, he also discredited the Marshall Plan by employing his traditional economic interpretation. He believed that the plan was supported by individuals with "interests in the export business" and Southern tobacco and cotton, who hoped to sell their products to the European nations "at the expense of American boobs like you and me who pay taxes."[76] A few months later, Beard, in a letter to George S. Counts, an authority on Soviet education, reflected pessimistically that "the sky is clear and ominous: only two mighty armed powers are on the horizon. What impends and with what portents? Day and night I wonder and tremble for the future of my country and mankind."[77]

But Beard could derive some personal pleasure from the brisk sale of his last book, which had five printings in April 1948, and from its presence on best-seller lists for many weeks.[78] He was also satisfied by the kind words of some friendly reviewers, even if, as in the case of the *Chicago Tribune* staff, there seemed to be scant support for Beard's views on domestic reform.[79] Finally, the sup-

75. Beard to Barton, June 5, 1948, Barton Papers; Beard to Barnes, January 14, July 9, 1948, Barnes Papers; Beard to Curti, January 19, 1948, Curti Papers, Box 4, Folder 13.

76. Beard to Curti, April 4, 1948, Curti Papers, Box 4, Folder 13.

77. Quoted by Counts, "Charles A. Beard, the Public Man," in *Beard Appraisal*, p. 235.

78. Beard to Barton, April 24, June 5, 1948, Barton Papers. According to Beale, 20,649 copies of *Roosevelt and the War* were sold: *Beard Appraisal*, p. 311.

79. George Morgenstern, "FDR Tactics Menace U.S., Beard Warns," *Chicago Tribune*, April 3, 1948, p. 1; Walter Trohan, "Historian Records Ruses that Got U.S. into Fight," *Chicago Sunday Tribune Books*, April 4, 1948, p. 3; "The Tangled Web," *Chicago Tribune*, April 5, 1948, p. 18.

port and encouragement he received from his devoted wife, Mary, undoubtedly buoyed his spirits considerably. The last month of his life was spent in the hospital, where, with dignity, he quietly and bravely accepted the inevitability of his declining health and, with his last breath, said to Mrs. Beard, "Mary, I have found—peace."[80]

80. M. R. Beard to Barnes, January 24, 1951, Barnes Papers.

9

Epilogue

GIVEN Beard's penchant for controversy, his peace of mind might have been sorely tested had he lived long enough to respond in full to his critics. Even before his death on September 1, 1948, "anti-Beard" and "pro-Beard" factions had aligned for a lingering, often acrimonious, debate over his last book and his qualifications as a historian. To be sure, word of Beard's death prompted an outpouring of respectful obituary notices, including many by liberal periodicals and historians. But there was no attempt to conceal their disappointment with Beard's final effort.[1] Harry Elmer Barnes, one of the most ardent defenders of Beard's revisionism and reputation, regarded some of these appraisals as "an obscene performance which reminded fair observers of jackals and hyenas howling about the body of a dead lion."[2]

Barnes' intemperate characterization of a number of Beard's critics was not limited only to those who wrote after the former "dean of American historians" had passed away. Among those who, according to Barnes, had applied "the smear technique" to Beard

1. See, for example, "Free Spirit," *Nation*, September 11, 1948, pp. 275–76; Perry Miller, "Charles A. Beard"; Max Lerner, "Charles Beard's Stormy Voyage"; Lerner, "Civilization and the Devils," *New Republic*, November 1, 1948, pp. 21–24.
2. Barnes, *Perpetual War for Perpetual Peace*, p. 38.

and his "two splendid books on American foreign policy"[3] was Samuel Eliot Morison, the noted historian of American naval operations in World War II. The very title of Morison's extensive review of Beard's last book, "Did Roosevelt Start the War? History Through a Beard," was considered by Beard's admirers to be an egregious slur on his character.[4] But Professor Morison, who lauded Beard as "an important historian and a fine man," was essentially disturbed by Beard's historical method, which included an "effective use of innuendo" and a technique of selection in which Beard jumbled "the multitudinous facts, opinions, surmises, and events of a vastly crowded and recent era into the pattern that he believes to be socially desirable."[5]

Most of the critical commentaries adopted a pattern similar to Morison's in evaluating Beard's second volume on FDR's diplomacy: a brief tribute to Beard's past accomplishments, a statement about the gravity of his allegations, and a section devoted to specific criticisms of his historical method, with illustrations of what the reviewers regarded as serious omissions, misinterpretations, and insinuations.[6] But the reviewer for the *American Historical Review*, though moderately critical of Beard's methodology and conclusions, also sought to appraise the significance of Beard's book in the historical perspective of liberal thought on American foreign policy: "the book is an isolationist treatise. It is, in all probability, the last isolationist book that will be written by a progressive democrat and loyal devotee of the liberal American tradition."[7]

The reviewer's prediction was reasonably sound, if the favorable reviews which greeted Beard's book and the subsequent works which cited Beard as an authority may be taken as valid reflections of the persistence of prewar isolationism or a postwar neo-

3. Ibid., p. 31.
4. Professor Morison later admitted that this was the most controversial piece he had ever published. Some of the letters he received in response to the review were indignant and some "even threatening," but most praised the review: Morison, *By Land and by Sea: Essays and Addresses*, p. 328.
5. Morison, "Did Roosevelt Start the War? History Through a Beard," pp. 92–93, 95, 97.
6. For a representative sampling, see the reviews of Arthur M. Schlesinger, Jr., in *New York Times Book Review*, April 11, 1948, p. 4; Walter Millis, in *New York Herald Tribune Books*, April 11, 1948, p. 5; Henry Pringle, in *Saturday Review of Literature*, April 24, 1948, p. 15; Mason Wade, in *Commonweal*, May 21, 1948, pp. 143–44.
7. Charles C. Griffin, in *American Historical Review* 54 (January 1949):382.

isolationism.[8] In many instances, however, those who endorsed Beard's revisionist conclusions on America's entrance into World War II were also of a conservative political persuasion, marked by antipathy toward the domestic social and economic reforms of the New Deal, reforms which Beard supported. Nevertheless, in their personal hostility to Roosevelt, some of them "hailed Beard as an ally" in his critical evaluation of the president's foreign policies.[9]

Beard was cognizant of this liberal-conservative divergence of views on domestic and foreign affairs, but felt he could rise above it. "Some woman," he informed George Morgenstern of the *Chicago Tribune*, "wants to know whether your noble institution approves Beard's article on Rugged Individualism and the doctrine contained therein."[10] Beard puckishly added, "It doth appear that if you agree with me on Roosevelt, Hull, Stimson, and Co., you must also approve my views on virgin birth, marginal utility, infant damnation . . . total immersion, transubstantiation, and compensatory financing. Though an exigent old cuss, I make no such demands upon my friends."[11]

The foremost anti-Roosevelt organ of isolationist sentiment in the Midwest, the *Chicago Tribune*, praised Beard's *President Roosevelt and the Coming of the War, 1941* for three consecutive days. One editor, in a front page column, observed that Beard's book was a warning that the tactics employed by the president were a menace to constitutional government. The next day, a reviewer described the volume as "the most important historical work of our day" and one that would "remain a standard authority on the subject for all time." An editorial the following day exhorted readers to acquaint themselves with Beard's book if they had "any

8. For discussions of the tenets and adherents of isolationism in the decade after World War II see Adlai E. Stevenson, "The Challenge of a New Isolationism," *New York Times Magazine*, November 6, 1949, p. 9; Hanson W. Baldwin, "Dissection of the 'Fortress America' Idea," ibid., August 17, 1952, p. 7; Arthur M. Schlesinger, Jr., "The New Isolationism," *Atlantic Monthly*, May 1952, pp. 34–38; Norman A. Graebner, *The New Isolationism: A Study in Politics and Policy since 1950* (New York: Ronald Press Co., 1956).
9. Strout, *The Pragmatic Revolt*, p. 135. Nearly two decades after Beard's death, his ideas on American society and economy were still anathema to ultraconservatives, who found him "guilty posthumously of ideological offenses against the youth of America": Peter A. Soderbergh, "Charles A. Beard and the Radical Right," p. 632.
10. See Beard, "The Myth of Rugged Individualism."
11. Beard to Morgenstern, April 12, 1948, Morgenstern Papers.

regard for preserving the Republic." "This factual and restrained
narrative," the editorial continued, "shows Roosevelt to have been
the greatest enemy that this Republic and its constitutional institutions ever had."[12]

The diplomatic historian Charles C. Tansill, who subsequently
published the revisionist and anti-Roosevelt work *Back Door to
War* (1952), characterized Beard's book "as an extended study in
presidential mendacity." "To the dwindling army of Roosevelt
zealots," Tansill added, "this book will be the subject of merciless
attack. It will be particularly distasteful to the 'war-hawks' of 1941,
so many of whom were invincible in peace but invisible in war."[13]

Raymond Moley, a member of the original Roosevelt "Brain
Trust" who broke with FDR by the late 1930s, reported that in
their last conversation shortly before Beard's death, Beard said to
him, "I have written two books about this war. I will write more
if I live." In spite of Beard's inability to fulfill this prophecy,
Moley was certain in 1949 that "there would be more books to
support his [Beard's] thesis before the whole story is told." Moley
was also convinced that Beard's challenge to the widely accepted
view that American participation in World War II was essential
and perhaps inevitable, although "momentarily unpopular, will
live."[14]

Moley was vindicated in his prediction about the continuing
presentation of the revisionist argument for at least a decade and
a half after Beard's death. It never became, however, a popular or
"orthodox" point of view. It is difficult to measure the precise
influence Beard and his thesis have had upon the revisionist, anti-
Roosevelt school of writers. Selig Adler maintains that Beard's
basic approach of depicting FDR as a dissembler was employed
by most revisionists but that the most seminal work for conclusions
on the immediate origins of the war and the Pearl Harbor attack
is George E. Morgenstern's *Pearl Harbor: The Story of the Secret
War* (1947), which appeared more than a year before Beard's second book on Roosevelt.[15] Even Harry Elmer Barnes considered

12. *Chicago Daily Tribune*, April 3, 1948, p. 1; *Chicago Sunday Tribune
Books*, April 4, 1948, p. 3; *Chicago Daily Tribune*, April 5, 1948, p. 18.
13. Review of *Roosevelt and the War*, in *Mississippi Valley Historical Review*
35 (December 1948):532, 534.
14. Quoted in Moley, *27 Masters of Politics*, pp. 15, 16.
15. Adler, *The Isolationist Impulse*, p. 424.

Tansill's *Back Door to War* to be "the definitive revisionist" work on America's entrance into World War II.[16]

Nevertheless, Beard has been something of a Nestor to many anti-FDR revisionists, who have included references to Beard's works as authoritative and reliable accounts of Roosevelt's duplicity and the events leading up to America's belligerent status in World War II. *Perpetual War for Perpetual Peace: A Critical Examination of the Foreign Policy of Franklin Delano Roosevelt and Its Aftermath* (1953), a collection of essays by such prominent revisionists as Barnes, Tansill, Morgenstern, Frederick R. Sanborn, and William Henry Chamberlin, was dedicated to Beard. Of the eight contributors to this symposium, however, only two—Barnes and the sociologist George A. Lundberg—cited Beard's volumes on Roosevelt or defended Beard against criticism. In attacking those critics who had cast doubt upon Beard's competence as a historian, Barnes listed a few of Beard's achievements as "a trained and venerable scholar" and expressed indignation over criticisms that referred to Beard's isolationist bias, even "though his facts and objectivity cannot be validly challenged."[17] Professor Lundberg called *President Roosevelt and the Coming of the War, 1941* a "meticulous analysis" which was "the most important study that has yet appeared about the political aspects of our participation in the war." Lundberg also claimed that, owing to Beard's reputable qualifications as a historian, his book, unlike some revisionist works, could not be dismissed because of "the polemical and *ex parte* character of the presentation."[18]

Throughout the decade of the 1950s, Beard's last volume was cited in works that were highly critical of Roosevelt's prewar and wartime diplomacy. In his *Myth of the Good and Bad Nations*, for example, René Wormser remarked that the story of the Pearl Harbor attack was "told with full documentation" in *President Roosevelt and the Coming of the War, 1941.*[19] The literary critic Edmund Wilson praised Beard's "two valuable books on American foreign policy." Beard's account of the way in which FDR decided "to push us into the general mess," wrote Wilson, "made of this chain of events what is really a horror story almost comparable to *The*

16. *Perpetual War for Perpetual Peace*, p. 25.
17. Ibid., p. 31.
18. Ibid., pp. 593–94.
19. Page 96.

Turn of the Screw, if we assume that in the latter the narrator has herself imagined the ghosts and is herself the tormenter of the children." Illustrating this literary allusion, Wilson pictured Roosevelt as "the gay Hudson River squire" and "the benefactor of the 'common man,'" who "surreptitiously and unconstitutionally" sent American boys overseas "to die and to inflict death by methods as cruel as any in use by the Nazis. . . ."[20]

The diplomatic historian Louis Martin Sears wrote glowingly of Beard's critique of Roosevelt's diplomacy. Beard, he said, "was leaving to his fellow-countrymen a testament. With no selfish axe to grind, he was pure patriot, like Clay and Webster in 1850."[21] In a similar vein, the journalist George N. Crocker eulogized Beard as "a man of vast human perspective," who saw that Roosevelt's diplomacy was motivated by grandiose ambition and a desire to escape the domestic problems of the Great Depression. Beard's last work, Crocker asserted, "thoroughly documented" the thesis that Roosevelt "goaded Japan into attacking Pearl Harbor."[22]

The thoroughgoing revisionist explanations of American involvement in World War II, in spite of Beard's prestige, have not enjoyed the wide acceptance accorded revisionist interpretations of World War I, such as Harry Elmer Barnes' *Genesis of the World War* (1926) and Walter Millis' *Road to War* (1935). Barnes conceded this in 1953, although he attributed it to a conspiratorial "historical blackout" on the part of publishers allegedly unsympathetic to the revisionist interpretation of World War II.[23] But he indirectly put his finger on a potentially more important reason for this lack of acceptance when he noted that revisionism would become "palatable" only if the United States suffered a military or political catastrophe, accompanied by the "disillusionment and realism required to produce any such result."[24] In 1968, Forrest McDonald, well known for his critique of Beard's *Economic Interpretation of the Constitution*, made the following observation: "A

20. *The American Earthquake: A Documentary of the Twenties and Thirties*, pp. 566–67.
21. "Historical Revisionism Following the Two World Wars," in *Issues and Conflicts: Studies in Twentieth Century American Diplomacy*, ed. George L. Anderson, p. 138.
22. *Roosevelt's Road to Russia*, pp. 18, 259n.
23. For a critique of some of Barnes' exaggerated claims on this score, see Richard T. Ruetten, "Harry Elmer Barnes and the 'Historical Blackout.'"
24. *Perpetual War for Perpetual Peace*, p. 57.

large part of the reluctance to accept Beard's argument rested upon reluctance to believe that a president of the United States, and particularly Franklin Roosevelt, could engage in large-scale and deliberate deception of the American people. In view of the 'credibility gap' that has developed during the Vietnam war, it seems likely that the present generation of students, inured to such deception, will find Beard's charge perfectly believable and will sooner or later revive the issue."[25] The issue has been partially revived through the writings of younger diplomatic historians, many trained by William Appleman Williams at the University of Wisconsin, who have engaged in what has been called "New Left" revisionist historiography. Their general attack, like Beard's during the 1930s, has been directed against imperialist episodes in American history, primarily expansion of foreign trade and investment—in other words, the Open Door policy. With respect to America's entrance into World War II, some of these historians imply that the pursuit of this policy, not totalitarian threats to the security of the United States, was the paramount reason for the conflict between the United States and the Axis Powers.[26]

In accounting for the general failure of revisionism during the first decade after World War II, however, Selig Adler persuasively argues that it was due, in large measure, to the fact that most Americans avoided many of the emotional excesses of World War I, both in the prosecution of the war and the expectations of the peace settlement. Moreover, the blatant aggressions of the Axis Powers were such that, after war came to America, only a few could "hold with the late Charles A. Beard that F.D.R. 'planned it that way.' "[27]

The fact that Beard should have embraced this conspiracy thesis even before Pearl Harbor and that he persisted in holding to it until his death has a direct bearing on the isolationist thrust of his thinking and the reason for his becoming such a confirmed revisionist on American involvement in World War II.

25. *The Torch Is Passed: The United States in the 20th Century* (Reading, Mass.: Addison-Wesley, 1968), p. 484.
26. Irwin Unger, "The 'New Left' and American History: Recent Trends in United States Historiography," pp. 1247–48. For one of the most recent works questioning the necessity of American belligerency in World War II, prompted by disillusionment with the Vietnam War, and partially stimulated by a review of Beard's attitudes toward World War II, see Bruce M. Russett, *No Clear and Present Danger: A Skeptical View of the U.S. Entry into World War II.*
27. Adler, "Isolationism since 1914," p. 339.

Among the more widely accepted explanations, some scholars have stressed historical relativism, the theoretical bases of which were thoughtfully investigated and accepted by Beard during the 1930s. Samuel Eliot Morison, for example, believed that Beard's conscious application of the tenets of historical relativism were evident in his study of FDR's diplomacy and that "when Beard set himself up as preacher and prophet, he was lost as a historian."[28] Yet, the same tenets could just as readily lead a historian to the adoption of an internationalist-interventionist "frame of reference." As I have tried to show, there were instances in Beard's career before he became interested in relativism when, in varying degrees, he "preached" or "prophesied" in his evaluation of historical events.

Somewhat related to the latter point is the engaging thesis of Forrest McDonald, who discerns a close connection between Beard's classroom style as a teacher and his writing style as a historian, apparent in many of his published works. When he employed the teaching technique of "playing the devil's advocate," Beard would defend a challenged interpretation "no matter how spurious Beard knew it to be, and . . . defend it with consummate intellectual dexterity." Despite Beard's resignation from Columbia University in 1917, McDonald is convinced "that in his heart Beard never left the classroom; instead, through his writings, he extended its boundaries a thousandfold. . . . his aim was to provoke thought, to jar people out of their clichés, to force them, by the brilliance of his own arguments and by deliberate sophistry, to look at things in a fresh way." But McDonald contends that in Beard's last work on FDR, he "employed complete sophistry" in a fashion that tended to intermix and confuse the role of teacher and historian.[29]

Another explanation has pointed to Beard's seeming isolation on his dairy farm in western Connecticut, after he left Columbia University, as a contributing factor. Divorced from the mainstream of academic life, Beard was not able to subject his controversial ideas to the constant scrutiny of his colleagues, with the suggestion that some of these ideas might have been significantly moderated, if not altered completely.[30]

28. "Did Roosevelt Start the War?" p. 93.
29. "Charles A. Beard," in *Pastmasters: Some Essays on American Historians,* eds. Marcus Cunliffe and Robin W. Winks, pp. 132–33, 139, 140–41.
30. Ibid., pp. 92–93; Lerner, "Charles Beard's Stormy Voyage," p. 20.

The thesis seems quite plausible, but loses much of its force in the face of contradictory evidence. Though residing in a rural community, the Beard family actually lived in a spacious house purchased in 1909 near New Milford, Connecticut. Beard's first farm, in South Kent, Connecticut, was not acquired until 1929, along with another farm at Sherman, Connecticut, that was bought in the 1930s but sold a few years later. Beard's daughter, Miriam Beard Vagts, claims that her "father never spent a night on either farm, or worked on them."[31] Mary Beard once wrote to a friend that they did not live in a "farm house" in the usual sense—the farm itself was twenty miles away—and that "one summer 94 people visited us."[32] Accordingly, Beard had many opportunities to hold a number of conversations and conduct a substantial correspondence with individuals in the academic world, some of whom did not share his views on American foreign policy.[33]

In addition, active membership in numerous professional organizations (including the presidency of the American Historical Association and the American Political Science Association) frequently found Beard on the lecture circuit of colleges and conventions throughout the country from the 1920s to the 1940s. Also, during the crucial years of the "great foreign policy debate," from 1939 to 1941, Beard was a visiting professor at Columbia University and Johns Hopkins University. Finally, Beard was well aware of the critical reviews of his works by well-known scholars and journalists before and during World War II. Most gave detailed objections to the type of methodology and arguments he employed in his two books on Roosevelt's diplomacy. Thus Beard, given the depth of his convictions, might not have been amenable to change even in a constant academic environment, for, according to a friend, "He knew his last two books would cost him many previously devoted ones. In full knowledge of the hurt and loneliness he was preparing for himself he went doggedly ahead."[34]

There have also been speculations as to Beard's possible senility —which presumably would have affected his intellectual vigor—and references to his deafness as it might have enhanced his sensitivity

31. Miriam Vagts to author, February 16, 1971.
32. M. R. Beard to Barnes, January 24, 1951, Barnes Papers.
33. Levin, "Charles A. Beard: Wayward Liberal," p. 39.
34. Beale, "Charles Beard: Historian," in *Beard Appraisal*, p. 153.

to criticisms.[35] One critic went so far as to charge that Beard's interpretation of Roosevelt's diplomacy constituted "superstitions that occupied Beard in his senility."[36] To be sure, Beard's correspondence during and after the writing of his last book reveals bitterness. But the contents of his letters also reflect the wit and ruminations of a keen mind to the end. While Beard's deafness, which afflicted him much of his life, was sometimes demanding of his energy, it was a handicap with which he learned to live.[37]

The most satisfying explanation for Beard's isolationism-revisionism is perhaps to be found in Beard's idée fixe, which imparted a logical consistency to his shifting views on American foreign policy, namely, the commitment throughout his adult life to a sweeping program of domestic reform. Before World War I, he helped to shape and was in turn shaped by the sort of advanced progressivism found in Herbert Croly's Promise of American Life (1909) and given historiographical expression in the "New History" Beard helped to formulate with James Harvey Robinson. In the 1930s, this persistent vision for American civilization was variously described by Beard as a "worker's republic" or a "collectivist democracy." Therefore, so long as Beard believed that the reform of American society could be attained, and possibly even accelerated, by significant American involvement in world affairs, he was a congenial internationalist. But when he believed the fulfillment of this ideal might be jeopardized by extensive foreign commitments, particularly of a commercial nature, he opted for an isolationist stance.

The depth of Beard's isolationism by the mid-1930s, however, was due largely to his anguish over the degrading and demoralizing human consequences of the Great Depression in a world increasingly afflicted by aggressively nationalistic, totalitarian movements. This private anxiety was revealed in The Idea of National Interest (1934) and The Open Door at Home (1934), in which the fundamental premises and conclusions of his "continentalist" thesis were outlined: the competition for foreign markets fostered international rivalries that inevitably result in wars; the American economy was

35. Levin, "Charles A. Beard," p. 39.
36. Michael Straight, review of Tansill, Back Door to War, in New Republic, June 16, 1952, p. 23.
37. Josephson, "Charles A. Beard: An Impression," in Beard Appraisal, p. 4.

not vitally dependent upon foreign commerce, most of which benefited the few at the expense of the many; the United States, in its national interest, therefore ought to significantly reduce these activities, remain aloof from any diplomatic quarrels or military confrontations in Europe and Asia, and dedicate itself to the massive effort of solving the nation's internal crisis in such a way as to furnish an ideal model of civilization for other nations to emulate.

Further reinforcing Beard's advocacy in the 1930s of strict neutrality, nonentanglement, and nonintervention was his complete conversion to the critical revisionist thesis of America's entry into World War I. Partly prompted by his earlier skepticism on the question of "war guilt," partly encouraged by the Nye Committee's inquiry into the activities of the so-called merchants of death, Beard's espousal of American belligerency on the side of the Allies before and after April 1917 made that much more poignant his later rejection of the necessity or desirability of American participation. It also placed him squarely in the liberal isolationist tradition of twentieth century America, which embraced an economicconspiratorial interpretation of World War I. A corollary was the prediction that America's involvement in a worldwide struggle would bring an end to domestic economic and social reform and would lead to a loss of civil liberties. Beard thus anticipated a replay of this scenario on a larger scale and with even more devastating consequences if the United States were drawn into another world conflict.

Another important element in explaining the intensity of Beard's isolationist convictions was his growing disillusionment with Roosevelt's leadership in general and his profound distrust of the president's motives in particular. The latter, Beard became convinced, involved moving the nation toward collective security and war in order to mask his failure to solve the domestic crisis.

Perhaps to partially vindicate his prewar criticisms of Roosevelt's diplomacy, and perhaps to validate his predictions that FDR was deliberately planning to plunge the nation into a war that Beard believed was contrary to American interests, he wrote *American Foreign Policy in the Making, 1932–1940* (1946) and *President Roosevelt and the Coming of the War, 1941* (1948). Though no stranger to criticism, Beard discovered to his disappointment that these two volumes provoked a storm of controversy, rivaled only by the conservative attacks on his *Economic Interpretation of the Consti-*

tution of the United States (1913). In this instance, however, most of the critics were of liberal political outlook, a number of them former admirers of Beard's trenchant critiques of American history. Ironically, then, Beard found himself apt to be most acclaimed by anti-FDR critics who did not share his abiding and noble dream of liberal reform.

Beard's volumes on Roosevelt also had the unfortunate effect of calling into question the validity of nearly the whole of his life's work. But the prospect that his entire career might become a matter of virtual antiquarian interest to historians was amply contravened by the substantial number of books, articles, and doctoral dissertations on one or more aspects of Beard's life that have been written since his death. The result perhaps has been what Richard Hofstadter regarded as "Beard's most enduring triumph: he no longer persuades, but he still sets the terms of the debate, even for those who are least persuaded."[38] In particular, Beard's overall interpretation of Roosevelt's diplomacy has yet to be accepted by most scholars, though particulars of his indictment have been conceded. My own analysis has reflected an endorsement of that consensus.

It must also be said, however, that some of Beard's general insights are of continuing scholarly value to diplomatic historians. *The Idea of National Interest* (1934), for example, was a sophisticated study that was a precursor to the post–World War II "realist" school of diplomacy advocated in the writings of Hans J. Morgenthau and George F. Kennan, and it has occasioned much scholarly commentary.[39] Some of Beard's criticisms of American foreign policy have been regarded by some scholars as relevant to the contemporary scene. *The Open Door at Home* (1934), though more of a "tract for the times," has been a special source of inspiration to some "New Left" historians, owing to its clarion call for placing comprehensive domestic reform ahead of any efforts to be the "world's policeman."[40]

38. *The Progressive Historians*, p. 225.
39. Wish, *The American Historian*, pp. 319–20; A. Vagts' introduction to the reprint of *The Idea of National Interest*, pp. xiii–xiv; Fred H. Harrington, "Beard's Idea of National Interest"; George A. Lundberg, "Conflicting Concepts of National Interest."
40. Unger, "The 'New Left' and American History," pp. 1242, 1247, 1248; "Revisionism: A New Angry Look at the American Past," *Time*, February 2, 1970, pp. 14–15; Lloyd C. Gardner, "From New Deal to New Frontiers: 1937–41," *Studies on the Left* 1 (Fall 1959):30, 43; Pinckney, "William E. Borah," pp. 49, 51–56; Hofstadter, *The Progressive Historians*, pp. 324–25.

Even in his last two works, Beard was interested in more than condemning FDR's diplomacy. For him, the entire episode was a transcendent history lesson bearing on the future of the United States. If particular features of his indictment fell short of proving his thesis, he did raise some searching questions of continuing concern to all Americans.

Of considerable importance was his preoccupation with the extraordinary powers of the president in foreign affairs. "At this point in history," Beard wrote with obvious displeasure in his last work, "the American Republic has arrived under the theory that the President of the United States possesses limitless authority publicly to misrepresent and secretly control foreign policy, foreign affairs, and the war power."[41] During World War II and for nearly two decades thereafter, many Americans—including politicians, military officers, scholars, and journalists—generally endorsed the principle of substantial presidential discretion in the conduct of American diplomacy. By the mid-1960s, however, and in the midst of heavy American involvement in a costly, controversial war in Indochina, many of the same Americans have echoed Beard's complaints about the ways in which executive authority has been exercised and have demanded action to curb the president in making foreign policy commitments, especially of a military nature, without full public debate and congressional approval.[42]

A similarly prophetic note seemed to be sounded by Beard in his criticisms of the "Big Navy Boys" and his fear that the United States might establish a military bureaucracy independent of effective civilian control. In so doing, he anticipated the substantial literature—from the polemical to the scholarly—dealing with a new arms race, strategic military planning, and the "military-industrial complex," whose "unwarranted influence" President Dwight D. Eisenhower warned against in his farewell address.[43] Beard, it would

41. *Roosevelt and the War*, p. 598.

42. One of the foremost liberal historians who was critical of Beard's interpretation of FDR's diplomacy, Arthur M. Schlesinger, Jr., has embraced this position in his study *The Imperial Presidency* (1973). Admitting his own contribution "to the rise of the presidential mystique," he now believes that "the American democracy must find a middle ground between making the President a czar and making him a puppet. The problem is to devise means of reconciling a strong and purposeful Presidency with equally strong and purposeful forms of democratic control" (pp. ix, x).

43. For the text of Eisenhower's address, see *New York Times*, January 18, 1961, p. 22.

appear, was a prophet without honor in his own time. It simply may be, however, that attacks on the military establishment of the United States since the early 1960s represent an instance of an idea whose time has finally come. The extensive military preparations begun in the Truman years were designed to cope with what many sincerely believed to be the challenge of the Soviet Union to American and Western European security. Nearly a quarter of a century later—with a balance of nuclear terror between the two superpowers, a relaxation of cold war tensions between the United States and its foremost adversaries, the USSR and the People's Republic of China, plus a new sense of urgency about the nation's social, economic, and environmental problems—the size of the military budget has struck many Americans as too large for adequate defense requirements and as a diversion of funds from essential domestic needs.

The latter developments suggest that more and more Americans may be prepared to heed some of the warnings and advice of Beard's concept of the "open door at home." If so, he was something of an intellectual harbinger of the sort of foreign policy, whether it be called "continentalist" or "neo-isolationist," that numerous Americans might one day embrace. But this would not necessarily validate Beard's critique of American diplomacy in the decade before Pearl Harbor. As previously noted, many of the postwar tribulations of the United States and the world stemmed from events and decisions before and during World War II, a number of which were clearly beyond the control of America's leaders and power. It is certainly arguable that these tribulations might well have been greater if the United States had not become a belligerent against the totalitarian menace by 1941.

Thus, while one might regard many of Beard's writings on American foreign policy principally as those of a publicist rather than a detached scholar, one should not dismiss them on that account. If Beard's writings during the last decade of his life provoked more dissent than approbation, he, nonetheless, contributed to a greater public self-consciousness about the assumptions and aims of American foreign policy. He also provided later students with some provocative ideas and principles which could be of value in assessing the record of American diplomatic history, and which might be pertinent to the present and future conduct of American foreign policy.

Appendix

(Beard's publications in this chronology have been limited to those discussed or referred to in the study.)

1874   Born near Knightstown, Indiana.

1880   Attended Spiceland Academy, Spiceland, Indiana.

1891   Graduated from Knightstown Academy.

1892   Published newspaper, *Knightstown Banner*, with brother Clarence.

1895   Enrolled at DePauw University, Greencastle, Indiana.

1896   Field trip to Chicago; visited Jane Addams' Hull House.

1897– Editor, *DePauw Palladium*. Attempted to enlist in U.S. Army
99   during Spanish-American War. Received Ph.B. from DePauw University, 1898. Trip to England: attended Oxford University; helped found the workers' college, Ruskin Hall.

1900   Semester of graduate study, Cornell University. Married Mary Ritter, also a graduate of DePauw University. Trip to the European continent.

1901   Published first book, *The Industrial Revolution*.

1902   Enrolled in Columbia University Graduate School.

1903   Earned M.A. at Columbia University.

1904   Earned Ph.D. in Political Science at Columbia University. Published dissertation: *The Office of the Justice of the Peace in England, in Its Origin and Development* (1904). Appointment to Department of Political Science, Columbia University.

1907   Published (with James Harvey Robinson) *The Development of Modern Europe.* Purchased first house north of New Milford, Connecticut.

1908   Delivered lecture on "Politics" at Columbia University.

1909   Purchased larger house closer to New Milford, Connecticut.

1910   Published first of ten editions of *American Government and Politics.*

1912   Associate Editor, *National Municipal Review.* Director, Training School for Public Service, 1912–17.

1913   *An Economic Interpretation of the Constitution of the United States.*

1914   *Contemporary American History, 1877–1914.*

1916   Presented lecture series at Amherst College, subsequently published as *The Economic Basis of Politics* (1922); 3d revised edition, 1945.

1917   January–
       February: called for more vigorous action against Germany.
       April: U.S. declared war against Germany.
       June: Honorary LL.D. degree from DePauw University.
       October: Resigned from faculty of Columbia University. Director of New York Bureau of Municipal Research (1917–22).

1918   Contributed articles and essays in behalf of the war effort to the Creel Committee and private journals. Membership in the League of Free Nations Association.
       November: World War I Armistice. Published (with Frederick A. Ogg) *National Governments and the World War.*

1919   Unjustly accused of pacifist activities during World War I. Helped to found New School for Social Research, New York City; presented lectures until 1921.

1921   Trip to Europe. *History of the United States,* first collaborative history by Charles and Mary Beard. Assisted in establishment of the Worker's Education Bureau of America.

Presented lecture series at Dartmouth College, a moderate revisionist account of the origins of World War I, published as *Cross Currents in Europe Today* (1922).

1922 Trip to Far East; advisor to the Tokyo Institute of Municipal Research.

1923 Second trip to Japan to assist in planning the rebuilding of Tokyo following earthquake. Published *Administration and Politics of Tokyo*.

1925 *Nation* article speculating on the possibility of war with Japan.

1926 President of the American Political Science Association. Purchased studio apartment in artists' cooperative in New York City; held until 1945.

1927 Published (with Mary R. Beard) *The Rise of American Civilization*. Trip to Europe; lectured in Hamburg and Berlin; winter in Yugoslavia under auspices of American-Yugoslav Society.

1928 *The American Party Battle.* Kellogg-Briand Pact.

1929 Published (with George H. Radin) *The Balkan Pivot: Yugoslavia, A Study in Government and Administration.* Served on American Historical Association's Commission on the Social Studies (1929–34). Purchased first dairy farm in South Kent, Connecticut.

1930 Purchased second farm in Sherman, Connecticut. (Sold after a few years, but retained parcel of land containing house still in the possession of Beard's heirs.) Published (with William Beard) *The American Leviathan: The Republic in the Machine Age.*

1931 September: Japanese invasion of Manchuria.
November: "A 'Five Year Plan' for America," in *America Faces the Future.*
December: Introduction to J. B. Bury's *The Idea of Progress.* Polemic, *The Myth of Rugged Individualism.*

1932 *The Navy: Defense or Portent?*, concurrent articles in the *New Republic* and *Harper's Magazine* on the "Big Navy Boys." President of the Association of History Teachers of the Middle States and Maryland. Vice-President of the American Historical Association.

1933 President of the American Historical Association; presidential address ("Written History as an Act of Faith") outlined tenets of historical relativism and announced faith in the fulfillment of a "collectivist democracy" in America. Published (with George H. E. Smith) *The Future Comes: A Study of the New Deal.* Member of the Consumers' Advisory Board, National Recovery Administration. Aided Governor Wilbur E. Cross in drafting milk law for Connecticut. Member (to 1935) of the Board of Directors of Social Science Research Council. Hitler's assumption of power.

1934   February: Attended dinner with President and Mrs. Franklin D. Roosevelt.

Two books (with George H. E. Smith): *The Idea of National Interest* and *The Open Door at Home.*

1935   February: *Scribner's Magazine* article containing first public allegation that Franklin D. Roosevelt might "maneuver" the country into war.

March: Congressional testimony against censorship of literature in the armed forces.

April: Congressional testimony, as head of Bondholders' Committee, opposing reorganization scheme of Missouri-Pacific Railroad.

October: Publication of "That Noble Dream," criticizing the principle of "objectivity" in the writing of history.

1936   *The Devil Theory of War,* concurrent articles in the *New Republic. The Discussion of Human Affairs* criticizing the theory of "causation." President of the National Association for Adult Education.

1937   Member of advisory board of the Institute for Propaganda Analysis.

1938   February: Congressional testimony against increased naval appropriations.

Completed (with Mary R. Beard) *America in Midpassage,* first detailed discussion of the "American continentalism" school of foreign policy.

1939   January: Membership in National Institute of Arts and Letters.

August: Nazi-Soviet Pact. *Giddy Minds and Foreign Quarrels.*

September: Visiting Professor of Government, Columbia University. German invasion of Poland—beginning of World War II.

1940 April: Germany's spring offensive.

May: *A Foreign Policy for America.*

June: Fall of France. Received First Annual Award of New York City Association of Teachers of Social Studies. On List of Sponsors and Initiators of the Emergency Rescue Committee (assisting refugee scholars from Europe).

September: Endorsed aims of America First Committee. *The Old Deal and the New* (with George H. E. Smith). One-year appointment as Professor of American History at Johns Hopkins University.

1941 February: Congressional testimony against lend-lease bill.

September: Condemned President Roosevelt's "shoot-on-sight" order. Visiting Professor of Government, Columbia University.

December: Japanese attack on Pearl Harbor.

1942 War-bond appeal. Introduction to *Voices of History. The American Spirit* (with Mary R. Beard).

1943 *The Republic: Conversations in Fundamentals.*

1944 Honorary degree from Columbia University. *A Basic History of the United States* (with Mary R. Beard). Wrote ten radio broadcasts for Office of War Information, beamed to Italy and the Balkans (to 1945).

1945 May: Surrender of Germany.

August: Letter congratulating President Harry S Truman on successful conclusion of war against Japan. Appeal for Congressional Pearl Harbor inquiry.

1946 Essay, "Grounds for a Reconsideration of Historiography," for Social Science Research Council. *American Foreign Policy in the Making, 1932–1940.* Elected member of Academy of Arts and Letters.

1947 March: Truman Doctrine announced.

June: Marshall Plan proposed.

October: Publicized "Court Historians" controversy.

1948 February: Awarded Gold Medal of National Institute of Arts and Letters in History.

April: *President Roosevelt and the Coming of the War, 1941.* Congressional statement against Universal Military Training Bill.

September: Died at New Haven, Connecticut.

POSTHUMOUS AWARDS AND TRIBUTES

1949 Honored on occasion of Fiftieth Anniversary of Ruskin College.
1951 Alfred A. Knopf established "Charles A. Beard Memorial Prize."
1954 Spiceland Academy dedicated Beard Building in his honor.

Bibliography

THE MAJORITY of the works listed are cited in either the text or the notes. Others were consulted in the course of research for pertinent background information. There are four works that give most comprehensive compilations of writings by and about Charles A. Beard, covering the many facets of his career and interests:

Jack Frooman and Edmund D. Cronon, "Bibliography of Beard's Writings," in *Charles A. Beard: An Appraisal*, ed. Howard K. Beale, pp. 265–86 (Lexington: University of Kentucky Press, 1954).
Richard Hofstadter, "Bibliographical Essay," in *The Progressive Historians: Turner, Beard, Parrington* (New York: Alfred A. Knopf, 1968).
Bernard C. Borning, *The Political and Social Thought of Charles A. Beard* (Seattle: University of Washington Press, 1962).
John C. Rule and Ralph D. Handen, "Bibliography of Works on Carl Lotus Becker and Charles Austin Beard, 1945–1963," *History and Theory* 5 (1966): 302–13.

WORKS OF CHARLES A. BEARD

Books, Pamphlets, and Edited Works

The Administration and Politics of Tokyo: A Survey and Opinions. New York: Macmillan Co., 1923.
Ed. *America Faces the Future*. Boston: Houghton, Mifflin Co., 1932.
——— and Beard, Mary R. *America in Midpassage*. 2 vols. New York: Macmillan Co., 1939.
American Foreign Policy in the Making, 1932–1940: A Study in Responsibilities. New Haven: Yale University Press, 1946.

176   *Bibliography*

American Government and Politics. 1st ed. New York: Macmillan Co., 1910.

—— and Beard, William. *The American Leviathan: The Republic in the Machine Age.* New York: Macmillan Co., 1930.

The American Party Battle. New York: Macmillan Co., 1928.

—— and Beard, Mary R. *The American Spirit: A Study of the Idea of Civilization in the United States.* New York: Macmillan Co., 1942.

—— and Radin, George. *The Balkan Pivot: Yugoslavia, A Study in Government and Administration.* New York: Macmillan Co., 1929.

—— and Beard, Mary R. *A Basic History of the United States.* New York: Doubleday, Doran & Co., 1944.

A Charter for the Social Sciences in the Schools. New York: Scribners Sons, 1932.

Contemporary American History, 1877–1913. New York: Macmillan Co., 1914.

Cross Currents in Europe Today. Boston: Marshall Jones, 1922.

—— and Robinson, James Harvey. *The Development of Modern Europe: An Introduction to the Study of Current History.* 2 vols. Boston: Ginn, 1907–8; rev. ed., 1929–30.

The Devil Theory of War: An Inquiry Into the Nature of History and the Possibility of Keeping Out of War. New York: Vanguard Press, 1936.

The Discussion of Human Affairs: An Inquiry into the Nature of the Statements, Assertions, Allegations, Claims, Heats, Tempers, Distempers, Dogmas, and Contentions Which Appear When Human Affairs Are Discussed and into the Possibility of Putting Some Rhyme and Reason into Processes of Discussion. New York: Macmillan Co., 1936.

The Economic Basis of Politics. New York: Alfred A. Knopf, 1922; 3d rev. ed., 1945.

An Economic Interpretation of the Constitution of the United States. New York: Macmillan Co., 1913.

European Sobriety in the Presence of the Balkan Crisis. New York: Association for International Conciliation, 1908.

A Foreign Policy for America. New York: Alfred A. Knopf, 1940.

Foreword to René Brunet, *The New German Constitution.* New York: Alfred A. Knopf, 1922.

Foreword to Alfred Rosenberg, *"Mythus": The Worship of Race.* London: Friends of Europe, 1936.

—— and Smith, George H. E. *The Future Comes: A Study of the New Deal.* New York: Macmillan Co., 1933.

Giddy Minds and Foreign Quarrels: An Estimate of American Foreign Policy. New York: Macmillan Co., 1939.

—— and Beard, Mary R. *History of the United States.* New York: Macmillan Co., 1921.

—— and Smith, George H. E. *The Idea of National Interest: An Analytical Study in American Foreign Policy.* New York: Macmillan Co., 1934.

The Industrial Revolution. London: Sonnenschein, 1901; corr. ed., George Allen and Unwin, Ltd., 1902.

Ed. *An Introduction to the English Historians.* New York: Macmillan Co., 1906.

Introduction to Brooks Adams, *The Law of Civilization and Decay: An Essay on History.* New York: Vintage Books, 1959.

Introduction to John B. Bury, *The Idea of Progress: An Inquiry into Its Origin and Growth.* New York: Macmillan Co., 1932.

Introduction to William E. Dodd, Jr., and Martha Dodd, eds., *Ambassador Dodd's Diary, 1933–1938.* New York: Harcourt, Brace, 1941.

Introduction to Silas B. McKinley, *Democracy and Military Power.* New York: Vanguard Press, 1934.

Introduction to Franklin Watts, ed., *Voices of History: Great Speeches of the Year 1941.* New York: Franklin Watts, 1942.

Issues of Domestic Policy. Chicago: University of Chicago Press, 1932.

The Myth of Rugged Individualism. New York: John Day Co., 1932.

―― and Ogg, Frederick A. *National Governments and the World War.* New York: Macmillan Co., 1919.

The Navy: Defense or Portent? New York: Harper & Bros., 1932.

The Office of the Justice of the Peace in England, in Its Origin and Development. New York: Columbia University Press, 1904.

―― and Smith, George H. E. *The Old Deal and the New.* New York: Macmillan Co., 1940.

―― and Smith, George H. E. *The Open Door at Home: A Trial Philosophy of National Interest.* New York: Macmillan Co., 1934.

―― and Robinson, James Harvey. *Outlines of European History.* 2 vols. Boston: Ginn, 1912-14.

Politics: A Lecture Delivered at Columbia University in the Series on Science, Philosophy, and Art, February 12, 1908. New York: Columbia University Press, 1908.

Preface to Melvin M. Knight, *Morocco as a French Economic Venture: A Study in Open Door Imperialism.* New York: Appleton-Century, 1937.

Preface to Ferdinand Lundberg, *Imperial Hearst: A Social Biography.* New York: Equinox Press, 1936.

President Roosevelt and the Coming of the War, 1941: A Study in Appearances and Realities. New Haven: Yale University Press, 1948.

Public Policy and the General Welfare. New York: Farrar and Rinehart, 1941.

Ed. *Readings in American Government and Politics.* New York: Macmillan Co., 1909.

The Republic: Conversations on Fundamentals. New York: Viking Press, 1943.

―― and Beard, Mary R. *The Rise of American Civilization.* 2 vols. New York: Macmillan Co., 1927.

"Statement of Dr. Charles A. Beard." *To Make Better Provision for the Government of the Military and Naval Forces of the United States by the Suppression of Attempts to Incite the Members Thereof to Disobedience: Hearings before the Committee on Military Affairs and Subcommittee No. 10, House of Representatives, on House Resolution 5845,* 74th Cong., 1st sess., March 19, 1935, pp. 49–54.

"Statement of Dr. Charles A. Beard." *Universal Military Training: Hearings before the Committee on Armed Services, United States Senate,* 80th Cong., 2d sess., April 3, 1948, pp. 1053–57.

"Statement of Dr. Charles A. Beard, Historian." *To Establish the Composition of the United States Navy: Hearings before the Committee on Naval Affairs, House of Representatives, on House Resolution 9218 to Establish the Composition of the United States Navy, to Authorize the Construction of Certain Naval Vessels, and for Other Purposes,* 75th Cong., 3d sess., February 10, 1938, pp. 2133–46.

"Statement of Charles A. Beard, New Milford, Conn." *To Promote the Defense of the United States: Hearings before the Committee on Foreign Relations, United States Senate, on Senate [Bill] 275,* 77th Cong., 1st sess., February 4, 1941, pp. 307–13.

Syllabus on the Expansion of the United States. New York: Teachers College, Columbia University, 1904.

Ed. *Whither Mankind: A Panorama of Modern Civilization.* New York: Longmans, Green, 1928.

Articles, Essays, and Book Reviews

——— and Beard, Mary R. "America and the Far East: The Issues of Pacific Policy." *Survey*, May 1, 1926, p. 189.
"America and the Next War." *New Republic*, June 14, 1939, pp. 148–50.
"America Debates War Plans." *Current History* 42 (June 1935):290–300.
"The American Invasion of Europe." *Harper's Magazine*, March 1929, pp. 470–79.
"America's 'Duty' to England." *Events*, November 1937, pp. 327–33.
"Awakening of Japanese Cities." *Review of Reviews* 69 (May 1924):523–27.
"A Bankruptcy Fire Sale." *American Mercury* 11 (July 1927):283–87.
"Behind the New Deal." *Saturday Review of Literature*, December 22, 1934, pp. 381–83.
"Bigger and Better Armaments." *Harper's Magazine*, January 1929, pp. 133–43.
"Big Navy Boys, I: Selling Increased Armaments to the Taxpayers." *New Republic*, January 20, 1932, pp. 258–62.
"Big Navy Boys, II: What is a Naval Expert and Why?" *New Republic*, January 27, 1932, pp. 287–91.
"Big Navy Boys, III: Who is Behind the Navy League?" *New Republic*, February 3, 1932, pp. 314–18.
"A Call upon Every Citizen." *Harper's Magazine*, October 1918, pp. 655–56.
"Captains Uncourageous." *Virginia Quarterly Review* 7 (October 1931):500–506.
"Challenge to the New Deal." *Current History* 43 (February 1936):513–20.
"City's Place in Civilization." *Survey*, November 15, 1928, pp. 213–15.
"Collective Security—A Debate: A Reply to Mr. Browder." *New Republic*, February 2, 1938, pp. 356–59.
" 'Collective Security' Begins at Home." In *War—What For?* New York: The Keep America Out of War Committee, 1938.
"A Communication: New Light on Bryan and War Policies." *New Republic*, June 17, 1936, pp. 177–78.
"Congress under Fire." *Yale Review* 22 (September 1932):35–51.
"Co-operation and the New Century." *Young Oxford* 2 (December 1900):96–100.
"Count Karolyi and America." *Nation*, April, 1, 1925, pp. 347–48.
"Creating the Good Life for America." *American Association of University Women Journal* 28 (June 1935):195–98.
——— and Vagts, Alfred. "Currents of Thought in Historiography." *American Historical Review* 42 (April 1937):460–83.
"Danger Spots in Europe." *Bulletin of the University of Georgia: Institute of Public Affairs and International Relations* 30 (November 1929):79–81.
"In Defense of Civil Liberties." *Current History* 54 (April 1936):66–72.
"In Defense of Congress." *American Mercury* 55 (November 1942):529–35.
"Democracy Holds Its Ground: A European Survey." *Harper's Magazine*, November 1928, pp. 680–91.
"Education under the Nazis." *Foreign Affairs* 14 (April 1936):437–52.
"Emerging Issues in America." *Current History* 41 (November 1934):203–9.
"The End of the War." *New Republic*, July 6, 1918, pp. 297, 299.
"Five Pages from Newton D. Baker." *New Republic*, October 7, 1936, pp. 247–48.
"A 'Five-Year Plan' for America." *Forum* 86 (July 1931):1–11.
"Forces Making for Peace." *Bulletin of the University of Georgia: Institute of Public Affairs and International Relations* 30 (November 1929):82–84.
"The Future of Democracy in the United States." *Political Quarterly* 8 (October 1937):495–506.

Bibliography 179

"German Annexations and Indemnities." *New Republic*, July 14, 1917, pp. 309–10.
"Germany up to Her Old Tricks." *New Republic*, October 24, 1934, pp. 299–300.
"Going Ahead with Roosevelt." *Events* 1 (January 1937):9–12.
"Government by Technologists." *New Republic*, June 18, 1930, pp. 115–20.
"The Great American Tradition." *Nation*, July 7, 1926, pp. 7–8.
"Grounds for a Reconsideration of Historiography." In *Theory and Practice in Historical Study: A Report of the Committee on Historiography* Bulletin 54, edited by Merle Curti, pp. 1–14. New York: Social Science Research Council, 1946.
"Heat and Light on Neutrality." *New Republic*, February 12, 1936, pp. 8–9.
"Heroes and Villains of the World War." *Current History* 24 (August 1926): 730–35.
"Historical Approach to the New Deal." *American Political Science Review* 28 (February 1934):11–15.
"Hitlerism and Our Liberties." Text of address presented at the New School for Social Research, New York City, April 10, 1934.
"Hot Lovers and Hot Haters." *Nation*, March 8, 1922, pp. 289–90.
"How to Stay Out of War." *Forum* 97 (February 1937):89–95.
"The Idea of History." *American Historical Review* 52 (July 1947):704–8.
"The Inside of Germany's War Politics." In *Essays in Intellectual History Dedicated to James Harvey Robinson*, pp. 107–24. New York: Harper & Bros., 1929.
"The Interpretation of Events." *Events* 2 (December 1937):441–46.
"Is Western Civilization in Peril?" *Harper's Magazine*, August 1928, pp. 265–73.
"Japan's Statesman of Research." *Review of Reviews* 68 (September 1923):296–98.
"Jefferson and the New Freedom." *New Republic*, November 14, 1914, pp. 18–19.
"Jefferson in America Now." *Yale Review* 25 (December 1935):241–57.
"Keeping America Out of War." *Current History* 43 (December 1935):290–98.
"The Key to the Mexican Problem." *New Review* 2 (June 1914):321–24.
"Labors of Congress." *Current History* 43 (October 1935):64–73.
"La Guerre Absolue." *New Republic*, September 21, 1921, pp. 109–10.
"Landlubbers on Foreign Seas." *New Republic*, March 29, 1922, pp. 144–45.
"The Last Years of Stephen Raditch." *Current History* 29 (October 1928):82–84.
"Lenin and Economic Evolution." *New Republic*, May 17, 1933, pp. 22–24.
"Letter of Resignation from Columbia University." *School and Society*, October 13, 1917, pp. 446–47.
"Light on the Franco-Russian Alliance." *New Republic*, February 22, 1922, pp. 375–76.
"A Living Empire. I." *Young Oxford* 3 (October 1901):24–25.
"A Living Empire. II." *Young Oxford* 3 (November 1901):39–43.
"Looking Forward to 1940." *Events* 5 (June 1939):401–4.
"Making a Bigger and Better Navy." *New Republic*, October 14, 1931, pp. 223–26.
"Making the Fascist State." *New Republic*, January 23, 1929, pp. 277–78.
"March and Countermarch." *Yale Review* 29 (September 1939):167–69.
"Men Who Have Helped Us. I: William Cobbett, Friend of Man." *Young Oxford* 2 (January 1901):171–74.
"Men Who Have Helped Us. II: Robert Owen." *Young Oxford* 2 (March 1901):206–9.
"Men Who Have Helped Us. III: Thomas Carlyle." *Young Oxford* 2 (April 1901):246–48.
"The Month in America." *Current History* 51 (March 1955):718–25.

"The Myth of Rugged American Individualism." *Harper's Magazine*, December 1931, pp. 13–22.
"National Politics and the War." *Scribner's Magazine*, February 1935, pp. 65–70.
"Neglected Aspects of Political Science." *American Political Science Review* 42 (April 1948):211–22.
"Neutrality: Shall We Have Revision?" *New Republic*, January 18, 1939, pp. 307–8.
"Neutrality Deadlock." *Events* 6 (September 1939):161–64.
"New Morgan Thesis." *New Republic*, January 20, 1937, pp. 350–53.
"On Keeping America Out of War." *Current History* 43 (March 1936):625–32.
"On the Advantages of Censorship and Espionage." *New Republic*, August 24, 1921, pp. 350–51.
"Our Choice in Foreign Policy." *Events* 1 (March 1937):161–65.
"Our Confusion over National Defense: Shall We Listen to the Pacifists or the Admirals?" *Harper's Magazine*, February 1932, pp. 257–67.
"Our Foreign and Domestic Policies." *Current History* 41 (February 1935):586–92.
"Peace for America." *New Republic*, March 4, 11, 18, 1936, pp. 100–102, 127–29, 156–59.
"Peace Loads the Guns." *Today*, June 29, 1935, pp. 3–4, 23.
"Pearl Harbor: Challenge to the Republic." *The Progressive*, September 3, 1945, pp. 1–2.
"The Perils of Diplomacy." *New Republic*, June 2, 1917, pp. 136–38.
"Politics of Our Depression." *Current History* 41 (October 1934):77–83.
"Preparedness: An American Issue." *Current History* 42 (May 1935):179–86.
"The Present Duty of Every American." Ms., Columbia University Library, 1902.
"The President Loses Prestige." *Current History* 42 (April 1935):64–71.
"Problems of Terminology in Historical Writing." In *Theory and Practice in Historical Study: A Report of the Committee on Historiography*, Bulletin 54, edited by Merle Curti, pp. 103–6. New York: Social Science Research Council, 1946.
"Propaganda in the Schools." *The Dial*, June 14, 1919, pp. 598–99.
"Prospects for Peace." *Harper's Magazine*, February 1929, pp. 320–30.
"Rebuilding in Japan." *Review of Reviews* 68 (October 1923):378–82.
"The Recent War." *New Republic*, December 22, 1920, pp. 114–15.
"A Reply to Mr. Browder." *New Republic*, February 2, 1938, pp. 357–59.
"Roosevelt and Realpolitik." *New Republic*, June 3, 1925, pp. 52–53.
"Roosevelt's Place in History." *Events* 3 (February 1938):81–86.
"Rough Seas for the Super-Navy." *New Republic*, March 30, 1938, p. 210.
"Ruskin and the Babble of Tongues." *New Republic*, August 5, 1936, pp. 370–72.
"Ruskin Hall and Temperance Reform." *Young Oxford* 2 (March 1901):221.
"Shooting It Out in Russia." *Events* 3 (March 1938):161–64.
"A Socialist History of France." *Political Science Quarterly* 21 (March 1906): 111–12.
"Solving Domestic Crisis by War." *New Republic*, March 11, 1936, pp. 127–29.
"Some Neglected Aspects of Political Science." *American Political Science Review* 42 (April 1948):211–22.
"Spooks: Made in Germany." *New Republic*, December 6, 1933, pp. 97–98.
"Statement of Experiences with the Administration of Columbia University." *New Republic*, December 29, 1917, pp. 249–51.
"The Supreme Issue for America." *Events* 3 (April 1938):275–77.

"The Tariff Campaign: The Last Gasp." *New Republic*, November 2, 1932, pp. 318–19.
"That Noble Dream." *American Historical Review* 41 (October 1935):74–87.
"That Promise of American Life." *New Republic*, February 6, 1935, pp. 350–52.
"Those Old-World Quarrels." *Events* 2 (October 1937):257–62.
"Transition in Politics." *Nation*, February 23, 1921, pp. 297–98.
"The University and Democracy." *The Dial*, April 11, 1918, pp. 335–57.
"Viscount Grey on War Guilt." *New Republic*, October 7, 1925, pp. 172–75.
"War—If, How, and When?" *Events* 2 (August 1937):81–86.
"War Springs from Peace." *Scholastic*, November 10, 1934, pp. 12 ff.
"War with Japan?" *Events* 8 (November 1940):321–23.
"War with Japan: What Shall We Get Out of It?" *Nation*, March 25, 1925, pp. 311–13.
"We're Blundering into War." *American Mercury*, April 1939, pp. 388–90.
"What I Expect of Roosevelt." *Nation*, November 14, 1936, p. 572.
"What Is a Statesman?" *American Mercury*, April 1924, pp. 394–96.
"What Is This Sea Power?" *Asia* 35 (January 1935):4–9.
"What Is Worth While in Education?" *Young Oxford* 1 (December 1899):16.
"What Price Must We Pay for Peace?" *New Republic*, April 15, 1936, p. 289.
"Whom Does Congress Represent?" *Harper's Magazine*, January 1930, pp. 144–52.
"Who Runs the Japanese Government?" *New Republic*, December 16, 1931, p. 137.
"Who's to Write the History of the War?" *Saturday Evening Post*, October 4, 1947, p. 172.
"Why Did We Go to War?" *New Republic*, March 10, 1937, pp. 127–29.
"Will Roosevelt Keep Us Out of War?" *Events* 2 (July 1937):1–6.
"The World as I Want It." *Forum* 91 (June 1934):332–34.
"Written History as an Act of Faith." *American Historical Review* 39 (January 1934):219–29.

WORKS ABOUT CHARLES A. BEARD

Adler, Selig. *The Isolationist Impulse: Its Twentieth Century Reaction*. New York: Abelard-Schuman, Ltd., 1957.
Agar, Herbert. "A Plea to Mr. Charles A. Beard: Review of *Open Door at Home*." *American Review* 4 (January 1935):297–309.
Asubel, Herman. *Historians and Their Craft: A Study of the Presidential Addresses of the American Historical Association, 1884–1945*. New York: Columbia University Press, 1950.
Barnes, Harry Elmer. *A History of Historical Writing*. Norman: University of Oklahoma Press, 1937.
———, ed. *Perpetual War for Perpetual Peace: A Critical Examination of the Foreign Policy of Franklin Delano Roosevelt and Its Aftermath*. Caldwell, Idaho: Caxton Printers, Ltd., 1953.
Beale, Howard K., ed. *Charles A. Beard: An Appraisal*. Lexington: University of Kentucky Press, 1954.
———. "The Professional Historian: His Theory and His Practice." *Pacific Historical Review* 22 (August 1953):227–55.
Beard, Mary R. *The Making of Charles A. Beard: An Interpretation*. New York: Exposition Press, 1955.
Beard, William, comp. *Charles A. Beard: The Economic Basis of Politics and Related Writings*. New York: Vintage Books, 1958.

Bibliography

Benson, Lee. *Turner and Beard: American Historical Writing Reconsidered.* Glencoe, Ill.: Free Press, 1960.

Berg, Elias. *The Historical Thinking of Charles A. Beard.* Stockholm: Almquvist & Wiksell, 1957.

Bliven, Bruce. "The Future of Foreign Policy." *New Republic,* February 24, 1937, pp. 63–66.

Blinkoff, Maurice. *The Influence of Charles A. Beard upon American Historiography.* University of Buffalo Studies no. 12. Buffalo, 1936.

Block, Maxine, ed. *Current Biography, 1941.* New York: H. W. Wilson Co., 1941.

Bolles, Blair. "Bearding FDR." *New Republic,* September 2, 1946, pp. 268–69.

Borning, Bernard C. "The Political Philosophy of Young Charles A. Beard." *American Political Science Review* 43 (December 1949):1165–78.

———. *The Political and Social Thought of Charles A. Beard.* Seattle: University of Washington Press, 1962.

Brown, Robert E. *Charles Beard and the Constitution.* Princeton: Princeton University Press, 1956.

Christman, Calvin L. "Charles A. Beard, Ferdinand Eberstadt, and America's Postwar Security." *Mid-America* 54 (July 1972):187–94.

Cohen, Warren I. *The American Revisionists: The Lessons of Intervention in World War I.* Chicago: University of Chicago Press, 1967.

Commager, Henry S. *The American Mind: An Interpretation of American Thought and Character since the 1880s.* New Haven: Yale University Press, 1950.

Cowley, Malcolm, and Smith, Bernard, eds. *Books that Changed Our Minds.* New York: Doubleday, Doran and Co., Inc., 1940.

Craig, Gordon. "Our Foreign Policy in 1941." *Yale Review* 37 (Summer 1948): 762–65.

Curti, Merle. "A Great Teacher's Teacher." *Social Education* 13 (October 1949): 263–66.

Davidson, Frank P., and Viereck, George S., Jr., eds. *Before America Decides: Foresight in Foreign Affairs.* Cambridge: Harvard University Press, 1938.

Degler, Carl N. *Out of Our Past: The Forces that Shaped Modern America.* New York: Harper & Bros., 1959.

Deininger, Whitaker T. "The Skepticism and Historical Faith of C. A. Beard." *Journal of the History of Ideas* 15 (October 1954):573–88.

Destler, Chester M. "Some Observations on Contemporary Historical Theory." *American Historical Review* 55 (April 1950):503–29.

Ducharme, Raymond A., Jr. "Charles A. Beard and the Social Studies: A Book of Readings." Ph.D. dissertation, Columbia University, 1961.

Ekirch, Arthur A., Jr. *The Decline of American Liberalism.* New York: Atheneum, 1967.

Feis, Herbert. "The Open Door at Home." *Foreign Affairs* 13 (July 1935): 600–611.

Ferrell, Robert H. "Pearl Harbor and the Revisionists." *The Historian* 17 (Spring 1955):215–53.

Gardner, Lloyd. "From New Deal to New Frontiers: 1937–1941." *Studies on the Left* 1 (1959):29–43.

Gideonse, Harry D. "Nationalist Collectivism and Charles A. Beard." *Journal of Political Economy* 43 (December 1935):778–99.

Glaser, William A. "Critique of Two Economic Interpretations of Politics: Charles A. Beard and A. M. Simons." Ph.D. dissertation, Harvard University, 1952.

Goldman, Eric F. "A Historian at Seventy." *New Republic*, November 27, 1944, pp. 696–97.
———. *Rendezvous with Destiny: A History of Modern American Reform*. New York: Alfred A. Knopf, 1952.
Harrington, Fred H. "Beard's Idea of National Interest and New Interpretations." *American Perspective: A Quarterly Analysis of Foreign Policy* 4 (Fall 1950):335–45.
Hepburn, Charles M. "Charles A. Beard and the Founding Fathers." Ph.D. dissertation, Stanford University, 1966.
Herring, Hubert. "Charles A. Beard: Freelance among the Historians." *Harper's Magazine*, May 1939, pp. 641–52.
Higham, John. "The Contours of William A. Williams." *Studies on the Left* 2 (1961):73–76.
———, ed. *The Reconstruction of American History*. New York: Harper & Bros., 1962.
Hill, Joe Baker, Jr. "An Interpretation of the Ideas and Opinions of Charles Austin Beard." Ph.D. dissertation, University of Georgia, 1961.
Hofstadter, Richard. *The Progressive Historians: Turner, Beard, Parrington*. New York: Alfred A. Knopf, 1968.
Hook, Sidney. "Charles Beard's Political Testament." *Nation*, October 23, 1943, pp. 474–76.
Hoxie, R. Gordon, et al. *A History of the Faculty of Political Science, Columbia University*. New York: Columbia University Press, 1955.
Jensen, Clarence G. "The Contributions of Charles A. Beard to American Education and Educational Literature." Ph.D. dissertation, University of Montana, 1967.
Jonas, Manfred. *Isolationism in America, 1935–1941*. Ithaca, N.Y.: Cornell University Press, 1966.
Josephson, Matthew. "Charles A. Beard: A Memoir." *Virginia Quarterly Review* 25 (October 1949):585–602.
———. *Infidel in the Temple: A Memoir of the Nineteen-Thirties*. New York: Alfred A. Knopf, 1967.
Kallen, Horace M. "In Remembrance of Charles Beard—Philosopher-Historian." *Social Research* 18 (June 1951):243–49.
Kennedy, Thomas C. "Beard vs. F.D.R. on National Defense and Rearmament." *Mid-America: An Historical Review* 50 (January 1968):22–41.
———. "Charles A. Beard and the 'Big Navy Boys.'" *Military Affairs*, Summer 1967, pp. 65–73.
———. "Charles A. Beard and the 'Court Historians.'" *The Historian* 25 (August 1963):439–50.
———. "Charles A. Beard in Midpassage." *The Historian* 30 (February 1968): 179–98.
Kirker, Harold, and Wilkins, Burleigh T. "Beard, Becker and the Trotsky Inquiry." *American Quarterly* 13 (Winter 1961):516–25.
Kraus, Michael. *A History of American History*. New York: Farrar and Rinehart, 1937.
LaFeber, Walter. "The Conscious Creation of a 'World-Wide Empire.'" *Studies on the Left* 2 (1962):103–7.
Lamm, Lucian, and Feins, Daniel M. "Charles A. Beard." *Social Education* 5 (April 1941):263–68.
Lerner, Max. "Charles Beard: Civilization and the Devils." *New Republic*, November 1, 1948, pp. 21–24.
———. "Charles Beard Confronts Himself." *Nation*, April 8, 1936, pp. 452–56.

——. "Charles Beard's Stormy Voyage." *New Republic*, October 25, 1948, pp. 20–23.

——. *Ideas Are Weapons: The History and Uses of Ideas*. New York: Viking Press, 1940.

——. "The Political Theory of Charles A. Beard." *American Quarterly* 2 (Winter 1950): 303–21.

Levin, Peter R. "Charles A. Beard: Wayward Liberal." *Tomorrow* 8 (March 1949):36–40.

Lundberg, George A. "Conflicting Ideas of National Interest." *American Perspective: A Quarterly Analysis of Foreign Policy* 4 (Fall 1950):359–72.

McDonald, Forrest. "Charles A. Beard." In *Pastmasters: Some Essays on American Historians*, edited by Marcus Cunliffe and Robin W. Winks, pp. 110–41. New York: Harper & Row, Publishers, 1969.

——. *We The People: The Economic Origins of the Constitution*. Chicago: University of Chicago Press, 1958.

McIlwain, Charles H. "The Historian's Part in a Changing World." *American Historical Review* 42 (January 1937):207–24.

Malin, James C. *On the Nature of History: Essays about History and Dissidence*. Ann Arbor: University of Michigan Press, 1954.

Mandlebaum, Maurice. "Causal Analysis in History." *Journal of the History of Ideas* 3 (January 1942):30–50.

Marcell, David W. "Charles Beard: Civilization and the Revolt against Empiricism." *American Quarterly* 21 (Spring 1969):65–86.

——. *Progress and Pragmatism: James, Dewey, Beard and the American Idea of Progress*. Westport, Conn.: Greenwood Press, 1974.

Marks, Harry J. "Ground under Our Feet: Beard's Relativism." *Journal of the History of Ideas* 14 (October 1953):628–33.

May, Henry F. *The End of American Innocence: A Study of the First Years of Our Own Time, 1912–1917*. Chicago: Quadrangle Books, 1964.

Miller, Perry. "Charles A. Beard." *Nation*, September 25, 1948, pp. 344–46.

Millett, Fred B. *Contemporary American Authors*. New York: Harcourt, Brace and Co., 1940.

Millis, Walter. *The Road to War, 1914–1917*. Boston: Houghton Mifflin Co., 1935.

Mitchell, Donald M. *A History of the Modern American Navy: From 1883 through Pearl Harbor*. New York: Alfred A. Knopf, 1946.

Moley, Raymond. *27 Masters of Politics*. New York: Funk & Wagnalls Co., 1949.

Morison, Samuel E. *By Land and by Sea: Essays and Addresses*. New York: Alfred A. Knopf, 1953.

——. "Did Roosevelt Start the War? History Through a Beard." *Atlantic Monthly*, August 1948, pp. 91–97.

——. "Faith of a Historian." *American Historical Review* 56 (January 1951): 261–75.

Mowrer, Edgar A. *The Nightmare of American Foreign Policy*. New York: Alfred A. Knopf, 1948.

Nevins, Allan. *The Gateway to History*. Boston: D. C. Heath and Co., 1938.

——. "Should American History be Rewritten?" *Saturday Review of Literature*, February 6, 1954, pp. 7–9.

Noble, David W. *Historians against History: The Frontier Thesis and the National Covenant in American Historical Writing since 1830*. Minneapolis: University of Minnesota Press, 1965.

Phillips, Clifton J., ed. "Charles A. Beard's Recollections of Henry County, Indiana." *Indiana Magazine of History* 55 (March 1959):17–23.
————. "The Indiana Education of Charles A. Beard." *Indiana Magazine of History* 55 (March 1959):1–15.
Phillips, Harlan B. "Charles Beard: The English Lectures, 1899–1901." *Journal of the History of Ideas* 14 (June 1953):451–56.
————. "Charles Beard, Walter Vrooman and the Founding of Ruskin Hall." *South Atlantic Quarterly* 50 (April 1951):186–91.
Pinckney, Orde S. "William E. Borah: Critic of American Foreign Policy." *Studies on the Left* 1 (1960):48–61.
Pixton, John E., Jr. "Ghost of Charles A. Beard." *Christian Century*, November 1, 1952, pp. 1120–22.
Rauch, Basil. *Roosevelt from Munich to Pearl Harbor: A Study in the Creation of a Foreign Policy.* New York: Farrar, Straus and Young, Inc., 1950.
Rodgers, Hugh I. "Charles A. Beard, the 'New Physics,' and Historical Relativity." *The Historian* 30 (August 1968):545–60.
Ruetten, Richard T. "Harry Elmer Barnes and the 'Historical Blackout.'" *The Historian* 33 (February 1971):202–14.
Russett, Bruce M. *No Clear and Present Danger: A Skeptical View of the U.S. Entry into World War II.* New York: Harper & Row, Publishers, 1972.
Sargent, Porter. *Between Two Wars: The Failure of Education, 1920–1940.* Boston: Porter Sargent, 1945.
Schlesinger, Arthur M., Jr. "Roosevelt and His Detractors." *Harper's*, June 1950, pp. 62–68.
Schmunk, Paul L. "Charles Austin Beard: A Free Spirit, 1874–1919." Ph.D. dissertation, University of New Mexico, 1957.
Sheehan, Donald, and Syrett, Harold C., eds. *Essays in American Historiography Presented in Honor of Allan Nevins.* New York: Columbia University Press, 1960.
Skotheim, Robert A. "Environmental Interpretations of Ideas by Beard, Parrington, and Curti." *Pacific Historical Review* 33 (February 1964):33–44.
Smith, Theodore C. "The Writing of American History in America from 1884 to 1934." *American Historical Review* 40 (April 1935):439–49.
Soderbergh, Peter A. "Charles A. Beard, the Quaker Spirit, and North Carolina." *North Carolina Historical Review* 46 (January 1969):19–32.
————. "Charles A. Beard and the Radical Right." *Teachers College Record* 68 (May 1967): 631–39.
————. "The Historian and the Schools: Charles A. Beard's Views and Influence on the Teaching of the Social Studies in Public Secondary Schools, 1909–1939." Ph.D. dissertation, University of Texas, 1966.
Soderlind, Arthur E. "Charles A. Beard and the Social Studies." Ph.D. dissertation, State University of Iowa, 1961.
Sorenson, Lloyd R. "Charles A. Beard and German Historiographical Thought." *Mississippi Valley Historical Review* 42 (September 1955):274–87.
Steinberg, Samuel. "Charles A. Beard: The Man and His Works." *Social Education* 19 (March 1955):101–3.
Stourzh, Gerald. "Charles A. Beard's Interpretations of American Foreign Policy." *World Affairs Quarterly* 28 (July 1957):111–48.
Strout, Cushing. *The Pragmatic Revolt in American History: Carl Becker and Charles Beard.* New Haven: Yale University Press, 1958.
————. "In Retrospect: Charles Beard's Liberalism." *New Republic*, November 17, 1955, pp. 17–18.

186   *Bibliography*

Vevier, Charles. "American Continentalism: An Idea of Expansion, 1845–1910." *American Historical Review* 65 (January 1960):323–35.

Wallace, Henry A. "Beard, the Planner: Review of *Open Door at Home.*" *New Republic*, January 2, 1935, pp. 225–27.

Ware, Alexander. "The Beards, Chroniclers of the Times." *Christian Science Monitor Magazine*, July 22, 1939, pp. 5 ff.

Whitaker, Arthur P. "Charles Austin Beard." *Revista de Historia de America* 26 (December 1948):419–23.

White, Morton. *Social Thought in America: The Revolt against Formalism.* Boston: Beacon Press, 1957.

Wilkins, Burleigh Taylor. "Frederick York Powell and Charles A. Beard: A Study in Anglo-American Historiography and Social Thought." *American Quarterly* 11 (Spring 1959):21–39.

———, ed. "Charles A. Beard on the Founding of Ruskin Hall." *Indiana Magazine of History* 52 (September 1956):277–88.

Williams, William A. "Charles A. Beard: The Intellectual as Tory-Radical." In *American Radicals: Some Problems and Personalities*, edited by Harvey Goldberg, pp. 295–308. New York: Monthly Review Press, 1957.

———. "A Note on Charles Austin Beard's Search for a General Theory of Causation." *American Historical Review* 62 (October 1956):59–80.

Wilson, Edmund. *The American Earthquake: A Documentary of the Twenties and Thirties.* New York: Doubleday-Anchor, 1958.

———. "What Do the Liberals Hope For?" *New Republic*, February 10, 1932, pp. 345–48.

Wish, Harvey. *The American Historian: A Social-Intellectual History of the Writing of the American Past.* New York: Oxford University Press, 1960.

Wishy, Bernard. "A New Appraisal of Charles Beard." *New Leader*, March 23, 1959, pp. 20–22.

Wormser, René. *The Myth of the Good and Bad Nations.* Chicago: Henry Regnery Co., 1954.

GENERAL WORKS

Adler, Selig. "Isolationism since 1914." *American Scholar* 21 (Summer 1952): 335–44.

———. "The War-Guilt Question and American Disillusionment, 1919–1928." *Journal of Modern History* 23 (March 1951):1–28.

Anderson, George L., ed. *Issues and Conflicts: Studies in Twentieth Century American Diplomacy.* Lawrence: University of Kansas Press, 1959.

Baker, Leonard. *Roosevelt and Pearl Harbor.* New York: Macmillan Co., 1970.

Barnes, Harry Elmer. *Pearl Harbor after a Quarter of a Century.* New York: Arno Press, 1972.

———. *The Struggle against the Historical Blackout.* 9th ed. New York: Devin-Adair Co., 1951.

Bartlett, Ruhl J. *The League to Enforce Peace.* Chapel Hill: University of North Carolina Press, 1944.

Billington, Ray A. "The Origins of Middle Western Isolationism." *Political Science Quarterly* 55 (March 1945):44–64.

Borg, Dorothy. *The United States and the Far Eastern Crisis of 1933–1938: From the Manchurian Incident through the Initial Stage of the Undeclared Sino-Japanese War.* Cambridge: Harvard University Press, 1964.

———, and Okamoto, Shumpei, eds. *Pearl Harbor as History: Japanese-American Relations, 1931–1941.* New York: Columbia University Press, 1973.

Bibliography 187

Bradley, Phillips, ed. *American Isolation Reconsidered*. Washington: American Council on Education, 1941.

Browder, Earl. "For Collective Security." *New Republic*, February 2, 1938, pp. 354–56.

Burns, James M. *Roosevelt: The Soldier of Freedom*. New York: Harcourt Brace Jovanovich, Inc., 1970.

Butterfield, Herbert. *History and Human Relations*. New York: Macmillan Co., 1952.

Cantrill, Hadley, ed. *Public Opinion, 1935–1946*. Princeton: Princeton University Press, 1951.

Carleton, William G. "Isolationism and the Middle West." *Mississippi Valley Historical Review* 35 (December 1946):377–90.

Chu, Power Yung-chao. "A History of the Hull Trade Program, 1934–1939." Ph.D. dissertation, Columbia University, 1957.

Cole, Wayne S. *America First: The Battle against Intervention, 1940–1941*. Madison: University of Wisconsin Press, 1953.

———. "American Entry into World War II: A Historiographical Appraisal." *Mississippi Valley Historical Review* 42 (March 1957):596–617.

———. *Senator Gerald P. Nye and American Foreign Relations*. Minneapolis: University of Minnesota Press, 1962.

Compton, James V. *The Swastika and the Eagle: Hitler, the United States and the Origins of World War II*. Boston: Houghton, Mifflin Co., 1967.

Creel, George. *How We Advertised America*. New York: Harper & Bros., 1920.

Crocker, George N. *Roosevelt's Road to Russia*. Chicago: Henry Regnery Co., 1959.

Current, Richard N. "How Stimson Meant to 'Maneuver' the Japanese." *Mississippi Valley Historical Review* 40 (June 1953):67–74.

———. *Secretary Stimson: A Study in Statecraft*. New Brunswick, N.J.: Rutgers University Press, 1954.

Davis, Forrest, and Lindley, Ernest K. *How War Came: An American White Paper; From the Fall of France to Pearl Harbor*. New York: Simon and Schuster, 1942.

Davis, George T. *A Navy Second to None: The Development of Modern American Naval Policy*. New York: Harcourt, Brace and Co., 1940.

DeConde, Alexander, ed. *Isolation and Security*. Durham, N.C.: Duke University Press, 1957.

Diggins, John P. "Flirtation with Fascism: American Pragmatic Liberals and Mussolini's Italy." *American Historical Review* 71 (January 1966):487–506.

Dillard, Hardy C. "The Treaty-Making Controversy: Substance and Shadow." *Virginia Quarterly Review* 30 (Spring 1954):178–91.

Divine, Robert A. "FDR and Collective Security, 1933." *Mississippi Valley Historical Review* 48 (June 1961):42–59.

———. *The Illusion of Neutrality, 1935–1939*. Chicago: University of Chicago Press, 1962.

Donovan, John C. "Congressional Isolationists and the Roosevelt Foreign Policy." *World Politics* 3 (April 1951):299–316.

Doyle, Wilson K. "Pre-War Democratic Control of Military Affairs." *Military Affairs* 6 (Winter 1942):207–18.

Drummond, Donald F. *The Passing of American Neutrality, 1937–1941*. Ann Arbor: University of Michigan Press, 1955.

Earle, Edward M. "A Half-Century of American Foreign Policy: Our Stake in Europe, 1898–1948." *Political Science Quarterly* 44 (June 1949):168–88.

Edman, Irwin, *Philosopher's Holiday*. New York: Viking Press, 1938.

Ekirch, Arthur A., Jr. *The Decline of American Liberalism.* New York: Atheneum, 1967.
Englebrecht, H. C., and Hanighen, F. C. *Merchants of Death: A Study of the International Armament Industry.* New York: Dodd, Mead & Co., 1934.
Esthus, Raymond A. "President Roosevelt's Commitment to Britain to Intervene in a Pacific War." *Mississippi Valley Historical Review* 50 (June 1963): 28–38.
Feis, Herbert. *The Road to Pearl Harbor: The Coming of the War between the United States and Japan.* Princeton: Princeton University Press, 1950.
———. "The Shackled Historian." *Foreign Affairs* 45 (January 1967):332–43.
———. "War Came at Pearl Harbor: Suspicions Considered." *Yale Review* 45 (March 1956):378–90.
Ferrell, Richard H. "Pearl Harbor and the Revisionists." *The Historian* 17 (Spring 1955):215–33.
Freeman, Joseph. *An American Testament.* New York: Farrar and Rinehart Co., 1936.
Frye, Alton. *Nazi Germany and the American Hemisphere, 1939–1941.* New Haven: Yale University Press, 1967.
Gallup, George, and Robinson, Claude. "American Institute of Public Opinion Surveys, 1935–1938." *Public Opinion Quarterly* 2 (July 1938):373–98.
Gentry, Richard H. "Liberalism and the *New Republic*, 1914–1960." Ph.D. dissertation, University of Illinois, 1960.
Goldman, Eric F. *The Crucial Decade: America, 1945–1955.* New York: Alfred A. Knopf, 1956.
Goodman, Jack, ed. *While You Were Gone: A Report on Wartime Life in the United States.* New York: Simon and Schuster, 1946.
Grattan, C. Hartley. "The Historians Cut Loose." *American Mercury,* August 1927, pp. 414–30.
Herzog, James H. *Closing the Open Door: American-Japanese Diplomatic Negotiations, 1936–1941.* Annapolis, Md.: Naval Institute Press, 1973.
Hirschfeld, Charles. "Nationalist Progressivism and World War I." *Mid-America* 45 (July 1963):139–56.
Hull, Cordell. *The Memoirs of Cordell Hull.* 2 vols. New York: Macmillan Co., 1948.
Huntington, Samuel P. "The Military Profession." *Daedalus: Journal of the American Academy of Arts and Sciences* 92 (Fall 1963):785–807.
Johnson, Alvin. *Pioneer's Progress: An Autobiography.* New York: Viking Press, 1952.
Johnson, Walter. *The Battle against Isolationism.* Chicago: University of Chicago Press, 1944.
Jones, Joseph M., Jr. *Tariff Retaliation: Repercussions of the Hawley-Smoot Bill.* Philadelphia: University of Pennsylvania Press, 1934.
Josephson, Matthew. *Infidel in the Temple: A Memoir of the Nineteen-Thirties.* New York: Alfred A. Knopf, 1967.
Kase, Toshikazu. *Journey to the Missouri.* New Haven: Yale University Press, 1950.
Kennan, George F. *American Diplomacy, 1900–1950.* Chicago: University of Chicago Press, 1951.
Kimmel, Husband E. *Admiral Kimmel's Story.* Chicago: Henry Regnery Co., 1955.
Koenig, Louis W. *The Presidency and the Crisis Powers of the Office from the Invasion of Poland to Pearl Harbor.* New York: King's Crown Press, 1944.
Langer, William M., and Gleason, S. Everett. *The Challenge to Isolation, 1937–1940.* New York: Harper & Bros., 1952.

Bibliography 189

———. *The Undeclared War, 1940–1941*. New York: Harper & Bros., 1953.

Leopold, Richard W. "The Mississippi Valley and American Foreign Policy, 1890–1941: An Assessment and an Appeal." *Mississippi Valley Historical Review* 37 (March 1951):625–42.

———. "The Problem of American Intervention, 1917." *World Politics* 2 (April 1950):405–25.

Levine, Harold, and Wechsler, James. *War Propaganda and the United States.* New Haven: Yale University Press, 1940.

Lubell, Samuel. "Who Votes Isolationist and Why." *Harper's*, April 1951, pp. 30–31.

Luce, Henry R. *The American Century.* New York: Farrar & Rinehart, Inc., 1941.

Lydgate, William A. *What Our People Think.* New York: Thomas Y. Crowell Co., 1944.

Mann, Arthur. "British Social Thought and American Reformers of the Progressive Era." *Mississippi Valley Historical Review* 42 (March 1956):672–92.

Marchand, C. Roland. *The American Peace Movement and Social Reform, 1898–1918.* Princeton: Princeton University Press, 1972.

Masland, John W. "The 'Peace' Groups Join Battle." *Public Opinion Quarterly* 4 (December 1940):664–73.

———. "Pressure Groups and American Foreign Policy." *Public Opinion Quarterly* 6 (Spring 1942):115–22.

May, Ernest R. *The World War and American Isolation, 1914–1917*. Cambridge: Harvard University Press, 1959.

Miles, Sherman. "Pearl Harbor in Retrospect." *Atlantic Monthly*, July 1948, pp. 65–72.

Millett, Fred B. *Contemporary American Authors.* New York: Harcourt, Brace, and Co., 1940.

Millis, Walter. *The Road to War, 1914–1917.* Boston: Houghton Mifflin Co., 1935.

Mock, James R., and Larson, Cedric. *Words that Won the War: The Story of the Committee on Public Information, 1917–1919.* Princeton: Princeton University Press, 1939.

Morgenstern, George. *Pearl Harbor: The Story of the Secret War.* New York: Devin-Adair Co., 1947.

Morgenthau, Hans J. *In Defense of the National Interest: A Critical Examination of American Foreign Policy.* New York: Alfred A. Knopf, 1951.

———. *Politics among Nations: The Struggle for Power and Peace.* New York: Alfred A. Knopf, 1948.

Morison, Elting E. *Admiral Sims and the Modern American Navy.* Boston: Houghton Mifflin Co., 1942.

Morison, Samuel E. *Rising Sun in the Pacific, 1931–April 1942.* Boston: Little, Brown and Co., 1948.

Morton, Louis. "Pearl Harbor in Perspective: A Bibliographical Survey." *U.S. Naval Institute Proceedings* 81 (April 1955):461–68.

Noble, David W. "The *New Republic* and the Idea of Progress." *Mississippi Valley Historical Review* 38 (December 1951):387–402.

Norman, John. "Influence of Pro-Fascist Propaganda on American Neutrality, 1935–1936." In *Essays in History and International Relations in Honor of George H. Blakeslee*, edited by Dwight E. Lee and George E. McReynolds. Worcester, Mass.: Clark University Press, 1949.

Osgood, Robert E. *Ideals and Self-Interest in America's Foreign Relations: The Great Transformation of the Twentieth Century.* Chicago: University of Chicago Press, 1953.

190

Bibliography

Bibliography

Paxson, Frederick L., Corwin, Edward S., and Harding, Samuel B., eds. *The War Cyclopedia*. Washington: Committee on Public Information, 1918.

Perkins, Dexter. "Was Roosevelt Wrong?" *Virginia Quarterly Review* 30 (Summer 1954):355–72.

Peterson, Horace C. *Propaganda for War: The Campaign against American Neutrality, 1914–1917*. Norman: University of Oklahoma Press, 1939.

Polenberg, Richard, ed. *America at War: The Home Front, 1941–1945*. Englewood Cliffs, N.J.: Prentice-Hall, Inc., 1968.

Puleston, William D. *Mahan: The Life and Work of Captain Alfred Thayer Mahan*. New Haven: Yale University Press, 1939.

Ransom, Harry H. *Central Intelligence and National Security*. Cambridge: Harvard University Press, 1958.

Rappaport, Armin. *The Navy League of the United States*. Detroit: Wayne State University Press, 1962.

Rauch, Basil. *Roosevelt from Munich to Pearl Harbor: A Study in the Creation of a Foreign Policy*. New York: Creative Age Press, 1950.

Read, Conyers. "The Social Responsibilities of the Historian." *American Historical Review* 55 (January 1950):275–85.

Ruskin, John. *Unto This Last: Four Essays on the First Principles of Political Economy*. London: Smith, Elder and Co., 1862.

Sanborn, Frederick R. *Design for War: A Study of Secret Power Politics, 1937–1941*. New York: Devin-Adair Co., 1951.

Sargent, Porter. *Getting Us into War*. Boston: Porter Sargent, 1941.

Schlesinger, Arthur M., Jr. *The Imperial Presidency*. Boston: Houghton Mifflin Co., 1973.

Shroeder, Paul. *The Axis Alliance and Japanese-American Relations, 1941*. Ithaca, N.Y.: Cornell University Press, 1958.

Stein, Roger B. *John Ruskin and Aesthetic Thought in America, 1840–1900*. Cambridge: Harvard University Press, 1967.

Stimson, Henry L., and Bundy, McGeorge. *On Active Service in Peace and War*. New York: Harper & Bros., 1948.

Taft, Robert A. *A Foreign Policy for Americans*. Garden City, N.Y.: Doubleday & Co., 1951.

Talbot, Melvin. "Beyond the Naval Treaties." *U.S. Naval Institute Proceedings* 61 (April 1935):465–74.

Tansill, Charles C. *Back Door to War: The Roosevelt Foreign Policy*. Chicago: Henry Regnery Co., 1952.

Thompson, J. A. "American Progressive Publicists and the First World War, 1914–1917." *Journal of American History* 58 (September 1971):364–83.

Togo, Shigenori. *The Cause of Japan*. New York: Simon and Schuster, 1956.

Trefousse, Hans L. *Germany and American Neutrality, 1939–1941*. New York: Bookman Associates, 1951.

Unger, Irwin. "The 'New Left' and American History: Recent Trends in United States Historiography." *American Historical Review* 72 (July 1967):1237–63.

Wector, Dixon. *The Age of the Great Depression, 1929–1941*. New York: Macmillan Co., 1948.

Weinberg, Albert K. "The Historical Meaning of the American Doctrine of Isolation." *American Political Science Review* 34 (April 1940):539–47.

Wheeler, Gerald E. *Prelude to Pearl Harbor: The United States Navy and the Far East, 1921–1931*. Columbia: University of Missouri Press, 1963.

Williams, Benjamin H. *The United States and Disarmament*. New York: McGraw-Hill Book Co., 1931.

Bibliography 191

Williams, William A. "The Legend of Isolationism in the 1920s." *Science and Society* 18 (Winter 1964):1–20.
———. *The Tragedy of American Diplomacy.* Cleveland and New York: World Publishing Co., 1959.
Wiltz, John E. *In Search of Peace: The Senate Munitions Inquiry, 1934–1936.* Baton Rouge: Louisiana State University Press, 1963.
Wohlstetter, Roberta. *Pearl Harbor: Warning and Decision.* Stanford: Stanford University Press, 1962.
Woodward, C. Vann. "The Age of Reinterpretation." *American Historical Review* 66 (October 1960):1–19.

UNPUBLISHED MATERIALS

DePauw University Archives, Greencastle, Indiana:
"A Collection of Materials on Charles A. and Mary R. Beard," Microfilm Number 139.
Franklin D. Roosevelt Library, Hyde Park, New York:
"Administrative Files";
"Selected Materials from the Papers of Franklin D. Roosevelt Concerning Charles A. Beard."
Harry S Truman Library, Independence, Missouri:
"Truman Papers, Official File 158, Miscellaneous."
The Houghton Library, Harvard University, Cambridge, Mass.:
Oswald Garrison Villard Papers.
John M. Olin Research Library, Cornell University, Ithaca, N.Y.:
Carl Becker Papers.
The State Historical Society of Wisconsin, Madison:
Bruce Barton Papers;
Merle Curti Papers.
Western History Research Center, University of Wyoming Library, Laramie:
Harry Elmer Barnes Papers;
George Morgenstern Papers.
Yale University Library, New Haven, Conn.:
Bernard Knollenberg Papers;
George H. E. Smith Papers;
Henry L. Stimson Papers.

Index

Adams, Brooks: *The Law of Civilization and Decay*, 111–13, 124
Adams, Charles F., 62*n*
Adler, Selig, 42, 157, 160
Alien Registration Act (1940), 121
America Faces the Future, 59–60
America First Committee, 100–101, 136
America in Midpassage, 90–93
American Committee against Conscription, 99
American Foreign Policy in the Making, 133–38, 142, 144, 164
American Government and Politics, 23–25
American Historical Association, 162
American Historical Review, 155
American Party Battle, 66
American Political Science Association, 139, 162
American Spirit, 109–10
American-Yugoslav Society of New York, 52
Association for International Conciliation, 22
Axis Powers, 76, 85, 134, 136, 147, 148, 160. *See also* Beard on

Balkan Pivot, Yugoslavia, The, 52
Bank for International Settlement, 55

Barnes, Harry Elmer, 43, 46*n*, 53, 87*n*, 111, 129, 139, 140–41, 154, 157–58, 159*n*; *Genesis of the World War*, 43, 159; *Perpetual War for Perpetual Peace*, 158
Barton, Bruce, 125, 138, 143*n*
Basic History of the United States, 118–23
Beale, Howard K., 142
Beard, Charles A.: on academic freedom, 37–38; and America First Committee, 100, 101; and American civilization, 45, 50, 53–54, 66, 67, 92, 93, 109–10, 127, 163, 164; on American Constitution, 16, 21, 23, 102, 107, 111, 113, 114, 147, 159, 164–65; on American imperialism, 6–7, 9–10, 13, 17, 49, 68, 90–91, 109–10, 118; Amherst College lectures (1916), 29; anti-Prussianism of, 10–11, 31, 33; on Axis Powers, 63, 85, 88, 94, 104, 105–6, 107, 115, 133–34, 136, 147, 148; on the Balkans, 22–23, 29, 52–53; on "Big Navy Boys," 62–63, 77, 166; and British trade union movement, 8–9; on capitalism, 3, 34, 35–36; career, multi-faceted, ix, 14, 15–16, 27; character of, 1–2, 3, 11, 16, 98, 163;

Beard, Charles A. *(con't.)*
on China and U.S. relations toward, 24, 48–49, 50, 51, 67, 91, 122; on civil liberties, 2, 36, 37–38, 39, 51, 119, 121, 122, 127, 143, 164; on William Cobbett, 11–12; on collective security, 82, 85, 87, 93, 94, 164; on "collectivist democracy," 14, 73, 163; and Columbia University, 12–14, 15–18, 21, 30–31, 37–38, 47, 73, 161, 162; on communism, 87, 91–92, 94, 122; on Congress, 102, 103, 106, 108–9, 113–14, 126–27, 133, 134; Connecticut farms of, 3, 161–62; and "Continental Americanism" ("continentalism"), x, 47, 49, 57, 58, 65, 92, 97, 98, 118, 125n, 163–64, 167; on Calvin Coolidge, 51, 54, 60, 62n; at Cornell University, 10; and "court historians" controversy, 138–42; critics of (including critiques of historical interpretations and methodology), ix–x, 25–26, 27, 46, 60–61, 68, 74, 75–76, 96, 98, 123–24, 136–37, 152, 154–55, 160–61, 162, 164–65; on Cuba, 6, 17, 23, 26, 72; Dartmouth College lectures (1921), 46–50; death of, ix, 153, 154, 165; decline in reputation of, ix, 154, 165; defenders of, 76, 84n, 95–96, 123, 137, 152, 154, 156–59; at DePauw University, 5–8; and "devil theory of war," 82–84, 98, 119; on "dollar diplomacy," 73, 91, 118; and economic interpretation of history (including war and imperialism), 3, 13, 16, 17–22, 26–27, 28, 34–36, 43, 44, 48–49, 59, 60, 66–67, 78, 82–84, 90–91, 111, 112–13, 116–17, 118–19, 124–25, 152, 163–64; in England, 8–12, 14; and English historians, 8, 18; on Ethiopian invasion (1935), 82; family background of, 1–3; on fascism, 54, 87, 88, 92, 120, 122; on FDR, ix, 23, 70–90 *passim*, 93, 95, 98, 101, 103, 107, 111, 113, 118, 120–21, 123, 125, 126, 130, 131n, 134–49 *passim*, 152, 156, 164–65, 166; and *Federalist Papers*, 7, 114; on Founding Fathers, 66, 97, 111, 113, 114; on France, 18, 22, 43, 46, 47, 49, 52, 80, 90, 94, 115, 120; on French Revolution, 17–18;

on Germany, 10, 29–43 *passim*, 52, 53, 63, 85, 86, 90, 94, 103, 104, 119, 123, 133, 144, 145; on Great Britain, 18, 22, 35, 43, 48–49, 52, 80, 86, 90, 94, 97, 101, 102, 103, 115, 119–20, 122; and Great Depression, 58, 59, 163; on Alexander Hamilton, 66–67, 72, 114; on Warren G. Harding, 48, 51, 119; on Hawaiian Islands, 49, 67, 92; historiographical concerns of (including causation, objectivity, and relativism), 8–16 *passim*, 27, 46, 58, 83, 106–7, 111–13, 132, 161; on Hitler, 85, 94, 144; at Hull House, 6; on immigration, 69, 116; on imperialism, 6, 7, 9–10, 13, 17, 18–22, 27, 34–36, 90–91, 97, 118, 120; influence of Brooks Adams on, 111–13, 124; influence of John Ruskin on, 7, 8; influence of thought on, ix, 27, 74–89 *passim*, 155–60, 165–67; internationalist views of, x, 20, 22–23, 29–30, 40, 41, 45, 54–56, 163; on international organizations, 29–30, 36, 42, 49–50, 51, 55, 64, 80, 110, 115, 117–18, 122; on international trade and finance, 9–10, 18–22, 27, 47, 55, 91, 117–18, 163; on isolationism, 13, 17, 24, 27, 42, 45, 55–56, 86, 100, 106, 133; isolationism of, x, 41, 44, 45, 47, 48, 49–50, 52, 56, 57, 58, 59, 71–73, 74, 85–103 *passim*, 155, 160, 163–64; on Italy, 44, 54, 63, 82, 94, 133; on Japan and U.S.-Japanese relations, 20, 48–49, 50–51, 63, 64–65, 67, 80, 81, 85, 93–94, 101, 104, 105, 120–21, 123, 126, 130, 133, 144, 148–51; on Thomas Jefferson and Jeffersonianism, 4, 5, 66, 71, 79; at Johns Hopkins University, 99, 162; on Kellogg-Briand Pact (1928), 53, 64; on laissez-faire, 59, 72, 122; on League of Nations, 42, 45, 49–50, 64–65, 114, 115; on Lend-Lease Act (1941), 101–3, 104, 107–8, 120, 144, 145; on James Madison, 21n; on Alfred Thayer Mahan, 81, 90, 109; on Karl Marx and Marxism, 27, 107, 112; and militarism, 6, 10–11, 19–20, 24–25, 31, 59, 121, 124–25, 126–27, 143–44, 166; on Monroe Doctrine, 6; on morality in foreign affairs, 115–16; on Mussolini, 44, 54, 85; on national interest (including defense and security), 16, 17, 19, 24–25, 39, 56, 60–72 *passim*, 83, 85, 89, 99, 102, 125, 135, 136, 145, 147; on national planning, 59–61; on naval expansion, 19, 60, 61–63, 65, 76–77, 81, 88–89, 90, 120, 144, 147; on Navy League, 77; on neutrality legislation, 78–85 *passim*, 93, 96, 120; on New Deal, 70–73, 87*n*, 99, 112, 122, 156; and the "New History," 13, 19, 163; on Nye Committee, 55, 78–79, 80; on official history, 36, 107–8, 129, 136, 137–43 *passim*; on Open Door policy, 48–49, 68, 72, 91; optimism of, 11, 29, 40, 54–56, 130; Oxford years of, 8–12, 14; on pacifism, 7*n*, 38; on Pearl Harbor, 104, 105, 120–32 *passim*, 144, 149–51; on Philippines, 10, 17, 49, 50–51, 62, 67, 72, 91; political partisanship of, 3, 5, 7, 156; on Populism, 5; on presidential powers, 16, 23–24, 80, 83, 84, 93, 102, 103, 113–14, 126, 166; idea of, 11, 29, 59; and Progressivism, 3, 25–26; on public opinion, 109, 115, 119, 135, 145; Quaker schooling of, 2; on "Quarantine" speech (1937), 86–89, 93, 120, 135; as reform-minded activist, 8–16 *passim*, 57, 59, 76, 152, 156, 163, 164; revisionist views of, 41, 46, 58, 78, 154–64 *passim*; and revolt against formalism, 13; on Theodore Roosevelt, 25, 90, 118; on "rugged individualism," 16, 61, 156; at Ruskin Hall, 8, 12; on Russia (Soviet Union), 22, 34, 43, 46, 47, 72, 115, 119, 122, 130; on secret diplomacy, 46, 56, 83, 136, 144, 166; on Spanish-American War, 6–7, 13, 17, 24, 26–27, 91, 118; on Spanish Civil War, 85; on tariffs, 61, 70; on technology, 11, 59; travels in Europe and Asia, 4, 8, 10–11, 44–45, 50–52; on universal military training, 125, 143–44; on urban civilization, 5–6; on U.S. foreign trade and investment, 6, 9, 17, 24–25, 26, 41–76 *passim*, 110, 163–64; on Versailles Treaty, 42, 45, 53, 114, 119, 133; on

war, 6, 7, 17, 24, 26, 31*n*, 46, 53, 54, 64, 81, 82–93, 99–100, 115, 143; on George Washington, 24, 90, 97; on Washington Naval Disarmament Conference (1921–22), 48–49, 64; on Woodrow Wilson, 30–31, 38, 41, 43, 44, 71, 78–79, 80, 83, 84, 115, 118–19, 120, 139; on World Court, 64, 80; *Young Oxford* essays of, 8–10, 11–12. *See also* individual works
—— on World War I: American intervention in, 30–32, 35, 38–46 *passim*, 58, 78–79, 83, 84, 86, 118–19, 164; causes of, 28–39 *passim*, 43–44, 46, 106, 119–20; war aims, 33–36, 41–42; war debts, 53, 60; "war guilt," 28–29, 33, 41–53 *passim*, 119–20, 164
—— on World War II: American intervention in, ix, 79, 80, 81, 84, 87, 88*n*, 89, 95, 101–5 *passim*, 120–21, 126–27, 134–36, 144–48; causes of, 94, 102, 106–7, 115, 133–34; postwar objectives of, 105–6, 108, 110, 114–18, 121–23, 125, 148
Beard, Mary Payne (mother), 1
Beard, Mary Ritter, 3, 7, 10, 12, 36, 44, 45, 50, 51, 52, 73, 81*n*, 90, 91, 92, 109, 118–23 *passim*, 141, 153, 162
Beard, Nathan (grandfather), 1–2
Beard, William, 44, 55–56, 105, 143*n*
Beard, William Henry Harrison (father), 1, 2–3
Becker, Carl L., 33, 58, 68
Bemis, Samuel Flagg, 74, 103–4
Bender, George, 101
Benson, Lee: *Turner and Beard*, 21*n*
Berdahl, Clarence A., 96*n*
Beveridge, Albert J., 90
"Big Navy Boys," 62, 63, 77, 166
Borah, William E., 95, 136
Borchard, Edwin C., 136*n*
Boxer Rebellion, 24
Brett, George P., Jr., 106*n*
Browder, Earl S., 87
Bryan, William Jennings, 7
Buell, Raymond L., 75
Burgess, John W., 13
Burnham, James: *The Managerial Revolution*, 112
Bury, J. B.: *The Idea of Progress*, 59*n*
Butler, Nicholas Murray, 37, 38
Butterfield, Herbert, 140

Byrnes, James F., 140*n*

Canby, Henry Seidel, 123
Carlyle, Thomas, 8, 107
Carnegie Corporation, 38, 65
Chamberlain, Neville, 94
Chamberlin, William Henry, 158
Chicago Tribune, 136, 141, 152, 156
China. *See* Beard on
City College of New York, 29
Cobbett, William, 11–12
Cold War, 148
Colegrove, Kenneth, 96*n*
Collective security, 82, 97, 98. *See also*
   Beard on
"Collectivist democracy." *See* Beard on
Columbia University, 12–13, 15, 16,
   18, 21. *See also* Beard and
Committee on Public Information, 32
Committee to Defend America by
   Aiding the Allies, 100, 135
Contemporary American History,
   25–27
"Continentalism." *See* Beard and
   "Continental Americanism"
Coolidge, Calvin, 51, 54, 60, 62*n*
Corwin, Edward S., 33
Council on Foreign Relations, 138
Counts, George S., 152
Creel, George, 32
Crocker, George N., 159
Croly, Herbert, 36, 42; *Promise of
   American Life*, 163
Cross-Currents in Europe Today,
   46–50
Crow, Carl: *Four Hundred Million
   Customers*, 91*n*
Current, Richard N., 149*n*
Curti, Merle, 76, 99, 111, 125, 152
Czechoslovakia, invasion of (1939), 94

Davis, Forrest: *How War Came*, 107–8,
   138
Dennett, Tyler, 74
DePauw University, 5, 6, 7, 8
Development of Modern Europe, 18–20
Deville, Gabriel, 18
Devil Theory of War, 82–84, 106
Dewey, John, 36
Division of Civic and Educational
   Publications, 32

Early, Stephen, 84*n*

Eberstadt, Ferdinand, 125
Economic Basis of Politics, 124–25
Economic interpretation of history.
   See Beard on
*Economic Interpretation of the Con-
   stitution*, 16, 21, 159, 164–65
*Economic Origins of Jeffersonian
   Democracy*, 66
Eisenhower, Dwight D., 166
Ethiopia, invasion of (1935), 82

Fay, Sidney B., 33; *Origins of the
   World War*, 47
Feis, Herbert, 76, 140*n*
Ferguson, Homer C., 128, 129–30, 131,
   132*n*
Ford, Guy Stanton, 32
Foreign Policy for America, 97–98
Forrestal, James, 125
Fourteen Points, 33
France. *See* Beard on
Frankfurter, Felix, 36
Future Comes, The, 99

Gallup Polls, 88*n*, 89*n*, 109, 115
Geneva Disarmament Conference
   (1932), 65
Geneva Naval Disarmament Confer-
   ence (1927), 62
German-American Bund, 101
Germany. *See* Beard on
Giddy Minds and Foreign Quarrels,
   95–96
Goldman, Eric F., 10, 40*n*, 53*n*, 78, 104
Goodnow, Frank J., 13
Goto, Viscount, 50*n*
Grattan, C. Hartley: *The Deadly
   Parallel*, 106
Great Britain. *See* Beard on
Great Depression, 40, 58, 62, 77, 163
Grew, Joseph C., 120
Grumbach, Solomon: *Das annexion-
   istische Deutschland*, 35

Hague Tribunal, 30
Hamilton, Alexander, 66–67, 72, 114
Harding, Warren G., 48, 51, 119
Harper's Magazine, 33, 55, 96
Hawley-Smoot Tariff (1930), 61
Hay, John, 90
Hayes, Carleton J. H., 21
Hepburn, Charles M., 87*n*
Herring, Hubert, 38

Historical relativism. *See* Beard, historiographical concerns of
History of the United States, 45
Hitler, Adolf, 85, 94, 97, 103
Hobson, John: *Imperialism: A Study*, 17
Hofstadter, Richard, 4, 11, 12, 15, 26, 79, 126*n*, 150, 165
Hoover, Herbert, 60, 62, 72
House, Edward M., 83
Howe, Quincy: *England Expects Every American to Do His Duty*, 86
Hull, Cordell, 71, 130, 140*n*, 146, 149–50
Hull House, 6

Idea of National Interest, 59, 65, 66–68, 70–80 *passim*, 163, 165
Imperialism. *See* Beard on
Industrial Revolution, 9, 11
Intercollegiate Socialist Society, 38
International organizations, international trade and finance, internationalism. *See* Beard on
Isolationism, 4, 40*n*, 64, 78, 106, 123*n*, 133, 155–56. *See also* Beard on
Italy. *See* Beard on

Jameson, J. Franklin, 33
Japan. *See* Beard on
Jay's Treaty (1794), 66
Jefferson, Thomas, 4, 5, 66, 71, 79
Johns Hopkins University, 99, 162
Johnson, Alvin, 21
Josephson, Matthew, 4, 101
Juarès, Jean, 18

Kase, Toshikazu, 150*n*
Kehr, Eckart: *Schlachtflottenbau und Parteipolitik, 1894–1902*, 63
Kennan, George F., 165
Keppel, Frederick P., 65
Kerensky, Alexander, 34
Keynes, John Maynard: *Economic Consequences of the Peace*, 42
Kimmel, Husband C., 126, 129, 131, 151
Knightstown Academy, 5
Knollenberg, Bernard, 104
Konoye, Premier (Prince), 50*n*, 148

Langer, William L., 138–39; *Our Vichy Gamble*, 139

Lansing, Robert, 83
League of Free Nations Association, 36
League of Nations, 40*n*, 42, 133. *See also* Beard on
League to Enforce Peace, 36
Lend-Lease Act (1941), 101, 103. *See also* Beard on
Lerner, Max, 39, 98
Life magazine, 111, 118*n*
Lindbergh, Charles A., 100, 136
Lindley, Ernest K., 73; *How War Came*, 107–8, 138
Lippmann, Walter, 130
Lodge, Henry Cabot, 90
London Economic Conference (1933), 71–72, 80
London Naval Treaty (1930), 62
Luce, Clare Boothe, 127*n*
Luce, Henry R., 109, 111, 126*n*, 127*n*; *The American Century*, 109–10
Ludlow, Louis A., 88
Ludlow Amendment, 88
Lundberg, George A., 158

McDonald, Forrest, 159–60, 161
MacDonald, Ramsay, 12
Mach, Edmund Von, 36
McKinley, William, 23, 26
Madison, James, 21*n*
Mahan, Alfred Thayer, 81, 90, 109
Manchuria, invasion of, 64–65
Marshall Plan, 143*n*, 148, 152
Millis, Walter, 74, 98; *Road to War*, 159
Moley, Raymond, 73, 81, 157
Moore, John Bassett, 13
Morgenstern, George, 141, 156; *Pearl Harbor: The Secret History of the War*, 141*n*, 157
Morgenthau, Hans J., 78, 165
Morison, Samuel Eliot, 6, 155, 161
Mumford, Lewis, 123–24
Munich Conference (1938), 90
Mussolini, Benito, 44, 54, 85

Nation, The, 25, 89
National Governments and the World War, 41–42
National Institute of Municipal Administration, 52
National Peace Conference (1939), 89
NATO, 148

Navy League, 62, 77
Neutrality Acts, 81–82, 84, 85, 86, 93, 94, 96, 120
"New History," 13, 19, 163
"New Left" historiography, 160, 165
New Masses, 25
New Republic, 25, 32, 33, 38, 42, 64
Newsweek, 7n, 137
New York Times, 30, 31, 96
Nye, Gerald P., 93n
Nye Committee, 55, 78–79, 80, 81, 164

Office of the Justice of the Peace in England, 13–14
Official Documents Relating to the Outbreak of the World War, 36
Ogg, Frederick A., 42n
Old Deal and the New, The, 99
Open Door at Home, 52, 59, 65, 68–70, 72–76, 163, 165
Open Door policy, 48–49, 91, 160
Osgood, Robert E., 78
Oxford University, 8, 11

Paxson, Frederick L., 33
Payne, Sarah Wilson (grandmother), 2
Pearl Harbor: attack on, 76, 85, 104, 105, 118, 120–21, 125, 126–27, 129, 144, 149–51, 159, 167; inquiry, 126–27, 128, 129, 130–32. *See also* Beard on
Philippines. *See* Beard on
Platt Amendment, 72
Poland, invasion of (1939), 94, 133
Political Science Quarterly, 21
Polk, James K., 23
Powell, Frederick York, 8, 11
President Roosevelt and the Coming of the War, ix, 144–59 *passim*, 164
Progress, idea of, 11, 29, 59
Progressive, The, 111, 126
Progressive Era, 15
Progressivism, 26

"Quarantine" speech (1937), 86–87, 88, 89, 93, 120, 135

Radin, George, 52
Raditch, Stephen, 52
Rand School of Social Science, 38
Ranke, Leopold von, 8
Rappaport, Armin: *The Navy League of the United States*, 77n

Relativism. *See* Beard, historiographical concerns of
Republic, The, 111–20
Revisionism, 41, 79, 87n, 136n, 140, 141, 157–58, 160
Rise of American Civilization, 44, 51–52, 123
Roberts Commission (1942), 131
Robinson, James Harvey, 13, 18–19, 21, 25, 28–29, 47, 55, 163
Rockefeller Foundation, 138
Roosevelt, Franklin D., ix, 23, 65, 66, 70–90 *passim*, 98–104 *passim*, 107, 111, 113, 118–28 *passim*, 134–52 *passim*, 155–62 *passim*, 163, 164, 165
Roosevelt, Theodore, 25, 90, 118
Roosevelt Library, 138, 142
Ruskin, John, 8
Ruskin Hall, 8, 10, 12

Sanborn, Frederick R., 158
Sargent, Porter, 123n
Saturday Evening Post, 138, 141
Saturday Review of Literature, 123
Schlesinger, Arthur M., 7
Schlesinger, Arthur M., Jr., 166n
Schneider, Herbert W.: *Making the Fascist State*, 54
Sears, Louis Martin, 137, 159
Selective Service Act: of 1940, 101; of 1948, 144
Seligman, E. R. A., 13, 21n
Senate Judiciary Committee Investigating German Propaganda, 38
Sharp, Walter R., 96n
Short, Walter C., 126, 129, 131, 151
Sino-Japanese War (1937–45), 85–86
Smith, George H. E., 66n, 71n, 73, 79, 88n, 99, 100, 103, 128–29, 130–32, 137
Social Science Research Council, 66, 132
Spanish-American War, 6, 7, 17, 24, 26, 68, 91, 118. *See also* Beard on
Spengler, Oswald, 112
Stalin, Joseph, 87
Stimson, Henry L., 62, 146, 149
Strong, Josiah, 109
Strout, Cushing, 104, 134
Stubbs, William, 8

Taft, William Howard, 118
Talbot, Melvin, 81n
Tansill, Charles C., 141, 143; *America*

Goes to War, 141; *Back Door to War*, 101n, 157, 158
Thompson, Dorothy, 53n
Time Magazine, 98, 109
Togo, Shigenori, 150n
Truman, Harry S, 126, 130, 140n, 144, 167
Tully, Grace G., 106n
Tyler, Moses Coit, 10

Universal military training bill (1948), 143–48

Vagts, Alfred, 39, 63, 101n
Vagts, Miriam Beard, 4n, 101n, 162
Vandenberg, Arthur H., 136
Versailles Treaty, 35, 42, 43, 45, 53, 114, 119, 133
Vietnam War, 160, 166
Villard, Oswald Garrison, 42, 89–90, 99, 111, 124, 130, 137
Vrooman, Walter, 8

Wallace, Henry A., 75
War Cyclopedia, The (1918), 32, 33n
Washington, George. *See* Beard on
Washington Naval Disarmament Conference (1921–22), 48
Washington Post, 139

Watts, Franklin: *Voices of History, 1941*, 107
Weaver, James Riley, 7
Weinberg, Albert K., 64
Welles, Sumner, 140n
Weyl, Walter: *The End of the War*, 35–36
White, Morton, 25
Whither Mankind, 54–55
Wilbur, Curtis, 51–52, 54
Wilhelm, Kaiser, II, 29, 43
Williams, William Appleman, 160
Willkie, Wendell, 99, 110n
Wilson, Edmund, 158–59
Wilson, Woodrow, 30–44 *passim*, 71, 115, 118–19, 120, 130, 139, 141
Wohlstetter, Roberta, 151n
Woodward, C. Vann, 56n
World Court, 64, 80
World War I, 28–39 *passim*, 43, 44–45, 53. *See also* Beard on
World War II, 94, 96–97, 157–58, 160, 166. *See also* Beard on
Wormser, René: *Myth of the Good and Bad Nations*, 158
Wright, Quincy, 96n

Yale University Press, 141
Young Oxford Magazine, 8, 11, 13
Young Plan (1929), 55